FROM 1450 TO THE PRESENT DAY
THE WORLD'S GREAT
HANDGUNS

FROM 1450 TO THE PRESENT DAY
THE WORLD'S GREAT
HANDGUNS

ROGER FORD

CHARTWELL
BOOKS, INC.

This edition published in 2005 by

CHARTWELL BOOKS, INC.
A Division of
BOOK SALES, INC.
114 Northfield Avenue
Edison, New Jersey 08837

Copyright © 1997 Amber Books Ltd

All rights reserved. No part of this publication may be
reproduced, stored in a retrieval system or transmitted, in
any form or by any means, electronic, mechanical, photo-
copying, recording or otherwise, without the prior written
permission of the copyright holder.

ISBN-13: 978-0-7858-1987-5
ISBN-10: 0-7858-1987-8

Editorial and design by
Amber Books Ltd
Bradley's Close
74–77 White Lion Street
London N1 9PF
United Kingdom
www.amberbooks.co.uk

PICTURE CREDITS:
Aerospace Publishing: 80, 93, 126–127, 149, 156, 157
The Bridgeman Art Library: 6–7, 12 (bottom left), 15, 21 (bottom right), 85
Corbis: 47, 60 (top left), 65
Ian Hogg: 130
The Hulton Getty Picture Collection: 113
Mary Evans Picture Library: 8 (centre), 10 (top and bottom right), 19 (top right),
24 (bottom), 32 (top), 34, 40 (centre right), 70 (top), 71 (top), 74 (top), 97
Novosti: 138 (bottom)
Peter Newark's Western Americana: 39, 41, 42, 62–63, 72, 105, 106, 117, 120
Peter Newark's Military Pictures: 124
Peter Newark's American Pictures: 166–167 (middle)
Rex Features: 151
Salamander Books: 8 (top left), 18, 24 (top left), 26 (bottom), 27, 33, 37, 38–39, 44,
49 (top), 50, 52 (top and bottom), 54, 58 (top and bottom), 66 (top left), 66–67,
68 (middle), 69 (top right), 70 (bottom), 73, 75, 76 (middle), 77 (bottom), 78,
79 (top right), 80 (middle),81 (bottom left), 83, 86 (bottom), 87, 91 (top and bottom),
93 (top), 94 (top and bottom), 98, 99, 100, 102, 122, 128, 131, 133, 136 (middle),
138 (top), 144, 160 (centre), 170 (bottom)
TRH Pictures: 88 (middle), 108, 111, 135, 146–147, 155 (top), 163 (top), 172 (middle)

Artwork credits
John Batchelor: 8–9, 11, 12 (top), 13, 14, 16 (top left), 16–17, 19 (bottom), 20,
21 (top right), 22 (top and bottom), 23, 25, 26 (top), 28, 29, 25, 36, 43, 51, 56, 59,
64, 68 (bottom), 79 (bottom), 80 (top), 82, 84, 89, 90, 93 (bottom),
95 (bottom), 96, 101, 103, 107, 109, 110, 112, 114, 115, 116, 119, 121,123, 125,
126 (top and bottom), 134, 136, 139, 141, 142, 145, 148, 149 (bottom right), 150,
152 (top and bottom), 154, 156 (top and bottom), 158, 159, 161, 163 (bottom), 164,
165, 166, 167, 168, 171, 172 (top), 173, 174
De Agostini: 149 (top right), 155 (bottom), 162
Jan Suermondt: 32 (bottom), 40, 45, 46, 48, 49 (bottom), 53, 55, 57, 60–61 (top right),
74 (bottom), 76, 81, 86 (top), 92, 95 (top), 118, 129, 132, 137, 140, 143, 169, 170 (top)

Printed in Singapore

CONTENTS

CHAPTER 1
FROM HAND CANNON TO HANDGUNS

The gun is so ancient that its origins are lost, quite literally, in the mists of time. We can put only an approximate date on its invention, though we can be sure that by the beginning of the fourteenth century, primitive firearms were already in common use in Europe.

These early guns were very simple devices indeed: a short, thick-walled tube with one end closed save for a small hole drilled through into the chamber at right angles, so that a red-hot wire or 'touche' could be inserted to ignite the charge packed inside. This 'gunpowder' was a recently invented explosive mixture of saltpetre, charcoal and sulphur. Early gunpowder was weak, and could occupy as much as three-quarters of the available space, although even the crudest black powder will produce something in the order of 100 times its volume in carbon dioxide gas. A more-or-less spherical projectile (the earliest 'pot-guns' fired loose stones), roughly sized to fit the bore of the 'barrel', rested atop a wooden plug which had been tamped down on top of the charge and was expelled by the subsequent sudden release of a very large volume of gas. Some of these proto-cannon were large, and rested in wooden cradles. Others, smaller, were fitted with cut-down pike-hafts and were carried by hand, the haft being planted in the ground and held under the gunner's arm for firing.

These earliest 'handguns' – they begin to appear in contemporary accounts before 1350 – fired projectiles less than 25mm (1in) in diameter. One of the oldest

■LEFT: **Swedish and Imperialist cavalry fight at the Battle of Lutzen on 16 November 1632. The effective range of wheel-lock handguns is indicated by the closeness of the combatants.**

examples yet found was cast in bronze and had a bore of about 18mm (.7in). Found in fragments; it seems to have burst in use, at the 1396 siege of Otepää, in what is now Estonia. Another, also in bronze, this time excavated in one piece at the site of a 1399 siege near Tannenberg, has a bore of just over 1mm (.5in). Similar-sized guns cast in iron or hammer-welded from sheet iron have also been found.

CRADLE-MOUNTED GUNS
Over the following century, as metalworking techniques improved, cradle-mounted guns, either welded from bundles of iron rods or cast, usually in easier-to-work bronze, got much bigger and more powerful. Even firing roughly shaped stone balls they soon put an end to the relative invincibility of the medieval fortress, and changed the nature of warfare for ever in the process. Stone projectiles stayed in common use until the end of the fifteenth century, not only because they were easier to manufacture than metal cannonballs, but also because they were lighter, and thus put less strain on the gun itself.

At the other end of the scale, portable firearms were also developing rapidly, the most important improvement being the addition of a serpentine (an S-shaped metal arm, pivoted in the middle) to hold the burning slowmatch. This was nothing more complicated than a piece of cord which had previously been soaked in a solution of saltpetre in spirits of wine,

Medieval Handgun

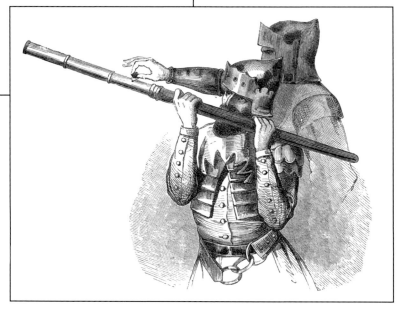

Calibre: 18mm (.7in)
Weight: 3.6kg (127oz)
Length: 1.2m (48in)
Barrel length: 0.6m (24in)
Effective range: 7m (23ft)
Feed: one shot
Muzzle velocity: 91mps (300fps)
Area of origin: Eastern Europe

■BELOW: Firing a fourteenth-century hand cannon was an elaborate manoeuvre. Two men were required for this process; one to hold and point the piece, the other to apply a match, or 'touche', to the crude charge. Such weapons were of limited use on the medieval battlefield, being inaccurate, unreliable and having a slow rate of fire.

and then allowed to dry, and which was used in place of the wire touche to ignite the charge. It allowed him to take some sort of aim before pulling back on the 'tricker' or trigger. This was no complicated spring-loaded mechanism but merely the lower arm of the serpentine. Pulling on it forced the lit end of the match down onto the priming charge contained in a small depression around the touch hole, in turn igniting the main charge in the chamber below and firing the piece. The innovation can be dated to before 1411, for an accurate description of a rudimentary matchlock appears in a manuscript of that date now in the Austrian National Library. Later guns had C-shaped serpentines, held off by a simple arrangement of leaf spring and sear, which became known as 'snap matchlocks'.

PREDECESSORS OF THE PISTOL

The forming of the rear of the gun's wooden stock into a rudimentary butt, allowing the gun to be brought up to the shoulder, also helped the aiming process. In competent hands the best of the late medieval matchlocks were surprisingly accurate, capable of hitting a playing card at 50m (164ft) and of killing a deer at twice that. Rifled versions – and while these were by no means common, they did exist from at least as early as 1520 – were accurate at up to twice those distances.

Early matchlocks are now widely known by their French name, 'arquebus'. The original form was the German 'hakbusche' (hook-gun), though it is by no means clear exactly what the 'hook' refers to. Other variants are 'arcabuco' in Spanish and 'hakbutt' and 'harquebus' in English. While easily carried by a single

man, they were still too heavy to be fired off-hand, and had to be propped up on anything convenient. Later they were often steadied by means of a forked rest. Handier versions, such as the shorter caliver and the breast-gun, or petronel, soon came into use, developed expressly for men mounted on horseback. These lighter weapons were the precursors of the handgun proper, though that final step had to wait until the problems of ignition by match had been overcome.

The slowmatch in its serpentine was certainly a real improvement over the hand-held touche, but the matchlock gun was still very clumsy and uncertain in use. The gunner had to light the match before going into action, and despite being removed from the serpentine and swung through the air when not in use, it was by no means guaranteed to stay alight, particularly through the lengthy and cumbersome reloading process or in bad weather. In a well-known incident, explorer Henry Hudson's party barely escaped with their lives when, during a

fight with Canadian 'Indians', rain put their slowmatches out. The match was inherently dangerous, too, for the glowing end was never far away from the priming charge. The arrangement never lent itself to the sort of firearm which could be carried in a holster or thrust through a

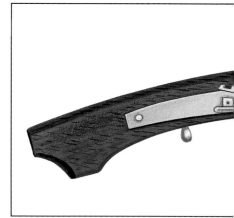

belt. Captain John Smith, the lover of Pocahontas, was badly burned when loose powder he was carrying in his pocket was ignited by his hakbutt's slowmatch. For that reason, there were very few matchlock pistols ever made, and it was not until the development of a successful friction ignition system that the handgun became truly feasible.

THE WHEEL-LOCK MECHANISM

Its inefficiency notwithstanding, the matchlock long arm stayed in use in Asia until well into the nineteenth century, particularly in Japan, where the industrial revolution was very slow in coming, and on the Indian subcontinent, where it was known as the 'bunduk' or 'bandukh' in the south and the 'jezail' in the northwest. This surprising longevity was due to the ease with which it could be manufactured with nothing but the simplest of tools. And an active 'equaliser' the long-obsolete weapon proved, too, under the right circumstances, as Rudyard Kipling reminded us in his poem *Arithmetic on the Frontier*, first published in *Departmental Ditties* in June 1886:

A scrimmage in a Border Station
A canter down some dark defile
Two thousand pounds of education
Drops to a ten-rupee jezail

It was well understood that gunpowder could be ignited by a single spark, and making fire from sparks caused by the action of stone against steel was already commonplace. By the end of the fifteenth century a search was underway to find a means of doing away with the slowmatch and igniting the powder in a gun's chamber by striking a spark at the breech. There is some evidence that the first successful spark ignition device, the wheel-lock, was actually devised by the incomparable Leonardo da Vinci. A design for such a mechanism was included in the catalogue of his inventions known as the *Codice Atlantico*, published around 1508. Even though modern-day replicas made to his specification have never quite worked reliably, the principle was sound enough, within the limits of the technology of the day. The mechanism used a spring-loaded serrated wheel to strike a spark off a piece of iron pyrites ('fool's gold'). The main drawback lay in its complexity, with as many as three dozen moving parts (and sometimes more, particularly in very expensive versions) being required to perform the apparently simple task of striking a spark at will and directing it into the priming pan.

FIRING THE WHEEL-LOCK

To the musketeer (or, more properly, the harquebussier) himself, the operation was relatively simple and straight-forward. The action was readied for firing by applying a square key to the shaft holding the serrated steel wheel, and turning it until a flat-link roller-chain, attached to the shaft and now wound around it, had fully compressed the folded spring which was attached to its other end. This allowed a horizontally acting sear pin, acting against another spring and capable of being released by the movement of the trigger, to fit into a recess on the side of the wheel to keep it from turning back. Pressure on the trigger not only released the serrated wheel to revolve against a pre-positioned piece of pyrites held in a dog's head clamp, but also moved the firing pan cover out of the way. The priming powder beneath was thus exposed to the shower of sparks produced, which ignited it and then the main charge. In practical terms, this meant that the gun could be set down somewhere convenient – holstered if it was a handgun – yet still be ready to use in an instant.

'DAGGEN' AND 'PISTOLETS'

Complex and expensive though it was (and it never replaced the matchlock in military use for that very reason), the wheel-lock made one-handed guns a practical possibility at last. By the middle of the sixteenth century, they were widespread, known in England as 'dags', in Germany as 'daggen' or 'pistolen', in France as 'pistolets' and in Italy as 'pistolette'. The latter name offers a firm clue as to the location of the seat of the new gunmaking industry: the Tuscan city of Pistoia, roughly halfway between Florence and Lucca. This theory has the name being a corruption of *un'arma pistoiese* (a Pistoian gun), with the addition of the diminutive ending. The suggestion isn't entirely far-fetched, and is supported by the *Oxford English Dictionary*. It even lends extra weight to the claim that Leonardo was the wheel-lock's inventor, this being the area in which he lived. By 1570 the modern form, 'pistol', had begun to appear in both German and English accounts.

In the just under 200 years in which handguns had been in existence, they had changed out of all recognition. Not only had they acquired a mechanism more complicated than that found in many contemporary clocks, but they had

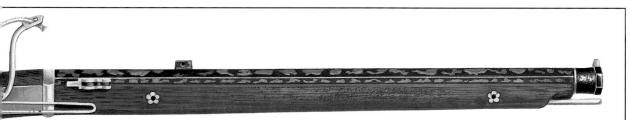

Early Matchlock

Calibre: 10.9mm (.42in)
Weight: 4.1kg (144oz)
Length: 1.2m (48in)
Barrel length: 800mm (32in)

Effective range: 45.7m (150ft)
Feed: single shot
Muzzle velocity: 137mps (450fps)
Country of origin: Germany

■RIGHT: German soldiers, circa 1600. Note in particular the long wheel-lock being held by the fully-armoured cuirassier, complete with plumed helmet, in the middle of the bottom row.

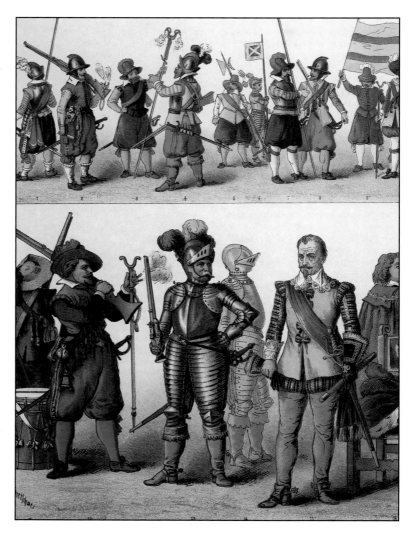

also become minor works of art, profusely decorated and inlaid with bone, horn, mother-of-pearl and precious metals. In their overall form, they differed in one major respect from more modern firearms: the grip or butt was set not at near right angles to the action and barrel, but almost in line with it. It was completed by a large pommel, usually spherical, lemon or pear-shaped. While the pommel probably served as a handy cosh or bludgeon on occasion, that wasn't its prime purpose; rather, it was there to improve the pistoleer's grip, particularly when drawing his weapon from a saddle holster. Most wheel-lock pistols were single-barrelled, but there are numerous examples of both over-and-under and side-by-side twins in existence. These pistols had paired locks – and very expensive they would have been, as is betrayed by the amount of decoration typically found on them.

THE SNAPHANCE
As the wheel-lock was so complicated, it was inevitable that it would be superseded in short order. The first attempts to devise a simplified action saw longer-lasting flint substituted for pyrites, the stone being held in a dog or clamp, very similar to that employed in the wheel-lock but now mounted atop a spring-loaded 'cock' moved back into the position the wheel itself had occupied, and turned through 180 degrees. The action of pulling the trigger first released the cock to revolve forwards, forcing the flint to scrape against a serrated steel striker plate located above the primer pan and held in place by a second, weaker leaf-spring. This same trigger pull moved the cover of the pan holding the priming powder. As the file-like steel (also known as the frizzen, battery, hammer and sometimes hen) was struck by the cock, it was pushed forwards, and the priming powder was exposed to the resulting sparks.

The new action had its origins somewhere in northern Europe – both Germany and Scandinavia have been suggested – but it came to the fore in the Netherlands. Known as snaphance or snaphaunce, it is believed to have taken its name from the Dutch: 'schnapp hahn',

or 'pecking cock'. This is a straight-forward description of the appearance and action of the flint holder, though some preferred to liken it to a barking dog, and named it accordingly. A persistent secondary explanation for the rather unusual name finds its way into every history: Dutch chicken thieves of the day were supposedly known either as 'schnapphahns' (cock-snatchers) or equally handily, by the nickname of 'Schnapphans' (Snatching Jack). One of this class, more mechanically minded

■RIGHT: German soldiers, early seventeenth century. This picture provides a good example of the cumbersome matchlock, which required a rest to operate effectively.

than his fellows, and being convinced of the need for any self-respecting chicken thief to go equipped with a firearm, invented the new action on the spur of the moment, the glowing end of a matchlock's slowmatch being something of a giveaway in a farmyard at night, and the wheel-lock proving far beyond his means. Whatever the origins of the name, there was no denying the practicality of the new mechanism and Holland, newly independent of Spain and already a major centre of maritime trade, was perfectly placed to exploit it. By the late sixteenth century, guns equipped with the Dutch snaphance lock became an important trade commodity, not just in northern Europe but as far afield as the western Mediterranean, Africa and the Far East. They established themselves as firm favourites in Scotland, for example, and remained in favour there even after the development of the flintlock.

At roughly the same time, guns with an outwardly similar new action made their appearance in Italy, in Tuscany and Emilia. There is no real evidence to suggest that one design influenced the other, or whether their contemporary appearance is just one more example of the coincidences which seem regularly to go hand-in-hand with technological development. Just as the Dutch snaphances became widely distributed through those parts of the globe which habitually traded with Amsterdam, so the Italian variant found long-standing favour in areas where the Italian influence predominated: the eastern Mediterranean, Near East, Balkans and Russia.

THE SPANISH LOCK
With at most a quarter of the number of components of the wheel-lock, the snaphance lock (in either of its forms) was both cheaper and easier to manufacture and repair. There was still one unnecessary complication in its design, however: the rather awkward method of clearing the priming pan cover, still linked mechanically to the action of the trigger by means of an articulated arm or plunger. This shortcoming was to be rectified in yet another of the gunmaking centres of the renaissance world: Spain.

Spanish gunmaking began relatively late, in 1530. In that year when Charles V, King of Spain, Holy Roman Emperor, the most powerful individual of his time and an avid collector of firearms, brought to Madrid brothers Simon and Peter Markhardt, master gunsmiths of

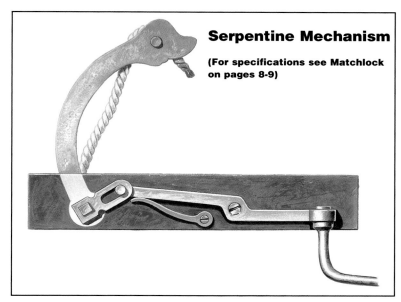

Serpentine Mechanism

(For specifications see Matchlock on pages 8-9)

Augsburg. To the son of one of them, by now known as Marquarte, usually goes the credit for having devised, sometime during the last quarter of the sixteenth century, a version of the snaphance with the pan cover forming an integral part of the steel. This removed the need for the cover to be displaced separately. There is some evidence that the simplified lock actually originated in southern Italy, and certainly it stayed in favour there, but it was the Iberian gunmaking centres which were its most serious adherents.

Simon Marquarte's invention eventually became known as the miquelet lock, but not until the time of the Peninsular Wars between Britain and France at the start of the nineteenth century. It had been known simply as 'the Spanish lock' over the intervening two centuries. Miqueletes were lightly armed irregular Spanish infantry employed by both sides; and who continued to use this lock long after it had given way to the simpler flintlock, both in the Spanish Army and outside Spain.

THE COMING OF THE FLINTLOCK
Just as the wheel-lock before them had done, snaphance and miquelet locks found their way into both long arms and single-handed guns. The wheel-lock remained in favour in some areas, notably among German sportsmen, though the last known pair of wheel-lock pistols to be manufactured were made in Paris by Le Page in 1829. In the same

way the snaphance and the miquelet have their adherents right up until the invention of the percussion cap at the beginning of the nineteenth century. They were overshadowed, though, by a simpler, more efficient and robust design – the flintlock. This was to become the standard action for both muskets and pistols.

BRITISH AND FRENCH GUNMAKING
So far in this brief introduction to the origins of firearms, two important names have been significant by their absence from the ranks of the world's great gunmakers, all the more curiously since they were those of two of the most prominent trading nations: Britain and France. The introduction of the simplest and most significant of the flint-and-steel actions was to rectify that omission with a rush, and Britain went on to become the acknowledged home of the best gunmakers of the day, while France was to give birth to the flintlock action itself. France continued to produce some of the best-decorated weapons ever seen, though in terms of technique and craftsmanship there is nothing to separate the work of the best French gunmakers, such as Nicolas Noel Boutet and Jean Baptiste Laroche, from their British peers. However, it is true that there were more really first-rate gunsmiths in England – and not a few in Scotland and Ireland, too – than there were on the other side of the Channel. The best north Italian gunmakers came from Brescia and the

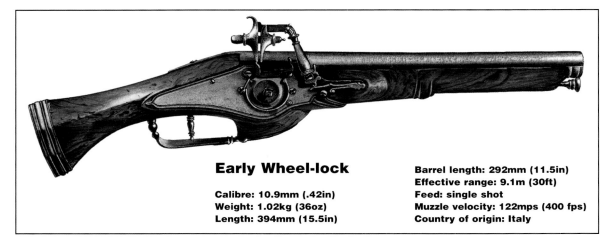

Early Wheel-lock

Calibre: 10.9mm (.42in)
Weight: 1.02kg (36oz)
Length: 394mm (15.5in)

Barrel length: 292mm (11.5in)
Effective range: 9.1m (30ft)
Feed: single shot
Muzzle velocity: 122mps (400 fps)
Country of origin: Italy

surrounding area, and they stuck, generally, to the snaphance variant perfected there. While in the south, around Naples and in Sicily and Sardinia, there was still a ready market for the Italian variant of the miquelet lock. But the one thing all the Italian workshops had in common was a fondness for decoration. And in Spain, Iberian gunsmiths continued to produce fine guns, particularly in Madrid, Barcelona and the Catalonian centre of Ripoll, in the Pyrenees, virtually all of them with miquelet locks. The infant industry of the new world didn't really get into its stride until later, and most eighteenth-century American firearms relied on imported components, particularly locks manufactured in Europe, with only the stock made locally. German gunsmiths, content to have devised the by-now long obsolescent wheel-lock, and still sticking with it, disregarded the French invention almost completely, and fell behind as a result.

LE BOURGEOYS' FLINTLOCK

We can say that France was the birthplace of the flintlock proper with absolute certainty, even though the evidence as to the inventor's identity is almost all circumstantial. Although there is no proof-positive of authorship, there is little doubt that the man responsible was one Marin le Bourgeoys, born into a family of sculptors, instrument and clock-

■LEFT: A seventeenth-century gentleman. He holds a wheel-lock pistol in his right hand. When mounted it was usual to carry these pistols in holsters positioned in front of the saddle.

makers in Lisieux, Normandy, around 1550. By 1598, le Bourgeoys was *valet de chambre* (the term has nothing to do with body servitude; its real purpose was to free le Bourgeoys from the control of the Paris craft guilds) to the French king, Henri IV, specialising in mechanical inventions such as moving globes and orreries. And sometime between then and 14 May 1610, the day his patron was assassinated, he presented him with a long arm utilising a hybrid of the snaphance. He took the internal mechanism of the snaphance, with the mainspring bearing on a tumbler, and from the miquelet he took the one-piece steel and pan cover, together with its spring actuation. His new lock had the sear operating between the trigger and the cock acting vertically, instead of horizontally as it had in all previous actions, both strengthening it and allowing the incorporation of a true 'safe' position, which became known as half-cock. By the mid-1630s, gunmakers all over France were copying le Bourgeoys.

English gunsmiths did, too, after briefly going down a false trail. At roughly the same time as le Bourgeoys was at work on the flintlock, a device which became known as the English dog lock became popular. This had a sear mounted on a vertical pin, like that of the wheel-lock, which acted horizontally through a hole in the lock plate upon the dog which gave the lock its name. This was a hooked catch which engaged in a recess cut in the tail of the cock. Though it looked outwardly similar at first glance, the dog lock was inferior to the true flintlock, which was both easier to produce and surer in operation, and it

was quickly superseded. At that time, the only significant differences between long arms and hand guns lay in the lengths of their respective barrels and the shape and dimensions of their stocks. The action employed was common to both, and remained so, even through the earliest types of repeating weapons. It was not until the development of the brass cartridge that the two types of personal firearm began to differ in their basic design. There were some experimental departures, of course, but that is all they were. The flintlock mechanism was the key to this de facto standardisation, and it mattered not at all that the very different nature of those two apparently very similar weapons was rapidly becoming clear.

EARLY HANDGUNS IN BATTLE
The first effective handguns were both large and heavy; they were not designed to be concealed about one's person or carried in a handy belt or shoulder-holster, but rather they were produced as a way of making a firearm that a mounted rider could use in one hand while gripping the reins with the other. They were the direct successor to the petronels, which were also intended for use on horseback.

Petronel is derived from the French word *poitrine*, the chest, against which their excessively curved butt was designed to be held. From the earliest times, firearms had a significant influence on the battle tactics of mounted men. There is certainly no doubt that cavalry, as first 'invented' by Charles II of France in 1445, was a regiment that was intended to be armed with guns, though

the first 'carabineers' (so-named from the carbines or short-barrelled guns they carried) probably rode with an infantryman mounted behind them.

CAVALRY PISTOLS
By the middle of the sixteenth century this practice had ceased; in 1554, Marshall de Brissac formed a corps of mounted infantry which he called dragoons, and who were intended to fight either on horseback or foot. The name is said to have been derived from the dragon's head carvings which adorned the muzzles of the pistols they carried as their primary armament. Within a generation, these troops had acquired the reputation of being the finest cavalry in Europe. They were drawn up in a single rank, advanced on the enemy, discharged their guns and turned away, to either reload or rearm at a safe distance. These tactics were soon supplanted – by the Spaniards and Germans, fighting in the Low Countries and northern France – by up to six or eight massed ranks of mixed gunmen and lancers. By the time of the Thirty Years War (1618-1648), the lance had all but disappeared and the carbine- and pistol-armed horsemen were employed, one rank after the other, to keep up a constant small-arms barrage against infantry formations. The size of such targets went a long way to make up for the inherent inaccuracy of the short-barrelled weapons of the day. From that time until the era of Frederick the Great (1712-1786), mounted troops were armed almost exclusively with guns; the *arme blanche* (sword or sabre) not taking over as the dominant cavalry weapon until the mid-eighteenth century. As the guns with

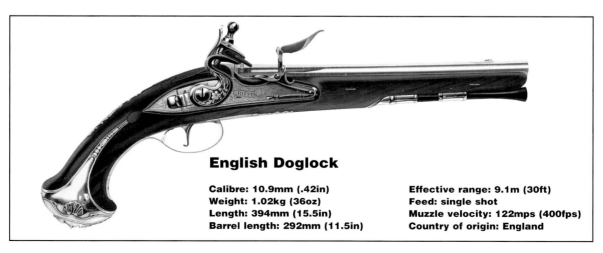

English Doglock

Calibre: 10.9mm (.42in)
Weight: 1.02kg (36oz)
Length: 394mm (15.5in)
Barrel length: 292mm (11.5in)

Effective range: 9.1m (30ft)
Feed: single shot
Muzzle velocity: 122mps (400fps)
Country of origin: England

which they were armed became more efficient and effective, so too did the cavalry formations themselves, but of course the same was true for the infantry against which they were pitted. Eventually, in the third quarter of the eighteenth century, new cavalry tactics evolved, which depended to a degree for their success on training, discipline and speed of execution. The sword (and the lance), deployed en masse and at speed, made a comeback, and played a major part in all the battles fought from then until the end of the next century.

Although by the mid-eighteenth century pistols were already losing much of what small military role they had ever had, the smooth-bore flintlock musket was going from strength to strength. It was becoming the only meaningful infantry weapon of the day, particularly when equipped with an effective removable bayonet. It was also being used as a flexible sporting and hunting arm.

The pistol's case should have been further retarded, if anything, by the poor quality of many of those produced. A poorly made handgun, perhaps more than anything, is likely to prove more of a danger to the person who uses it than to anyone else, and that was just as true in the eighteenth century as it is today. But there's no denying the equalising effect of firearms in combat, and that, far outweighing anything else, has been responsible for the popularity of the handgun down the ages. Cheap to produce, simple and straightforward to use and undoubtedly deadly at close quarters, the flintlock pistol was adequate proof of that, particularly since it could be made small enough to fit

comfortably into a coat pocket. Many individuals, particularly officers, were not slow to resort to them at need; indeed, soldiers and sailors often went to considerable lengths – and paid out large amounts of money – to equip themselves with something better than the standard service pistols provided by their governments. And even if handguns were finding decreasing favour with the military, they found a ready home in civilian hands at a time when law and order was a shaky concept at best. It is no exaggeration to suggest that any traveller out of town was at considerable risk, and that walking even the main streets of a busy city at night was fraught with danger. Any man of any means would have owned at least a brace of pistols as a matter of course, and would no more have gone unarmed outside his own home than he would have gone bare-headed.

THE QUEEN ANNE PISTOL

One popular form of pocket pistol of the eighteenth century seems, at first glance, to be a major innovation: a breech-loaded weapon long before they were commonly available. In fact the 'turn-off' or 'Queen Anne' pistols, with barrels which screwed off just in front of the chamber, were only halfway towards that desirable goal. The powder charge was still loaded from ahead of the action, though the ball, which was pressed into the breech end of the barrel as it was mated up with the lock again, could be said to have been breech-loaded. Nonetheless, turn-off pistols were consistently more accurate and hard-hitting than conventional muzzle-loaders for two reasons. First, the

projectiles they fired were a much closer fit in the barrel. Thanks to the need to ram them down having been removed, a ball of slightly over the nominal bore could be employed. Second, their propellant charge could be more accurately measured, more evenly compressed and better contained, the latter being one of the most important factors in improving the explosive performance of gunpowder.

BOX LOCKS

Turn-off pistols were not an eighteenth century invention; they had been around for some time – but their greater efficiency meant that small models, which would fit in a pocket, were as effective as much bigger, clumsier muzzle-loaders. These popular pistols were fitted with simplified actions known as box locks. Similar in concept and operation to the conventional side-mounted lock, the box lock's cock was centrally mounted between two sideplates. It required no intermediate tumbler, since the tail of the cock itself was notched to hold the trigger sear. The steel and pan had also to be centrally placed, and thus cock and steel intruded into the sight-line, precluding effective aiming. This was no drawback in pocket flintlock pistols, which were only roughly pointed, but the centre-line action didn't achieve wider acceptance until the introduction of percussion revolvers, with their hammers acting horizontally and thus able to be located much lower.

Muzzle-loaders, be they pistols or muskets, were still readied for firing by the old, cumbersome method, virtually unchanged for 300 years and more. The

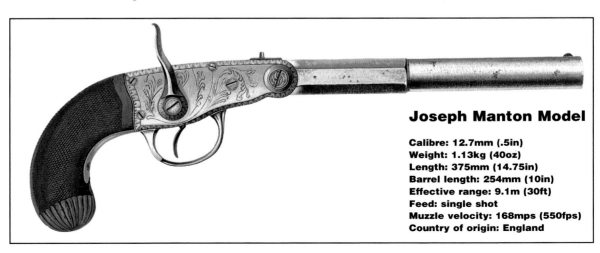

Joseph Manton Model

Calibre: 12.7mm (.5in)
Weight: 1.13kg (40oz)
Length: 375mm (14.75in)
Barrel length: 254mm (10in)
Effective range: 9.1m (30ft)
Feed: single shot
Muzzle velocity: 168mps (550fps)
Country of origin: England

user first had to pour a measured charge of powder down the barrel, normally one-and-a-half times the volume of the ball it was to propel. He then had to ram a wad of some sort down on top of it, often the remains of the paper 'cartridge' the charge came in. Next he rammed down the ball, often wrapped in an oiled linen patch where accuracy was a consideration. The cock was then pulled back to the safe half-cock position, exposing the pan. A small amount of rather better-quality powder was poured in from a separate flask or horn, and the cover and steel ensemble returned to battery (the firing position). The gun was now both ready to fire and safe, and all that remained was to pull the cock right back to its fullest extent and press the trigger. Much has been made of the length of time needed to load a flintlock arm, long or short. In actual fact, 15 or 20 seconds was quite sufficient (it took considerably longer to load a turn-off gun), and a trained soldier would certainly have attained that, and probably improved on it by a useful margin. The loading procedure followed for target guns, duelling pistols and the like was lengthier, with much greater care being exercised. Up to 15 seconds is a very long time in the face of a determined enemy, and a great deal of thought went

into producing weapons which had increased stopping power and a reduced requirement for the shooter to aim straight. Perhaps the most fearsome of those was the blunderbuss, which started life as a short-barrelled long arm (carbine) but soon became available in handgun form.

THE BLUNDERBUSS PISTOL

This was a heavy barrelled gun with a greater than usual bore which, instead of being parallel, opened out sharply at the muzzle. In fact, as modern-day tests have shown, the spread of shot fired from such a weapon has nothing whatsoever to do with the dimensions of its bell mouth, but rather with the size of the charge, the length of the barrel, the initial bore at the chamber and a steady increase in diameter all the way from chamber to muzzle. At best, all the exaggerated bell-mouthed muzzle of the early blunderbusses did was make the piece rather easier to load under difficult conditions. Later versions, with almost parallel bores, were certainly more effective. Another myth commonly attached to this fearsome though short-lived weapon was that it could function equally well with 'expedient' ammunition such as small pieces of scrap iron, nails,

broken glass, sharp gravel and the like. Doubtless there were cases of such loads being used in an emergency, but the weapon performed so much better when loaded with pistol balls or shot about the size of a pea that it would have been madness to have regularly charged it with anything else.

Another popular way to increase one's firepower was by means of multiple barrels. Over-and-under and side-by-side twin-barrelled pistols with one lock per barrel had been available for many years before the emergence of the flintlock, but now, with the considerable reduction in cost brought about by the new lock's relative simplicity, they became more common. Single-lock versions, with either a sliding block or a simple tap-like device to give access to one barrel at a time, or to both simultaneously, from a common supply of priming powder, also started to appear. These variations were sometimes combined, to produce four and even six-barrelled pistols. Twin and four-barrelled 'turnover' guns were notably popular in

■BELOW: A cavalry skirmish in the Thirty Years War. As well as being used in the mêlée, pistols were also employed by cavalry at this time to deliver volley fire against infantry.

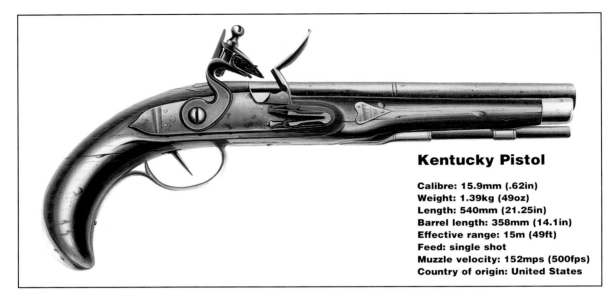

Kentucky Pistol

Calibre: 15.9mm (.62in)
Weight: 1.39kg (49oz)
Length: 540mm (21.25in)
Barrel length: 358mm (14.1in)
Effective range: 15m (49ft)
Feed: single shot
Muzzle velocity: 152mps (500fps)
Country of origin: United States

France and Holland. These had their barrels mounted on an axial pin and free to revolve, each with its own steel and priming pan. The user merely rotated the charged one into the firing position to replace one which had been discharged. Such weapons were the precursor of the 'pepperbox' revolvers.

A rather less obvious solution was to superimpose loads in the gun's single barrel and fire them in succession, either by means of multiple locks or by one rearwards-sliding lock. This technique relied on the ball of any subsequent load acting as a barrier and preventing premature ignition by flash-over from the first firing. Examples exist from as early as the sixteenth century (Glasgow Art Gallery has a German three-shot wheel-lock pistol dating from that time), though such flintlock versions as have survived, with a few notable exceptions, are usually sporting long arms. And to increase firepower further, superimposed guns also existed in multi-barrel versions.

EARLY REVOLVERS

Multi-chambered single-barrel guns were also available in the seventeenth and eighteenth centuries, although they were seldom regarded as anything but oddities. There exists a drawing, for example, of a German 10-shot revolver matchlock, dating from the first quarter of the sixteenth century, though sadly the gun itself has disappeared. And the British Royal Armoury boasts a seven-shot revolver wheel-lock carbine, circa

1620, and a similar model can be found in the *Musée de l'Armée* in Paris. There are also surviving examples of snaphance revolver pistols, the earliest of which is in the Tower of London. Dated at about 1680, it is attributed to London gunmaker John Dafte. Dafte's revolver, though it excited little more than curiosity at the time, was eventually to prove a very significant gun indeed.

The British Royal collection also houses two fine four-shot revolver flintlock muskets, but the principle, while

not fatally flawed, was never widely applied to the design of pistols. Their manufacture was technically demanding, and the result cumbersome and sometimes unreliable, as can be seen from the few examples which have survived. It wasn't until the very end of the flintlock era, in the early nineteenth century, that satisfactory revolvers were produced, such as those made in London by Evans to the design of a Bostonian engineer, Elisha Collier, who had in turn appropriated it from Artemus Wheeler of

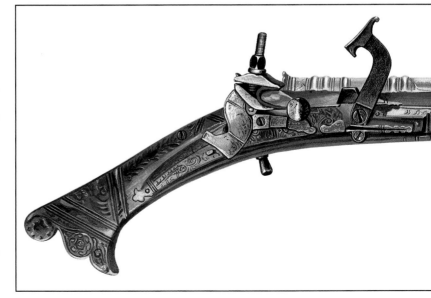

Concord. And it was not until the percussion cap had solved the problem of how to keep the priming powder to hand safely that the revolver found any real favour. Flintlock 'pepperbox' revolvers were short-lived oddities. These were pistols with a concentrically-mounted array of barrels arranged to step-rotate around either a longitudinal axial pin or another barrel, each with its own chamber and priming pan. If there was a centre barrel, it was fired along with one of the others. The pepperbox design proved of considerably greater, though short-lived, interest only after the invention of the percussion cap.

LORENZONI'S REPEATING PISTOL

Another ingenious system saw powder and projectiles stored in separate magazines, usually found within the butt. It never achieved public acclaim, but proved sufficiently interesting for some eminent seventeenth century gunmakers (notably H.W. Mortimer, one of the best of the day and noted for his duelling pistols) to experiment with it. The long arm versions, most often based on a system designed by Peter Kalthoff in Denmark, were made in both wheel-lock and flintlock versions. They frequently had rifled barrels, and are of as much interest for their being breech-loaders as they are for being repeaters. Many gunsmiths were searching diligently for a breech-loading system which worked, since loading a rifled gun via the muzzle was

not an easy or quick procedure. Pistols were rarely the subject of such experiment, but many and varied were the attempts made to perfect the breech-loading flintlock rifle. The Kalthoff guns were very complex indeed, and prone to failure as a result.

The best known repeater pistols of this type used the much simpler Lorenzoni system, said to have been devised by Michele Lorenzoni in Florence in the mid-seventeenth century. There were two compartments in the butt, one containing powder and the other balls, which were connected to the breech via a rotating block. With the gun held muzzle-down this breech-block, turned through 90 degrees, admitted one ball and a measure of powder; turned back, it transferred them successively to the breech. A smaller second powder magazine charged the priming pan when the block was counter-rotated (this action also returned the steel to battery and brought the piece to full-cock).

THE ROYAL NAVY'S VOLLEY GUNS

More commonplace than the early repeaters were so-called volley guns, though the term is relative; they were never widespread. These had multiple barrels which fired simultaneously, and the most successful of these were carbines, such as the version with seven concentric barrels which James Wilson designed and Henry Nock manufactured in 1780 for Britain's Royal Navy. But

there were volley firing pistols, too, such as the 'duckfoot' guns with their horizontal array of four barrels splaying out like the fingers of an outstretched hand from a common lock and priming pan. Nock's gun was withdrawn from service when it became apparent that, at £15 each when a sea service musket cost £2, it was far from cost effective. It was also widely rumoured that the real reason for its disappearance was that few men could survive firing it with their shoulder and collarbone intact; the effect on anyone firing a duckfoot pistol must have been equally shattering, though there is no doubt that either was stunningly effective at close quarters.

The volley gun, be it single-barrelled, like the blunderbuss, or multi-barrelled, was perhaps the best 'equaliser' of them all, since it removed even the need to aim the gun accurately. However, during the period of the flintlock's currency another lethal way of deploying firearms came into vogue: duelling.

DUELLING PISTOLS

For centuries the duel had been only a slightly formalised alternative to a fight to the death with whatever weapons happened to come to hand. The introduction of firearms was eventually to have the effect of turning such encounters into the most macabre form of performance art imaginable. Where previously, a would-be duellist would have been advised to measure the extent of an opponent's skill-at-arms before deciding whether to issue a challenge, now all that was required for a sporting chance of success was nerve and a gun which shot straight and 'pointed' naturally. (By way of a simple test, point your finger at an object not in your direct line of sight; now 'sight' down your finger. Achieving that same degree of accuracy when holding a pistol is by no means as straightforward, and whether or not a gun 'points' naturally and accurately depends largely on its balance.)

Pistols began to take over from swords as the duellists' weapon of choice as early on as the late seventeenth century. Over the course of the next 100 years the demand for more reliably accurate pistols, from gentlemen determined to settle their differences by this means, grew. Specialist gunmakers began to turn out better-quality 'holster pistols' in response. By about 1780 the transition was complete, and the first pistols made for duelling and no other purpose made

Dutch Snaphance

Calibre: 17.1mm (.675in)
Weight: 1.67kg (59oz)
Length: 400mm (15.75in)
Barrel length: 208mm (8.2in)
Effective range: 15m (49ft)
Feed: single shot
Muzzle velocity: 137mps (450fps)
Country of origin: Netherlands

their appearance, though it is no simple matter to tell a true duelling pistol from a weapon made for wider use purely by sight alone. The first and best indication is the level of decoration: true duelling pistols had little or none, their makers concentrating instead on fine workmanship where it really mattered. Chequering was often applied to the grip to help prevent a sweating hand from slipping, while the barrel was worked to so fine a tolerance that there was not a degree of divergence between the line of pointing and the flight of the projectile. Most duelling pistols came complete with a ball cast and finished to match it absolutely. The main point of distinction between pistols produced on different sides of the English Channel was in the barrel. English custom was for smooth-bore pistols, the French for rifling. Those few Englishmen who held that rifling produced a truer flight, but who wanted to appear to hold to tradition, went to master gunmaker Joseph Manton, who had perfected a 'blind' rifling system which stopped some 50mm (2in) before the muzzle's mouth, and was undetectable except by serious expert investigation.

FINE BALANCE

In fact, there was no real improvement in accuracy to be achieved over the distance in question by rifling the barrel. A duelling weapon would also have an adjustable trigger mechanism set up so that a pressure of mere ounces would release it; priming pans and touch-holes lined with gold or platinum to reduce the chances of corrosion and a resultant misfire; trigger-guard spurs, to allow the

second finger a steadying role, and 'saw-handle' grips with thumb-spurs to assist in keeping the muzzle down. But the crucial feature was an overall balance so judged that the pistol was nothing less than an extension of the hand and arm, and one which 'pointed' as effortlessly and accurately as one's finger, for this deadly game allowed no time for the deliberate taking of aim.

NOTABLE DUELS

The code duello was slowly refined in a process which rather paralleled the development of the pistols most commonly used for such affairs. By the end of the seventeenth century, sword duels had turned into organised gangfights, the two antagonists' seconds being expected to join in. Eventually the duel fell out of favour in both France and Italy thanks to the severe punishment handed out to anyone caught duelling. The practice flared up again briefly during and just after the French Revolution, then gathered momentum as the pistol replaced the sword.

By that time the British had also come to embrace the practice, and it crept back into popularity, particularly among army officers. This was despite the draconian penalties it attracted: Major Campbell killed his man, Captain Boyd, in 1808, and was hanged for it; a duel fought between two officers in 1813, in which Lieutenant Blundell was killed, resulted in not just his opponent but both the seconds being found guilty of murder and sentenced to death, although they were later reprieved. Nonetheless, there were very few prominent British politicians and members of society who did not 'go

out' at least once in the course of their lives. Even the Duke of Wellington, who was an outspoken opponent of the practice, and did much to expunge it from the Army, himself fought the Earl of Winchelsea in 1829. A list of the names of other participants is straight out of *Who's Who*. William Adam and Charles James Fox fought in earnest after metaphorically crossing swords during a Parliamentary debate, and other politicians found themselves in the same circumstances: William Pitt faced George Tierny; Lord Castlereagh faced George Canning; and Sir Francis Burdett fought James Paull, to name but a few.

AMERICAN DUELLISTS

By the 1840s, the situation was verging on the absurd again. Curiously, the British military code still authorised duelling, and it took two prominent affairs to get the situation changed. The Earl of Cardigan shot and killed Captain Harvey Tucker on 12 September 1840, was tried for murder in the House of Lords and was acquitted. On 1 July 1843, Lieutenant Alexander Munro killed (most reluctantly, it is reported) his brother-in-law, Colonel David Fawcett. This latter affair, in particular, attracted considerable public attention and led to the Queen 'conveying her desire for reform'. A change to the Articles the following year made duelling a military offence, but didn't succeed in halting the practice altogether – committed duellists met in Boulogne or Calais instead.

Though the War of Independence had succeeded in separating America from the mother country, there was still a great deal of European influence to be felt,

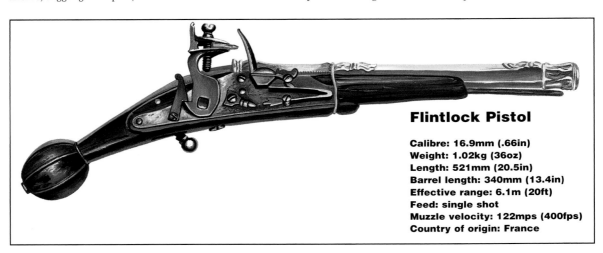

Flintlock Pistol

Calibre: 16.9mm (.66in)
Weight: 1.02kg (36oz)
Length: 521mm (20.5in)
Barrel length: 340mm (13.4in)
Effective range: 6.1m (20ft)
Feed: single shot
Muzzle velocity: 122mps (400fps)
Country of origin: France

particularly in Washington. So, not surprisingly, there were duels between prominent men fought here, too. On 30 May 1806, Andrew Jackson – who was to become the seventh President of the United States – fought Charles Dickinson in Logan County, Kentucky, after the two had argued about a gambling debt. Dickinson fired first, and hit Jackson in the chest, but thanks to a heavy coat the latter was wearing, much of the force of the .70-calibre ball was spent, and he was only wounded. Displaying considerable phlegm, Jackson straightened up, took aim and despatched his opponent. Two years earlier, on 12 July 1804, on the banks of the Hudson River at Weehawken, New Jersey, Aaron Burr killed Alexander Hamilton in an affair which had overtones of deliberate homicide. Hamilton had certainly done all he could to damage the political career of a man whom he believed wished to subvert the republican system; he helped Jefferson to beat him to the presidency in 1800, and was largely responsible for him being denied the governorship of New York four years later. This was too much for Burr, who settled on Hamilton's accusation that he was a traitor to his country as reason to call him out. When the two met it is clear that Hamilton did so very reluctantly: not out of fear but out of distaste for the

■RIGHT: The American naval hero John Paul Jones shoots one of his sailors who had attempted to strike the colours. Even eighteenth-century flintlocks were accurate at this range!

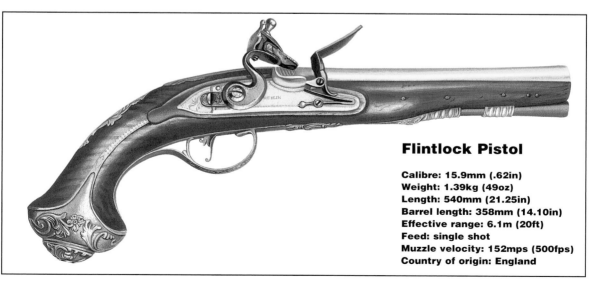

Flintlock Pistol

Calibre: 15.9mm (.62in)
Weight: 1.39kg (49oz)
Length: 540mm (21.25in)
Barrel length: 358mm (14.10in)
Effective range: 6.1m (20ft)
Feed: single shot
Muzzle velocity: 152mps (500fps)
Country of origin: England

Flintlock Pistol

Calibre: 15.9mm (.62in)
Weight: 1.42kg (50oz)
Length: 552mm (21.75in)
Barrel length: 368mm (14.48in)

Effective range: 6.1m (20ft)
Feed: single shot
Muzzle velocity: 152mps (500fps)
Country of origin: United States

entire practice; it had cost the life of his son, Philip, three years previously. Hamilton announced to his second that he would not take aim at Burr, but would fire in the air. This he did, but Burr was made of different stuff; he took careful aim and shot his adversary dead.

FRENCH DUELS

If duelling was rife in the English-speaking world, it was endemic in the French, and got more prevalent, particularly between politicians, as the nineteenth century progressed. Napoleon is known to have been against duelling, and said that a man skilled in it was apt to make a bad soldier, but nonetheless it persisted; the Code Civile of 1810 made no mention of it. Léon Gambetta, one of the most influential men of his time, met the French ex-minister of the interior, F.O. Bardy de Fourtou in 1878, and General Georges Boulanger, until lately minister of war, was wounded when he 'went out' against Charles Floquet, president of the chamber of deputies, in 1888. Gambetta died in 1882 from the result of 'an accidental wound in the hand from a revolver', while Boulanger shot himself with a pistol in 1891, continuing the thread which links the use of handguns with death by them. And though the practice was almost entirely confined to men, French ladies sometimes felt themselves so wounded by a rival's insults that only a challenge to a shooting match would satisfy their honour. Thus did two women whose names have not survived the passing of time meet at Bordeaux in 1868. The victrix (by virtue of wounding her rival in the thigh) was sent to prison for 15 days, to prompt her to mend her ways. No such inconvenience threatened the Princess Pauline

Metternich or the Grafine Kilmannsegg, when they met in the Grand Duchy of Lichtenstien in 1892, though on this occasion no blood was drawn.

As to the duel itself, there were no hard and fast rules, though there was most certainly a structure or framework within which the combat had to take place. Details were usually worked out beforehand, usually between the two parties' seconds. The object was to produce 'a level playing field', on which neither man had an unfair advantage, and at the same time to introduce enough of an element of skill to avoid charges of murder should all go for the best (or worst). In all truth, there seems little reason for committed antagonists not simply to have stood toe-to-toe with a pistol at each other's head or breast and for each to have pulled the trigger on a given signal – and there is little doubt that just that scenario, or one very much like it, was also enacted from time to time. Most frequently, however, the two men faced each other at a distance of 10 to 15 paces, each one half-turned away so as to present the slimmest profile, stomach drawn in and pistol arm shielding as much of the chest as possible (which led to the bent-arm position favoured by the best pistol shots of the day). The hand and the pistol held in it pointed at the sky or down at the ground. On a given signal – a dropped handkerchief, perhaps – the men would level their pistols, take aim and fire. Speed was of the essence, and thus the need for the pistol one used to 'point' naturally and accurately. Lethal though the practice was designed to be, it wasn't necessary to kill, or even wound an opponent; having gone out against him was quite enough to satisfy honour. There

are many examples of men like Alexander Hamilton, who deliberately fired wide of the mark, but if for every Hamilton there wasn't a Burr, there were certainly enough like-minded men to make such a practice very dangerous.

We need not linger over the standard military issue flintlock pistol of the eighteenth century, largely because none of them qualified to be called 'great'. Indeed, the genre only has a role in the broader field of military history at all as an example of how the early application of an incomplete theory of mass production resulted in a general lowering of standards. Only one aspect of this premature attempt to bring an element of uniformity to military hardware had a widely beneficial outcome, and that was the standardisation of the size of projectiles, a most important factor in battle-readiness. For previously, each individual soldier had to cast his own bullets, and those cast for one gun might well not fit another.

CALIBRES AND BORES

The contemporary method of describing a weapon's calibre used a system which bears no direct relationship to the dimensions of a gun's bore. It can be somewhat confusing since it seems to work in reverse: the number of the bore ('gauge' in the USA) increases as the real diameter of the barrel decreases. The nominal bore is in fact the number of true spherical balls of given diameter which could be cast from 0.45kg (1lb) of pure lead. Thus, a 20 bore gun fired a ball weighing 23gm (.8oz) and 15.6mm (.6in) in nominal diameter. A ball of 120 bore with a weight 3.7gm (.1oz) and diameter 8.1mm (.3in) was widely held to be the smallest ball with any sort of stopping power, and most military small arms fell somewhere between 12 and 24 bore. Firearms intended for civilian use soon came to accept these standard calibres, too, if only so that shooters could use 'army surplus' ammunition. The same measuring system is still used today to classify shotguns.

THE SLIPPING OF STANDARDS

The principle of standardisation went further than this, and in theory at least, all British pistols for example, of a given model had interchangeable components. The drawback to this predecessor of mass-production was the poor overall quality of workmanship, which acted as a lowest common denominator and resulted in the production of a vast number of not very good guns. As time went on, manufacturing methods improved and so did quality control, and individual weapons achieved a much higher standard as a result.

It was not until the coming of the era of the machine tool in the mid-nineteenth century that mass-produced guns even approached the quality attained by the

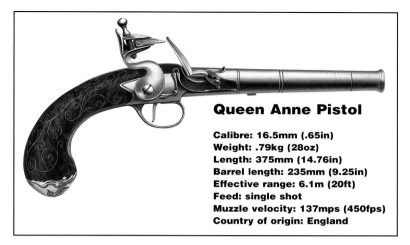

Queen Anne Pistol

Calibre: 16.5mm (.65in)
Weight: .79kg (28oz)
Length: 375mm (14.76in)
Barrel length: 235mm (9.25in)
Effective range: 6.1m (20ft)
Feed: single shot
Muzzle velocity: 137mps (450fps)
Country of origin: England

craftsman-gunsmiths of the eighteenth century. At their best, the guns of the seventeenth and eighteenth centuries were not only things of considerable beauty, but were practical, effective weapons, capable of hitting what they were aimed at more often than not. The phrase 'more often than not' is

■BELOW: The capture of the pirate Blackbeard in 1718, a rather fanciful interpretation, but one that indicates combatants had to get as close as possible with flintlock pistols. Their range was so limited that discharge was pointless, 'till you feel your antagonist's ribs with the muzzle'.

Blunderbuss Pistol

Calibre: 16.5mm (.65in)
Weight: 1.3kg (46oz)
Length: 444mm (17.49in)
Barrel length: 229mm (9in)
Effective range: 3m (10ft)
Feed: buckshot
Muzzle velocity: 152mps (500fps)
Country of origin: England

significant. Though they improved almost out of all recognition over the hundreds of years they were current, both in design and in execution, all flint-and-steel guns were lamentably unreliable. They were hit-or-miss affairs, and their failure to work meant at best a missed duck or pheasant, at worst an untimely death.

FRAILTIES OF THE FLINTLOCK

In order for a flintlock arm to function properly, a complex set of conditions had to be met. First, the flint had to be properly shaped and positioned, which usually meant a new stone had to be fitted after every 30 to 50 rounds had been fired. Second, the steel had to be kept clean and properly tempered, and its serrations sharp; another operation which had to be carried out periodically, and one which normally involved a visit to the gunsmith. Third, the pan and touch-hole had to be kept free of carbon deposits and corrosion. Fourth, the gunpowder in the pan and in the chamber had to be kept dry and the

mixture properly homogenous. This latter problem had largely been solved as early as the sixteenth century by the introduction of 'corned' or 'mealed' powder, which consisted of made-up granules composed of the whole saltpetre/carbon/sulphur mixture in the right proportions.

The chain of disparate operations leading to the projectile leaving the muzzle caused its own problems. When pulled, the trigger released the sear, which in turn released the cock, either directly or via a tumbler. Propelled by a spring, the cock travelled forwards through about an eighth of a turn before the flint clamped in its jaws hit the steel, striking sparks off it as it continued its downwards journey. At the same time the flint pushed the steel and the priming pan cover connected to it, forwards out of the way, overcoming the pressure of another spring and opening the pan itself to expose the priming charge. The shower of sparks from the action of flint against steel, which have a measurable, though short, life, fell upon this charge, igniting it (if it were perfectly dry). This caused the propellant charge proper, exposed to the flash via the touch-hole, to ignite in turn (pre-supposing that it, too, was perfectly dry). Contained by the chamber and the projectile, this ignition resulted

Pocket Pistol

Calibre: 12.7mm (.5in)
Weight: .34kg (12oz)
Length: 168mm (6.62in)
Barrel length: 76mm (3in)
Effective range: 1.5m (5ft)
Feed: single shot
Muzzle velocity: 107mps (350fps)
Country of origin: United States

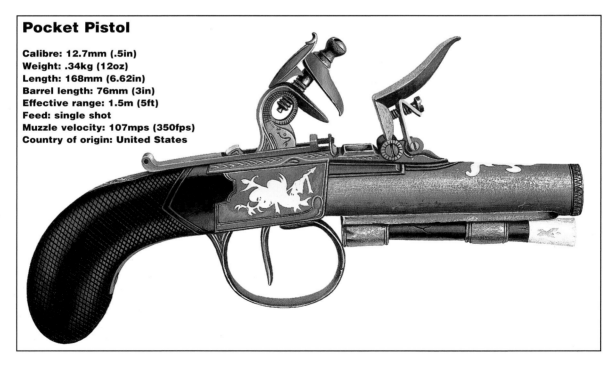

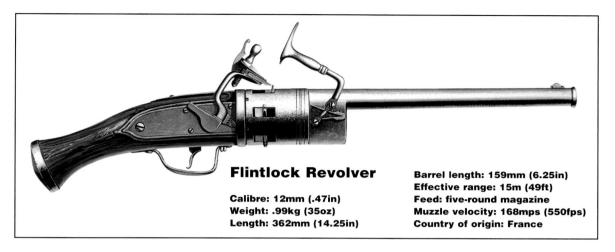

Flintlock Revolver

Calibre: 12mm (.47in)
Weight: .99kg (35oz)
Length: 362mm (14.25in)

Barrel length: 159mm (6.25in)
Effective range: 15m (49ft)
Feed: five-round magazine
Muzzle velocity: 168mps (550fps)
Country of origin: France

in an explosion and a sudden, though not quite instantaneous, release of copious quantities of gas. This gas promptly obeyed Boyle's Law and took the route of least resistance, which was to propel the projectile up and out of the barrel.

SEARCH FOR NEW PROPELLENTS

Modern experience with flintlock weapons – and they have an enthusiastic following, particularly in the United States – shows that in a good-quality gun in pristine condition, the action of pulling the trigger and the gun discharging will seem as one. This assumes that every one of the set of conditions described above is met absolutely. Naturally enough, that was very often not the case at all. In the field, improperly maintained and in less than expert hands (just the sort of conditions under which a weapon of war, in particular, was most likely to be used), the eighteenth century gun was a fallible piece. In a soldier's hands it would fire on average seven times out of 10. Even if it did fire successfully, there was often a noticeable delay between the cock falling and the discharge taking place; during that delay the gunman often faltered and allowed his weapon to drift away from the point of aim or, worse still, an animate target, seeing the spark, could actually get out of the line of fire.

Historical tradition has it that it was frustration at thus being eluded – by wildfowl – which led a Scots clergyman, Alexander John Forsyth, to reflect upon the nature of the gun's operation. Forsyth, a widely read man of catholic interests, among them both chemistry and mechanics, knew of the existence of a set of unstable explosive salts known as

fulminates, obtained by dissolving metals in acids. Fulminate of gold, for example, is mentioned in Samuel Pepys' diary of 11 November 1663. Fulminate of silver, so volatile that 'when it has been once obtained it can no longer be touched' was produced by the French chemist Claude Louis Berthollet in 1788, two years after he had synthesised potassium chlorate and shown how it could be used as a substitute for saltpetre in gunpowder. Following Edward Howard's fabrication of the more docile fulminate of mercury in 1800, Forsyth began to experiment with it and with potassium chlorate, hoping, it seems, to produce a new faster-acting and self-detonating propellant to supplant gunpowder.

FORSYTH'S INVENTION

These early experiments came to nothing, and Forsyth turned to the notion of using the mixture as priming, rather than propellant, still without much success. While a spark would set it off, there was no certainty that it would ignite the main charge, and the new mixture proved inferior in this respect to fine gunpowder. However, it would detonate when struck a direct blow, which gunpowder will not, and Forsyth's good fortune was to realise that this property, previously seen as one of the fulminates' biggest drawbacks, was in fact the key to their usefulness. After experimenting with a simple iron tube, he produced a gun action with a hammer in place of the flintlock's cock and replaced the priming pan with a small dispenser, in shape and operation much like a perfume flask. When tipped up, this flask fed a measured quantity of powdered fulminate directly into the touchhole and onto an

enclosed 'anvil' adjacent to it.

Forsyth used a gun fitted with his new 'lock' against wildfowl throughout the winter of 1805, and the following year demonstrated it in London to Lord Moira, Master General of Ordnance. Moira was sufficiently impressed to invite Forsyth to set up a workshop within the Royal Armoury in the Tower of London, but before the Scot could produce a perfected version of his invention, Moira was replaced by John Pitt, 2nd Earl of Chatham and Prime Minster William Pitt the Younger's brother. Pitt, fearful that the fulminate Forsyth was working with would cause a massive explosion, immediately ordered him 'to take himself and all his rubbish from the Tower'. Forsyth returned home greatly displeased, but soon ventured out again, in order to consult his friend, James Watt, on how to word an application for letters to patent and protect his invention from commercial piracy in the widest possible way. The patent, Number 3032, for igniting a charge of gunpowder by a revolutionary means, was granted on 11 April 1807. It would seem that Watt's advice was valuable, for Forsyth did have to fight off would-be pirates and did so successfully.

Though he remained a practising cleric until he died in 1843, Forsyth was not unwilling to enter into commerce. In 1808, with a *locum tenens* installed in his Scottish living, he set up in business at 10 Piccadilly, in London's newly created 'West End', with one James Purdey, lately apprenticed to Joseph Manton, as his assistant. They produced 'scent-bottle' locks and a later 'sliding magazine' lock which performed the same function in a rather more efficient manner, suitable for

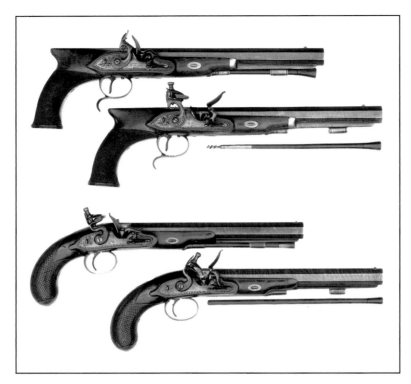

■LEFT: Nineteenth-century duelling pistols, which almost invariably came in pairs. The top pair are Mortimer duelling guns, while those underneath are Joseph Manton models.

both pistols and long arms. He remained there until 1819, subsequently returning to his parochial duties while Purdey continued work on his behalf. He also licensed other gunmakers to produce the patent lock; Innes of Edinburgh was one. After Forsyth's death, Purdey struck out on his own and became famous in his own right. The shotguns his family firm still produces by the old methods are widely held to be the best in the world, and are the most sought-after.

Many gunmakers purchased locks from Forsyth and his licensees and used them to convert otherwise-sound flintlock weapons to the new system, but the Scot made no attempt to improve on the means of delivering the detonating

■BELOW: A typical nineteenth-century duel. Duelling pistols had barrels worked to fine tolerances to ensure total accurancy with the first, and only, shot.

fulminate to the breech. A particular problem was that the fulminate was very corrosive, and the use of it in powder form necessitated regular cleaning of the lock. Some means of enclosing it was also needed. Improvements were left to others, and soon a variety of new methods were on offer. Patch primers had a quantity of fulminate enclosed between two sheets of paper to be stuck to the nose of the hammer and exploded against a hollow tube or nipple at the breech. Tape locks used fulminate charges which were enclosed between two strips of stiff paper and fed as a tape between hammer and nipple. Pill locks used minute quantities of fulminate made up into tiny pellets by the addition of a little gum arabic, which were inserted into a recess at the top of the touch-hole and struck by a sharp point on the hammer's nose. Tube locks, as devised by Joseph Manton in 1818 and improved by William Westley Richards in 1831, made use of short tubes of soft metal, filled with fulminate, crimped at each end and inserted into the touch-hole itself with one end slightly protruding and resting upon the anvil.

THE PERCUSSION CAP
Best of all was the percussion 'cap', so named because it was shaped to fit over a nipple similar to that found in a patch or tape lock. There are a number of claimants to the title of inventor of the percussion cap. Some of the more likely candidates include sporting writer Colonel Peter Hawker, gunmakers Joseph Egg, James Purdey and Joseph Manton in London, a French plagiarist named Prélat in Paris, and an English emigrant to the USA, the artist Joshua Shaw. Shaw obtained a patent for the percussion cap in the USA in 1822, but always maintained that he had actually perfected the invention some five years earlier. His claim is widely accepted and, if true, marks the first time an important step forward in the state of the gunmaker's art was made outside Europe, and the first of many to be made in the United States. Shaw's original caps were made of steel, but he quickly switched first to pewter and then to copper. It was soon clear that the percussion cap was a notable improvement over other percussion systems and, save for Maynard's 1854 tape primer system, few examples of the others have survived.

It was equally clear that the percussion system solved all the problems flintlocks were heir to. The new system was embraced by sportsmen and other gun owners throughout Europe and the United States with growing enthusiasm through the 1820s and 1830s. The military establishment was slower to accept the innovation, and it was the middle of the nineteenth century before flintlock smooth-bore, muzzle-loading weapons gave way to percussion muzzle-loaders. The Prussian Army was the first to adopt percussion arms generally, in 1839, one year before the Swedes. Both the British and United States Armies switched over to percussion weapons in 1842. Such tardiness meant that military percussion muzzle-loaders had a brief life, as within 20 years effective metal composite cartridges had made breech-loading a practical proposition.

THE TAPE PRIMER SYSTEM
The US Government switched from percussion caps to Maynard's tape primer system in 1855, and employed it in a heavy pistol-carbine (with a detachable shoulder stock) and a musket, both manufactured at the Springfield Armory in considerable quantities. It was also used in converted Model 1842 percussion cap muskets. By 1861 these guns had been superseded, the tape primer system proving unreliable in wet weather. Maynard – a Washington dentist – received $60,000 from the US Government for his invention, while Shaw, by a special Act of Congress 'For the Relief of Joshua Shaw', got $18,000. In contrast, Forsyth received only a nominal payment from his government, and most of it posthumously.

Civilians and individual military officers who still relied on pistols for self-defence had no such reticence in adopting

Duckfoot Pistol

Calibre: 15.9mm (.62in)
Weight: 1.2kg (42.3oz)
Length: 254mm (10in)
Barrel length: 127mm (5in)

Effective range: 6.1m (20ft)
Feed: single shot, four barrels
Muzzle velocity: 152mps (500fps)
Country of origin: England

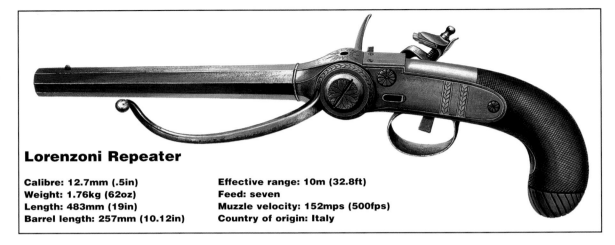

Lorenzoni Repeater

Calibre: 12.7mm (.5in)
Weight: 1.76kg (62oz)
Length: 483mm (19in)
Barrel length: 257mm (10.12in)

Effective range: 10m (32.8ft)
Feed: seven
Muzzle velocity: 152mps (500fps)
Country of origin: Italy

Shaw's percussion system, even if it could still be said to be untried. Gunsmiths were inundated, both with requests to convert still-usable flintlock pistols to percussion operation, and with orders for new guns. Converting a flintlock was not a difficult task. A hammer replaced the cock, and a nipple the priming pan; the only other modification involved the

■BELOW: Pistol designs in the nineteenth century. A pair of double-barrelled holster pistols (left), a four-barrelled turnover pistol (top right) and an over-and-under pistol (bottom right).

removal of the spring which positioned the frizzen and pan cover and those two components themselves. The sear and tumbler which had connected the trigger with the cock functioned perfectly in tripping the hammer. The new simplified action, which solved once and for all the problem of containing the priming powder within the pan, meant that pocket pistols lost much of their clumsiness. In particular the smaller, more streamlined hammer having replaced the cock, they were easier to take out without their catching in one's clothing, while single-lock turnover

pistols and 'pepperboxes' suddenly became much more reliable and practical.

The pistol was still losing ground as a weapon of war, though. Such was the strength of feeling against it in the British Army that when, in 1837, a further attempt to standardise calibre was made, no less a personage than the Duke of Wellington himself suggested that this was a good time to withdraw these 'ineffectual weapons' from service. Pistols were actually abolished as cavalry armament the following year, though officers still carried them, and lancers were allowed to retain them.

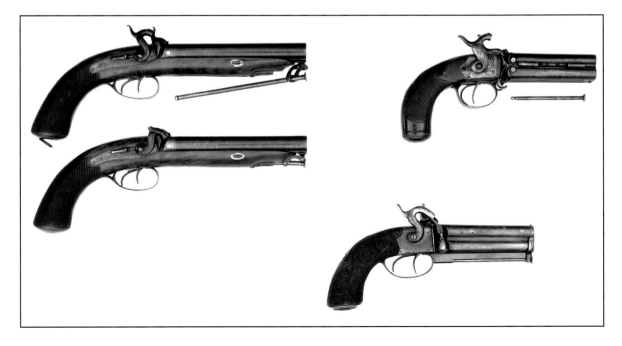

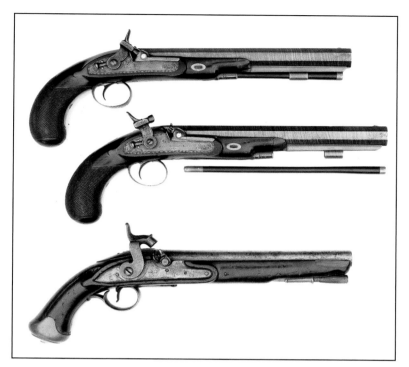

■LEFT: Three nineteenth-century pistols utilising the percussion cap firing system. John Manton models (top and middle) and a converted flintlock pistol (bottom).

designs were evolved in one or the other of them, until the Harper's Ferry Armory was destroyed in 1861, never to be rebuilt. Even so, a number of civilian gunmakers received contracts to manufacture the new pistols, including Henry Aston, who made over 30,000 between 1846 and 1850 at a cost of $6.50 each. Among these gunmakers one who was unwittingly to give his name to a whole class of small pocket pistols: Henry Deringer of Philadelphia, who had been making both smoothbore and rifled pistols since 1806.

BARREL MANUFACTURE

Aston's achievement demonstrates very clearly how wholeheartedly and rapidly American manufacturing industry – and the armaments industry in particular – had adopted machine tools and the twin concepts of mass production and interchangeability of parts. 'Industrial' gunmakers such as Ames, Aston, Simeon North (who had won the first US Government contract to manufacture pistols, in 1799, and who was to produce an estimated 100,000 guns for the US Army and Navy before his death in 1852), Eli Whitney (Senior and Junior), Samuel Colt, Elisha King Root, Francis Pratt, Amos Whitney, Charles Billings and Christopher Spencer, are now recognised as pioneers in the wider field of production engineering.

The development of machine tools such as lathes, profile cutters, multiple-spindle drills and vertical and horizontal milling machines made the mass-market arms industry possible. And the inexorable pressure from that greedy industry, along with such diverse interests as agricultural implement makers and manufacturers of sewing machines and other textile-related machinery, impelled the machine tool industry itself. Thus, the modern-day United States of America can be said to have been created by the gun. British and European gunmakers (and their engineering industries in general) failed to follow the American lead and clung to out-dated 'craft' practices. This, basically, was the cause of industrial dominance passing across the Atlantic from Great Britain, the cradle of the Industrial Revolution.

George Lovell, who had suggested the new attempt at calibre standardisation, and who supported Wellington's proposal, became Inspector of Small Arms in 1840. Lovell was subsequently responsible, paradoxically, for producing the best pistols the British Army and the Royal Navy (not to mention police forces up and down the country) had been given up until that time. He was also largely responsible for the switch from smooth-bore to rifled pistols in the mid-1850s, by which time a successful derivative of the Minié bullet had been accepted. The Minié was a slightly under-calibre conical 'round' with a hollow base, within which was located a small iron cup. The first result of the explosion of the propellant charge was to push the cup into the hollow, causing the skirt of the bullet to expand and grip the barrel's rifling grooves, although it was later determined that the iron 'expander' was redundant. Lovell went on to design other pistols and had an influence on the far side of the Atlantic, too, where the firearms industry was just getting into its stride.

The United States Government's attitude toward the acceptance of percussion cap arms was not dissimilar from the conservatism displayed in London. The Pattern 1832 pistol was the last smooth-bore flintlock to be accepted for service, its successor being the Model 1842 Navy percussion pistol calibre. Designed by Nathan Peabody Ames, this pistol also owed much to Lovell, particularly its back-action lock and enclosed hammer, a feature the British master had unashamedly 'borrowed' from Henry Nock. There was also a conventional exposed-hammer model, in the same calibre but with a longer barrel, adopted that year for the US Army. Apart from their locks, both pistols were much closer to contemporary French and German designs, with their half-stock and securing brass barrel band. British practice was to fix the stock to the barrel by means of pins or a screwed-through lug. The first official US Government pistol, the Model 1799 flintlock, had been a direct copy of a French design of 1777, and that had set the pattern.

AMERICAN WEAPON PRODUCERS

Much of the US Government's need for arms was being supplied from the national armories at Springfield, on the Connecticut River, and Harper's Ferry, on the Potomac. These were established as early as 1794, and the first pistol made in a Government armory was the Model 1805, produced at Harper's Ferry. New

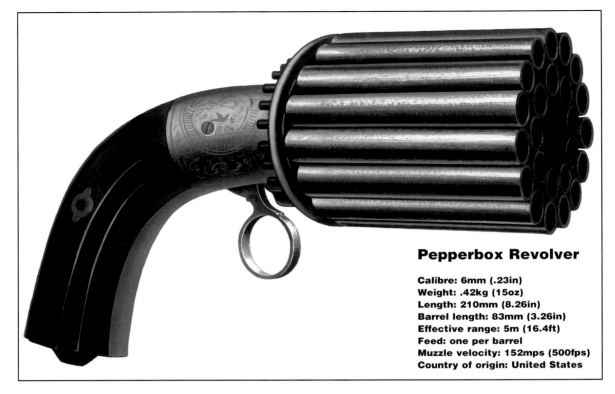

Pepperbox Revolver

Calibre: 6mm (.23in)
Weight: .42kg (15oz)
Length: 210mm (8.26in)
Barrel length: 83mm (3.26in)
Effective range: 5m (16.4ft)
Feed: one per barrel
Muzzle velocity: 152mps (500fps)
Country of origin: United States

One of the farthest-reaching changes in working practice caused by the coming of industrialisation to gunmaking concerned the manufacture of barrels. It had become clear very early on in the gun's history that simple castings were not good enough for small arms. Similar methods to those employed to forge the finest sword blades came into use to work the iron used to make gun barrels. Soft, malleable iron, often in rod form, was gathered into bundles called faggots, and was heated and twisted, beaten and turned back upon itself. The process would be repeated as many as three dozen times before the resulting strip, now consisting of thousands of strata welded into an homogenous whole, was wound round a mandrel in a spiral and welded by hand into a seamless tube. The iron for handmade gun barrels often came from waste and scrap metal, since the more times it had been worked over, the less impurity would remain. Old horseshoes and horseshoe nails were particularly prized, as was scrap steel from spring and bayonet makers. Where composites of iron and steel were used, the careful application of etching acid to the finished barrel brought out the

characteristic 'damascene' pattern thus created, a common feature of the finest guns of the day and often falsely created by the unscrupulous to seduce the unwary. The first stage of industrialisation saw machine-forged iron, now in bar form, being passed through bending rollers to turn it into a tube, which was then reheated and passed through welding rollers; later still, solid forgings were simply drilled.

Another important change occurred in the manufacture of wooden gun stocks. They were no longer shaped by hand, first by rough sawing and then, painstakingly, with spokeshave and plane, but were now produced on copying lathes derived from a prototype Thomas Blanchard constructed at the Springfield Armory. This complex machine used a master stock as a pattern, and was so accurate that the overall standard of the Armory's metalworking machinery and practice had to be improved to match it.

THE PEPPERBOX PISTOL
Percussion priming did nothing to speed up the lengthy process of loading a gun with separate charge and projectile via the muzzle. In fact, it slowed it down

somewhat, as clumsy fingers now had to fumble for a tiny cap and place it upon the nipple, where before they simply shot a small measure of powder into a pan. However, it did do away with the need to expose loose powder in an open pan at the appropriate moment, and gave a considerable boost to the few makers of repeating arms then in business.

DAFTE'S SINGLE BARREL
John Dafte had already shown, over a 100 years earlier, that single-barrelled 'revolvers' were feasible, with chambers parallel with the axis, which rotated into battery when the gun was cocked, even though the construction of them, on the snaphance or flintlock system, was complicated. Elisha Collier, exploiting the work of an American gunsmith, Artemus Wheeler, had also demonstrated that, with 'modern' workshop practice, they were practical, too. But it was the coming of the percussion cap which really made the difference, reducing the work necessary to set the pistol up for the next shot by removing the need to return the frizzen to battery, either manually or by means of a difficult-to-engineer mechanical link. There was a short-lived

Pepperbox Revolver

Calibre: 10mm (.39in)
Weight: .42kg (15oz)
Length: 279mm (11in)
Barrel length: 127mm (5in)
Effective range: 12.2m (40ft)
Feed: one per barrel
Muzzle velocity: 168mps (550fps)
Country of origin: United States

interim step before the revolver as we know it, though: the percussion 'pepperbox' pistol. Its one simple advantage over the single-barrelled cylinder revolver was that there was no need to ensure that the chamber coming to battery was accurately aligned with the barrel. Flintlock pepperboxes, thanks to their clumsiness, had gained little favour by the middle of the eighteenth century. Between shots, all but a few required the barrel assembly to be rotated by hand against a ratchet. It has been suggested that a hand-rotated pepperbox was probably the first revolving percussion pistol seen in England in about 1820. Certainly pistols of this type came to be popular over the following few decades, being effective in use and inexpensive to make.

THE COCKING ACTION

The next step was to link the revolution of the barrel group to the cocking of the action. There was nothing new in this; 'single action' flintlock pepperboxes and cylinder revolvers, in which the cylinder or barrel group was rotated so that a fresh charge was brought into battery by cocking the action, while not widely available, would certainly have been known to the major gunsmiths throughout the eighteenth century. As a result, the action could not be patented (or not, at least in Britain, where most contemporary developments were taking place), and there is no documentary evidence of exactly who first produced such a pistol.

Benjamin and Barton Darling succeeded in obtaining a US patent for a single-action pepperbox pistol on 13 April 1836, which seems rather late. The following year, Ethan Allen, of Worcester, Massachusetts (not the Revolutionary War hero, nor any relation to him), obtained a US patent for a double-action pepperbox revolver, in which the action was cocked and the barrel group revolved by taking up the first pressure on the trigger. Allen's pistols, which became very popular in the United States over the next decade, used a top-hammer action, the nipples which held the percussion caps being set at right angles to the bore of the chamber. This same arrangement was also to be found in many of the other revolvers, both cylinder and pepperbox, produced over the following two decades. It was not universal, however, as a design with in-line nipples and an enclosed striker was produced in Belgium in 1837, and was patented there as the Mariette pistol. An English gunsmith, J.R. Cooper, began production, too, and even claimed to have obtained a British patent, though there is no sign of that in the records of the London Patent Office.

Popular as they were, percussion pepperbox revolvers shared a dangerous tendency to fire more than one barrel at a time, owing to insufficient separation between one percussion cap and the next, resulting in flash-over and multiple ignition. In a pepperbox this was disconcerting; in a cylinder revolver,

where there was no clear path for the unintended discharge to follow, it was potentially disastrous. In addition, despite the concept of mechanical indexing having existed for over 200 years, there were still problems concerning the revolver's operation.

DOUBLE-ACTION SYSTEM

A double-action system only made matters worse in that respect, and not surprisingly, considering the mass of the moving parts and the mechanical disadvantage inherent in the linkage. These pepperboxes required a considerable force to be exerted on the trigger to simultaneously bring the new barrel into battery and cock the action, which ensured that they would never be really effective at anything much greater than point-blank range. In order to make the repeating pistol perform as well as its single-shot counterpart and to reduce it to a more manageable size, the revolver would have to become much lighter. This meant a return to the single-barrel cylinder revolver concept, the enduring problems besetting it notwithstanding. In particular, the difficulty of locating the chamber precisely in line with the barrel, the need to achieve something like a gas-tight seal between chamber and barrel, and the potentially disastrous flash-over problem had to be solved once and for all. And these problems were all sorted out, by one of the most influential gunmakers of them all: Samuel Colt.

CHAPTER 2
THE MUZZLE-LOADING PERCUSSION REVOLVER

Legend has it that Samuel Colt was inspired to design his first revolver during the autumn of 1830, whilst sailing to England on the brig *Corlo*. Supposedly, he observed the way in which the steering wheel turned, and could be prevented from turning, by the action of a simple dog clutch. His application of the system forms the basis of the modern revolver.

On his return to the United States, he tried to obtain a patent for a revolver action, using a crudely carved wooden model to demonstrate its innovations, and had his application refused by William P. Elliott.

In 1831, Anson Chase, a gunmaker in Hartford, Connecticut, where Colt was born, translated Colt's concept into a working model revolver rifle. The first model blew up on being fired, due to the nipples not being properly isolated and the flash from one percussion cap setting off the charge in a number of chambers at once. Notwithstanding, the young inventor persisted, raising money to fund his experiments by any means he could, the most effective being the demonstration of newly discovered nitrous oxide – laughing gas – to paying customers. Finally, with satisfactory working models made by John Pearson of Baltimore, the necessary drawings and a written application, he travelled to England in October 1835 and obtained British Patent Number 6909 for

■**LEFT: American troops battle Indians under Tecumseh, chief of the Shawnees in 1813. Their weapons are flintlocks, soon to give way to guns with percussion caps and self-contained cartridges.**

a revolver repeating action. He then secured similar protection in France and Prussia before returning to the USA and taking out American Patent Number 138 on 25 February 1836. By a quirk of British law, had he taken out his American patent first, his British application would not have been accepted, and that would have left Colt open to imitation in what was still, in the 1830s, a significant market for firearms.

COLT'S REVOLVER PRINCIPLE
He had solved the problem of lining up chamber and barrel by means of much-improved engineering to finer tolerances, and by devising a means of locking the cylinder at the moment of discharge. He also prevented flash-over by locating the nipples (set in line with the chambers) in deep individual recesses. The action was indexed simply by returning to the old method of rotating the next chamber into battery by pulling back directly on the hammer. Thus there was little or nothing actually new about Colt's design; rather, he had modified elements which already existed, and in doing so, made them work. He also produced a pistol which looked and felt 'right', where existing revolvers seemed clumsy and unfinished.

As for the manner in which the Colt pistol indexed its cylinder, the action bore a striking resemblance to that of the flintlock revolvers John Dafte had produced over 150 years earlier. Whether or not Colt had seen one of Dafte's guns and modelled his own on it is open to speculation. The similarity could just have been a coincidence, particularly as there are only a limited number of ways a simple mechanical operation can be carried out with any degree of efficiency. Colt's system used a pawl linked to the breast of the hammer and engaged in a ratchet machined into the rear face of the cylinder, the ratchet having one tooth for each chamber and the pawl's location being spring assisted. As the hammer was drawn back to engage the trigger sear, the pawl advanced the cylinder by one 'click' of the ratchet, rotating it through an arc such that a fresh chamber was brought into line with the barrel. The cylinder was locked into line with the barrel only at the moment of firing, by means of a lever bolt attached to the trigger, and acting vertically from it.

COLT'S COMPANY
On 5 March 1836, Colt formed The Patent Arms Manufacture Company at Paterson, New Jersey, with premises on the banks of the Passalc river. He began to turn out what are now known as the Paterson revolvers, primarily single-

■RIGHT: Samuel Colt (1814-62), the father of the modern revolver. He apparently dreamt up the idea of the revolver when voyaging between Boston and Europe as a mere boy.

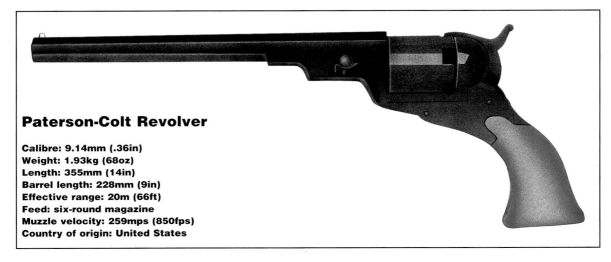

Paterson-Colt Revolver

Calibre: 9.14mm (.36in)
Weight: 1.93kg (68oz)
Length: 355mm (14in)
Barrel length: 228mm (9in)
Effective range: 20m (66ft)
Feed: six-round magazine
Muzzle velocity: 259mps (850fps)
Country of origin: United States

action five-shot pistols with folding triggers and no trigger guard, in three different models and four calibres. Heaviest was a large holster pistol of .36 calibre; a smaller holster pistol was available in .31 and .34 calibre, while a pocket pistol was available in .28, .31 and .34 sizes. In addition, Colt produced a variety of revolver carbines and rifles. It has been suggested that Colt, still in his early twenties, and with little in the way of commercial experience to balance his drive and enthusiasm, was somewhat over-ambitious in trying to produce such a variety of guns before an established market existed, and that contributed to the failure of his first business venture.

LOADING THE PATERSON-COLT
Like most revolvers of the day, the cylinder of the Paterson guns had to be removed in order for the chambers to be charged. This operation first necessitated the removal of the barrel, which was located and fixed to the axial cylinder pin by means of a simple and easy-to-remove rectangular cotter or key. To speed up the process, Colt delivered with each gun a custom-made five-necked powder flask, which fitted over the cylinder, each nozzle corresponding to the position of a chamber. Later models – the subject of further important patents, granted in 1839 – were redesigned so that the chambers could be charged one at a time with the cylinder in situ through a pronounced rebate in the frame on the lower right-hand side. A powder flask with an offset neck was used, and the charge packed down tightly with an integral double-hinged compound

ramming lever. This was in two parts, its handle lying under the barrel and retained there by a clip, and the rammer itself housed within the lower part of the forward frame, in line with the bottom cylinder. The recoil shield which formed the rear of the frame behind the cylinder was cut away on the right-hand side to expose the nipple and allow the fitting of a fresh percussion cap. Since Colt's revolvers rotated their cylinders clockwise, as seen by the shooter, it would have been more logical to have made this provision on the left hand side, so that a new cap could be fitted to the recharged chamber after the cylinder had been rotated through one step.

Colt's venture foundered, perhaps due to his over-ambition, but also certainly as a result of military conservatism and economic depression in the USA, coupled with the $130 price tag on each pistol, at a time when a pepperbox revolver could be bought for a tenth of that amount. His heavy holster pistol was tested by the US Army at West Point in 1837, and rejected as too complex, though the US Government did buy 50 eight-shot revolver rifles during the war with the Seminole Indians in Florida. A small number of heavy holster pistols were also sold to the navy of the Republic of Texas, and thus became known as the Texas Model. In 1842 the Paterson plant closed, the company's assets liquidated at the year's end, and Colt turned to other things, notably the perfection of the submarine telegraph cable and the supervision of the laying of one, between Manhattan and Staten Island. He continued to develop his firearm

designs, as well as keeping his precious patents alive and bringing would-be pirates to court. Five years later his efforts and his faith were justified when the US Government ordered 1000 revolvers, to a modified design, to be used during the war with Mexico which had been declared on 13 May 1846.

THE TEXAS RANGERS
That somewhat belated order came about despite the conservatism of the army establishment, as a result of the enthusiasm with which a small number of men had adopted the Paterson pistols. Many of these men who were to become somewhat influential within the ranks of the US armed forces when their skill as guerrilla fighters, honed in battles with bands of Comanche Indians, were called up against Mexican forces. They became known as the Texas Rangers. The best-known example of the invincible qualities of Colt's early guns in combat cites a Ranger patrol, 15 men under Captain Jack Hays, holding off a Comanche band which outnumbered them five to one. They are reported as killing 35 enemy in the process, though that number varies. When they were mustered into US service, on the annexation of Texas in December 1845, the Rangers brought with them not just their revolvers but their enthusiasm for them, and this soon proved to be infectious.

Captain Samuel H. Walker had ridden with Jack Hays, and it was he who was sent out to negotiate with Samuel Colt in the hope of persuading him back into the firearms business; one can imagine that Colt didn't need much persuasion. He

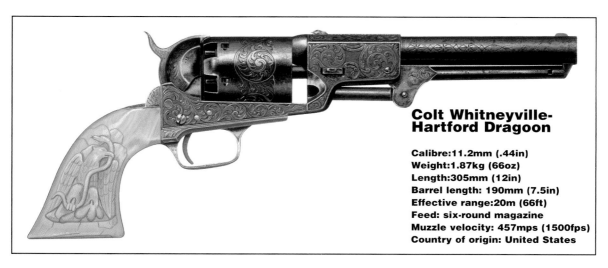

Colt Whitneyville-Hartford Dragoon

Calibre:11.2mm (.44in)
Weight:1.87kg (66oz)
Length:305mm (12in)
Barrel length: 190mm (7.5in)
Effective range:20m (66ft)
Feed: six-round magazine
Muzzle velocity: 457mps (1500fps)
Country of origin: United States

■ABOVE: Texas Rangers in action during the US-Mexican War (1846-48). The Rangers carried Paterson-Colt revolvers as side-arms, finding them to be ideal cavalry weapons.

needed little encouragement to accept Walker's suggestion for refinements to his design, either, although he had no manufacturing capability of his own.

THE COLT DRAGOON

When the new gun went into production in 1847, at Eli Whitney Jr.'s Whitneyville, Connecticut, plant, it was as the Colt Whitneyville-Walker Dragoon Model. The Dragoon was a big gun by any standards, 343mm (13.5in) long, of which 330mm (13in) was barrel, and weighing over 2kg (4.4lb). It was a six-shot revolver in .44, a calibre heavier than any Colt had employed before. These first Colt Dragoon pistols (so-called because they were intended for use by men on horseback) can be distinguished from later models by their oval or lozenge-shaped locking slots. This was still not a perfect system, but a considerable improvement on the circular recesses which were all that served to lock the Paterson revolvers' cylinders.

Whether this was a Colt or a Walker innovation is unclear. They also had a distinctive square-cut recurve to the back of the trigger guard which, along with the butt-strap, was made of brass. They cost the US Government a much more reasonable $28 each, and one might imagine that the price of the guns had a good deal to do with their acceptability.

Only about 1000 Whitneyville-Walker guns were produced in all, and as a result surviving specimens are very expensive today. On 13 July 1847, the US Government ordered a further 1000 guns, and these Colt produced at a plant he set up himself, in Pearl Street in Hartford, using tools and machinery provided by Whitney under the terms of their earlier contract. Both the Whitneyville and the Whitneyville-Hartford guns, as the latter came to be called, were produced by a combination of mechanised and craft methods, and so there was not complete interchangeability of parts between individual specimens, but this was the last time that criticism could be levelled. Indeed, Colt, together with his associate and successor, Elisha Root, occupies a proud place in American industrial history, on a par with Henry Ford and for

many of the same reasons. What Ford later did for the production of motor vehicles, Colt did for firearms. The main difference between the Whitneyville-Hartford Dragoons and the earlier model was a reduction in barrel length to 190mm (7.5in), and a 198gm (7oz) weight saving which went with it. There were detailed changes, too, to the ramming lever and the way the barrel was fixed, though that was still nothing more complex than a plain steel wedge pushed home through matching slots in the barrel extension and the cylinder pin over which it fitted.

COLT'S GLOBAL SUCCESS

Over the next eight years, Colt offered the Hartford Dragoon in three slightly different versions, including one with a 203mm (8in) barrel. The most effective modification saw the substitution of square-cut rectangular cylinder locking slots and an appropriately shaped bolt. The square-backed trigger guard gave way to a rounded pattern which was offered in an alternative larger size more suitable to gloved hands, and the V-shaped mainspring housed in the butt was replaced by a simple leaf, which now

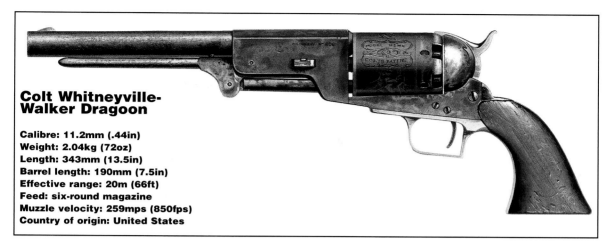

Colt Whitneyville-Walker Dragoon

Calibre: 11.2mm (.44in)
Weight: 2.04kg (72oz)
Length: 343mm (13.5in)
Barrel length: 190mm (7.5in)
Effective range: 20m (66ft)
Feed: six-round magazine
Muzzle velocity: 259mps (850fps)
Country of origin: United States

acted on the hammer through a roller bearing. The second and third Model Dragoon pistols came with provision for a shoulder stock, and one was customarily supplied with each pair of pistols. Colt made a version for the English market, which was sold in London with locally made wooden cases and accessories.

Production was also licensed in Liege, Belgium, using parts made in Hartford or in a factory set up in London in 1853. Belgian-made guns are occasionally to be found with fluted, rather than the traditional octagonal, barrels. The design being relatively simple, handmade imitations were still being produced long after Colt himself stopped manufacture in 1860, many of them made in Texas during the Civil War.

The second-generation Colt pistols set the standard for military percussion revolvers, not just in their native USA, but abroad, too, despite competition from local gunmakers, particularly in Britain. Colt went from strength to strength, augmenting the heavy Dragoons with lighter 'Little Dragoon' pocket pistols, .31 calibre five-shot revolvers with 76mm (3in), 100mm (4in), 127mm (5in) or 150mm (6in) barrels. The Little Dragoon was superseded by the Model 1849 pocket pistol, sometimes known as the 'Wells Fargo', which stayed in production until 1873, by which time almost 350,000 had been produced. It was joined two years later by the Model 1851 Navy, a lighter six-shot holster pistol at 1.02kg (2.25lb), in .36 calibre. This pistol was also an immediate success in commercial terms – the British Government ordered 41,500 (and a further 22,000 heavy Dragoons) in 1854. This was largely due to Samuel

Colt's presence in London and his having opened a factory there, but the British switched to the home-produced Adams revolver as the official Service Pistol the following year. Better yet was a New Army Model of 1860, the first of Colt's revolvers with a 'streamlined' look to them. The block which formed the breech end of the barrel and housed the rammer was sculpted, with its sharp corners smoothed off, and the rebate in the frame below, which allowed the chambers to be loaded without removing the cylinder, was cut away further. The frame was completely pierced, allowing access to the bottom chamber from either side.

A new pocket pistol, a side-hammer design patented in 1855, by Root, proved less successful, even though it introduced two important improvements: a rigid top strap over the cylinder and a screw-in barrel. Its most distinctive feature was the stud trigger, a form with which both Colt and the company which was eventually to challenge for overall supremacy in the firearms market, Smith and Wesson, were to persist until well into the twentieth century.

THE DOUBLE-ACTION MECHANISM

Two years previously, Root, acting for the Colt company, had patented another less-than-satisfactory design, for a 'self cocking' (i.e. double action) revolver. This made an attempt to overcome the gross mechanical disadvantage which had been a poor feature of the early double-action pepperboxes, by means of helical slots machined into the cylinder, into which a dog attached to the trigger was located. Pulling the trigger back through the first pressure thus not only propelled the

hammer back to the full-cock position, but also acted on the cylinder to turn a new chamber into battery by a means completely independent of the pawl-and-ratchet method which had been used up until then. Colt did not develop the idea, but German gunsmith Paul Mauser incorporated a similar idea into his 'zig zag' revolver of 1878. An Englishman, Colonel George Fosbery VC, also used this idea in the more ambitious 'automatic revolver' he designed later, it entering limited production by Webley & Scott in 1900. In fact, even a basic theoretical knowledge would have led its protagonists to realise that this method was more inefficient, in mechanical terms, than the pawl-and-ratchet that it sought to supersede.

THE CIVIL WAR BOOSTS DEMAND

The six-shot .44-calibre Army Model Colt revolver of 1860, and .36-calibre Navy Model, which followed the next year, proved popular and sold in large numbers, despite the fact that Colt's patent protection had expired in 1857 and the market was now completely swamped by competitors using the features he had designed and developed. Five-shot .36-calibre Pocket and Police Models of 1862, which were available with a range of barrels from 114mm (4.5in) to 165mm (6.5in) in place of the 19mm (7.5in) item which was standard for the service revolvers, also sold well, largely through circumstances outside Samuel Colt's control. Fortuitously for the arms trade, 1861 saw the start of the war between the States, which boosted the demand for guns of all types to an unheard-of level. The US and

Colt Navy 1851

Calibre: 9.1mm (.36in)
Weight: 1.02kg (36oz)
Length: 328mm (12.91in)
Barrel length: 190mm (7.5in)
Effective range: 20m (66ft)
Feed: six-round magazine
Muzzle velocity: 213mps (700fps)
Country of origin: United States

Confederate Governments bought some 375,000 pistols between 1861 and 1865, from around 20 different manufacturers, and private sales were probably at least as high. Model 1860 Army Colts alone accounted for 34 per cent of the Union's procurement, and over the 12 years of that pistol's currency, over 200,000 were produced. The 1862 Police Model differed from the Pocket Model in having a fluted cylinder, and was the last of the Colt percussion revolvers, though many of this type – and the contemporary models it so closely resembled – were later converted to accept unitary metal centre-fire cartridges.

Colt's revolvers were so successful and so popular that some of his post-1857 competitors, notably the Manhattan Fire Arms Manufacturing Co. and the Metropolitan Arms Co., both of New York, did little more than copy his designs line-for-line. Other gunsmiths were more interested in developing viable products of their own, albeit using Colt's now – unprotected ideas and developments, and the best of them – Remington, Starr, Savage did produce fine pistols, even if some were rather odd in certain areas.

REMINGTON'S NEW MODEL ARMY

Eliphalet Remington started out as a blacksmith in Ilion, New York, and made rifles as a hobby; by 1826 his sideline had turned into his main line of business. In that year he opened a gun factory in his home town, gaining his first government contract in 1845. It was not until 1857 (the year Colt's main patent expired) that he first started to manufacture pistols, designed by Fordyce Beals. Remington's New Model Army and Navy revolvers of

1860, in .44- and .36- calibres respectively, were, after Colt's own, the second most popular sidearms during the Civil War. Also Beals-designed, the guns included an aesthetic element which was conspicuously absent from most other pistols of the day save for Colt's. In the case of the Remington, the most obvious feature was a fine tapered web extending along the ramming lever, which continued the general line of the pistol's frame almost up to the muzzle. Its purpose was to prevent it catching in a holster but the effect was to impart a streamlined appearance. At 350mm (13.75in) long and weighing 1.25kg (2.75lb), it was not the sort of gun one could carry in one's pocket. Even after the changeover to brass cartridges, when the ramming lever had given way to a spring-loaded ejector rod located in the same position, Remington continued the streamlining rib; it had become something of a feature.

The Remington New Model Army pistol was a fine, sturdy gun, its strongest feature, both literally and metaphorically, being its solid top strap frame – a feature of all Beals' designs, even that of the otherwise rather outlandish 'Walking Beam' semi double-action pistol he had designed for Whitney. He himself had earlier patented a solid frame revolver but had unfortunately neglected to include the top strap in his description, thus allowing an important development to pass into the public domain, in the USA at least. The Whitney Beals, as the pistol was properly known, employed a double ratchet acting on notches at each end of the cylinder; the trigger – a ring – was first pushed forward, then returned to the normal

position to rest against the sear, this action rotating the cylinder by half-steps; the hammer was cocked manually. Needless to say, though perhaps only obvious with the benefit of hindsight, it attracted few customers, and the only substantial factor in its favour was that it circumvented Colt's patent.

Despite having been rendered obsolescent by the brass cartridge (and superseded even by Remington's own

Colt Navy 1851 (Replica)

(For specifications see Colt Navy 1851 above)

Army Model of 1875), the New Model pistols continued in production until 1888. They were joined by lighter, more compact guns with shorter barrels, down to 89mm (3.5in) and in smaller calibres of .31 and .36, the former's capacity being reduced to five rounds.

STARR'S BREAK-OPEN ACTION

In the interests of saving space, the New Model Pocket Revolver did away with a trigger guard, a trigger sheath being provided in its place. Remington also produced two double-action models, the short-lived first of which used an action patented by Rider in 1858 and 1859, which involved a curious mushroom-shaped cylinder. The second was a more conventional double-action variant of the lightened version of the New Model Navy, outwardly indistinguishable from the original save for its trigger having been moved forward substantially. Such a forward-located trigger is a feature common to all double-action revolvers, and is an easy means of telling them from single-action guns even at first sight.

Third in the league table of manufacturers of percussion revolvers in the United States during the genre's last two decades was the rather longer-established firm of Nathan Starr and Sons, of Middletown, Connecticut, one-time employers of Henry Aston. The most significant feature of the Starr revolvers was their break-open action, as best exemplified in the Single Action Model, in .44 calibre, of 1864. The top/front section of the frame, on which were located the barrel and the rammer, was connected, by a lateral pin which formed a hinge, to the lower/rear section, which comprised the butt and contained the action proper. The top strap terminated in a fork, the arms of which passed each side of the hammer and hooked over the recoil shield behind the cylinder, the two parts being drilled and tapped to take a retaining screw with a large knurled head which fixed them firmly together. No tools were required to remove the retaining screw, and on the pistol being broken open, the cylinder – located on a stub pin at the front, and by the advancing ratchet at the rear – could be easily removed. Those other parts of the gun susceptible to fouling were also exposed, which simplified cleaning. These pistols, forerunners of a whole genre of British revolvers of a later period, were rather misleadingly marked 'STARR'S PATENT JAN 15 1856'; the patent in question actually refers to a locking system developed for a self-cocking pepperbox revolver. The important patent – that which protected the hinged solid frame, as well as describing an improvement to the self-cocking action – wasn't awarded until 4 December 1860 (though once again, the American letters were predated by a successful application made in London some eight months earlier). The patent for the Starr Single Action itself was granted in April 1864.

DOUBLE-ACTION REVOLVERS

Starr had previously produced double-action pistols of a sort, in both .36- and .44-calibres, though it is probably safer to refer to them by another name, perhaps 'selective double-action', as one eminent authority suggests. Starr's double-action revolvers had a selector lever behind the trigger to switch from single-to double-action, with all the benefits in terms of accuracy of the former and speed of operation of the latter. Even so its double-acting mechanism was by no means as refined as that of the Beaumont-Adams Revolver, which had appeared in England some years earlier. The double-action was complex in its mechanism, and that was reflected in the

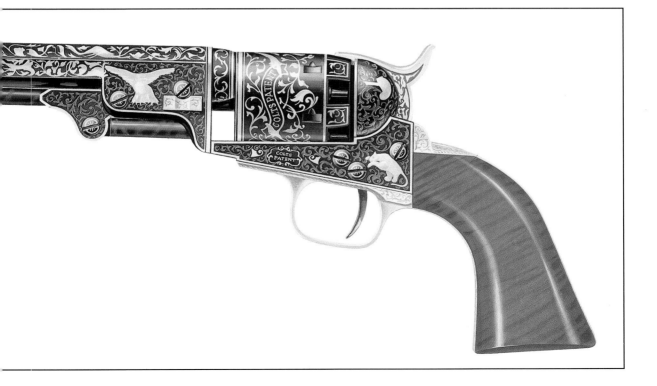

price of the pistols; there is little doubt that the company's decision to switch over to single-action was market-driven at a time when there were considerable amounts of money to be made from government contracts, particularly if the price was right.

SAVAGE'S TOP-MOUNTED HAMMER

The fourth force in the pistol market in the USA in the 1860s certainly understood those constraints. The Savage Revolving Fire Arms Company was formed by Henry S. North and Edward Savage of Middletown, Connecticut, in 1860, after they had been awarded patent protection for yet another cumbersome self-cocking action. In some ways the .36 calibre Savage Model 1861 pistol which followed was anachronistic – and it certainly looked it – particularly since its top-mounted hammer acted vertically on nipples set at right-angles to the axis of the chambers. This did simplify access to the nipples themselves, for the purpose of fitting new percussion caps, although that had never been much of a problem with in-line nipples. The top hammer was mounted to the right of the centre-line of the frame, in order to allow the user to take some sort of aim, and struck the nipple via a hole in the top strap. This

gave a rather clumsy line to the pistol, which was accentuated by the enlarged trigger guard necessary to house the two superimposed triggers. The lower – a ring – was used to cock the action and bring a new chamber into battery, first withdrawing the cylinder from the breech end of the barrel, where matched chamfers provided not only positive location but also a gas seal. It was a heavy gun – 1.6kg (3.5lb) – when Colt and Remington pistols of similar calibre were about 0.5kg (1lb) lighter. Despite this, and its distinctly old-fashioned appearance, the gun sold in appreciable quantities, largely due to its very reasonable price. The Union Army alone bought 10,000 at a cost of $20 each, including accessories.

A number of gunmakers adapted the Maynard tape primer system to the revolver, perhaps the best known of them being the Massachusetts Arms Company (MAC). This company locked horns with Colt in 1851 when it produced a six-shot revolver which, Colt insisted, contravened his patent covering mechanically rotated cylinders, even though the bevelled gears method used was nothing like the pawl-and-ratchet mechanism he himself employed. Somewhat surprisingly, although the geared action designed by

Wesson and Leavitt really was substantially different from anything Colt had designed, the case went against MAC, who not only had to pay substantial damages, but also had to withdraw the pistol in question from sale. The basic defects of the tape primer system notwithstanding, a revolver employing it seemed to have some advantages over one using percussion caps, if only in terms of ease of loading. The Massachusetts Arms Co. put it back on the market in 1857 after Colt's patent had expired but it was never a commercial success.

A BITTERLY FOUGHT BATTLE

The Civil War between the States put pistols into the hands of many who had never been accustomed to carrying them, and at the same time introduced desperation into many lives – a dangerous and volatile combination. Under a thin veneer of gentility, the war was as vicious as any of its kind; in the states of Kansas and Missouri, in particular, much of the fighting took the form of guerrilla warfare, and this, largely undisciplined as it was, was to become the seedbed of an entire genre of violent crime. Both the guerrillas and the outlaws who came after them depended largely on handguns. All too often they

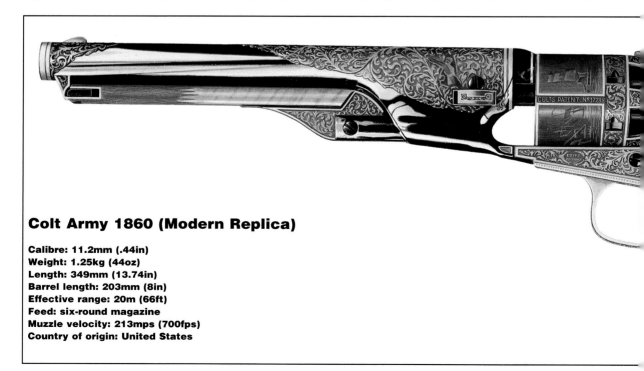

Colt Army 1860 (Modern Replica)

Calibre: 11.2mm (.44in)
Weight: 1.25kg (44oz)
Length: 349mm (13.74in)
Barrel length: 203mm (8in)
Effective range: 20m (66ft)
Feed: six-round magazine
Muzzle velocity: 213mps (700fps)
Country of origin: United States

were one and the same men – Frank and Jesse James and their gang, including their cousins the Youngers, being prime examples. The most notorious of the guerrilla leaders were William Quantrill on the Confederate side, and Jim Lane and Charles Jennison on the other. A biographer of Quantrill, William Elsey Connelley, described the importance he placed on the handgun, and the skill with it which he expected his men to display:

'The arms of the guerrilla consisted principally of Colt's navy revolvers of .44 calibre. Some of them carried cavalry carbines which they had captured, a few had Sharps rifles and there were even shotguns and old muskets among them. The main reliance of the guerrilla, however, was upon the revolver. And the guerrilla was usually a dead-shot, either afoot or on horseback. Quantrill became very expert with the revolver. There has been much said about his teaching his men to shoot by drilling them and insisting upon compliance with some certain formula or routine of action.

■**RIGHT: A Colt advertisement of 1852 showing the cylinder engraving of the Walker Colt (top) of 1847, the Navy Model of 1851 (middle) and the Pocket Pistol of 1849.**

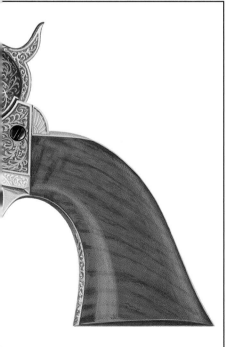

He did nothing of the kind. He urged constant practice at first, but each man could shoot as he liked if he shot well. Quantrill required results in pistol firing and the guerilla understood this art much better than any other soldier. The powder charge of the Union soldier was made up for him and these charges were uniform in size. The guerilla made up his own charge. He was compelled to be economical of his ammunition. He discovered that a small powder charge enabled him to shoot more accurately than he could with a heavier charge. His pistol did not 'bounce' when fired, and the aim was not spoiled. And the ball ranged as far and penetrated as deeply as did that fired by a heavy charge. Every guerrilla carried two revolvers, most of them carried four and many carried six, some even eight. They could fire from a revolver in each hand at the same time. The aim was never by sighting along the pistol barrel, but by intuition, apparently without care, at random. But the ball rarely missed its mark – the centre. Many a guerrilla could hit a mark to both the right and left with shots fired at the same time from each hand.'

GUERRILLA FIREARMS TACTICS
Connelley was Secretary of the Kansas State Historical Society and a confirmed Unionist; his biography of Quantrill, written in 1909, is a very clear attempt to portray the Confederate guerrilla leader as 'a fiend incarnate', as one commentator has put it. There is good reason to believe that Connelley was no firearms expert, but he drew on first-hand accounts, and his work is accurate where it is not horribly biased. But some of his assertions have to be weighed carefully. His comment on the undiminished range and penetrating power of a 'short' charge, for example, is

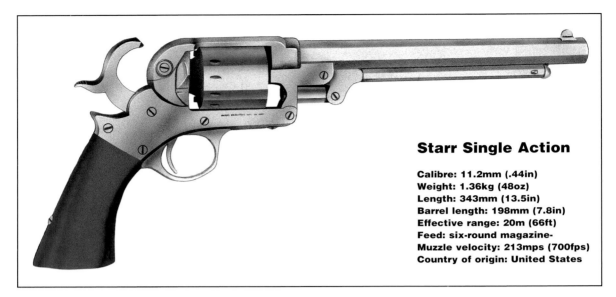

Starr Single Action

Calibre: 11.2mm (.44in)
Weight: 1.36kg (48oz)
Length: 343mm (13.5in)
Barrel length: 198mm (7.8in)
Effective range: 20m (66ft)
Feed: six-round magazine-
Muzzle velocity: 213mps (700fps)
Country of origin: United States

nonsense, and he missed the salient point that most pistol work took place at close range, where a reduced charge is indeed often no drawback. As to his comments on 'intuitive' aiming, there is much anecdotal evidence to support him, even though reason suggests that very short ranges and pure luck had more to do with a man's chances of hitting a target precisely when firing from the hip, particularly in two directions at once.

QUANTRILL'S RAIDERS

Reference to Quantrill turns on an interesting sidelight – the age of the average American gunman. Quantrill was just 24 years old when he formed his guerrilla band, and at that, he was one of its senior members. Jesse James, at 15, was deemed too young to participate in Quantrill's most effective enterprise, the notorious raid on Lawrence, Kansas, in August 1863, which resulted in $2,000,000 worth of damage and the deaths of 142 townspeople (and just one guerrilla). Frank James, at 19, was not, and went along, at the side of his 18-year-old cousin Thomas Coleman (Cole) Younger. All the celebrated gunfighters were in their teens or twenties when they started on their bloody careers, and few saw 30, though some of the most eminent of the lawmen lived surprisingly long lives, considering their chosen profession. Bill Tilghman, for example, was reckoned to be one of the most effective, and was still at work as a law enforcement officer at the age of 70. He was Town Marshal of

■RIGHT: A Union soldier photographed during the American Civil War. His left hand is resting on a Colt Dragoon revolver. The trigger guard and butt-straps were made of brass.

a lawless, oil-rich community called Cromwell, in Oklahoma, and had gone there in 1924 to clean it up at the express request of the state Governor when he was shot to death (from behind) by a colleague of a sort, a drunken prohibition enforcer named Wylie Lynn. A true companion, Chris Madsen, who served with Tilghman as Deputy Marshal of Oklahoma Terrritory, and had also more than his fair share of narrow escapes, outlived him by more than a few years – Madsen died in his home in Guthrie, Oklahoma, at the age of 92 in 1944. Few outlaws lived to enjoy their old age, however, though Frank James and Cole Younger both did.

EUROPE LAGS BEHIND

War gives a great impetus to trade, particularly the arms trade. There is no doubt that the Civil War between the United and Confederate States of America boosted the American armaments industry, particularly, of course in the north; the south had no industrial base to speak of. This came just at a time when the introduction of machine tools and mass production techniques had made it possible to produce guns at a rate previously unimaginable, while both maintaining uniformly high quality and

keeping prices down. European arms manufacturers benefited too, and quantities of British-and French-made guns found their way across the Atlantic, sometimes by devious means. By and large, however, the European manufacturers were still an entire generation behind their American counterparts, in execution if not in the quality of their ideas. This was true even though they had good reason to step up their rates of production during a period when the race to lay claim to huge areas of territory and cement them into empires had just come under starter's orders.

The 'craft' gunsmiths in London, in particular, around the time that Colt was lodging his first successful patent application, were also producing cylinder percussion revolvers. Most of them were self-cocking double-action pieces based very firmly and clearly on the pepperbox pistols which were then very much in vogue. Indeed, the guns were frequently little more than pepperboxes with their barrels cut down to chambers, with no top or bottom strap and the barrel fixed on to a suitably shortened cylinder spindle, and often located by nothing more positive than a grub-screw. These crude, cheaply made weapons made no provision to lock the cylinder with a chamber in line with the barrel save by means of the ratchet which indexed it, and must, as a result, have been quite terrifying to the user as well as to anyone threatened with one.

This is not to say that there were no good revolvers produced in Europe during the period, but rather to emphasise the difference in attitude there and in America. By the mid-point of the nineteenth century, inexpensive, effective, well-made repeating pistols were readily and widely available in the United States, while in Europe, if you wanted a properly made gun, you still had to go to a craftsman gunsmith and pay an inflated price for a weapon which was still largely handmade.

TRANSITIONAL REVOLVERS

The industrialisation of the British armaments industry was still some way off when the first major improvement in the European pistol came, with the addition of a bottom strap to provide a second anchorage for the barrel. This improved the gun's rigidity somewhat, though in no case was this element of the frame as substantial as in Colt's contemporary designs. It had no need to be; the European adherence to the top hammer acting vertically on radial nipples meant that the trigger had to be placed well to the rear of the plane of the cylinder, below the toe of the hammer. Thus the bottom strap did not have to serve double duty as the location for the trigger mechanism, and could, in fact, be dispensed with entirely. It was only in the 1850s, when the Europeans switched over to horizontally acting hammers and cylinders with axial nipples, that the overall appearance of their pistols

■ABOVE: The outlaw Jesse James (1847-82), here photographed at the age of 17 as a Confederate guerrilla in Quantrill's raiders. His weapon is a Colt 1860 Navy Model.

changed and became more like those being manufactured in the USA.

Ever since the first attempts to produce a single-barrelled repeater with multiple cylinders, propellant gas leaking at the junction between chamber and barrel had been a persistent problem. Not only did the escaping gas reduce the propellant force, and therefore the velocity of the projectile, but it also presented the risk of flash-over igniting the powder in adjacent chambers. Collier addressed the problem in his flintlock revolver of 1820 by machining truncated conical recesses into the mouths of each chamber and a corresponding truncated cone onto the breech end of the barrel. The cylinder was thrust forward by means of a wedge propelled by the forward action of the cock as it fell, which also had the very desirable secondary effect of co-locating the barrel and the chamber. Makers of English 'transitional'

revolvers, as the top-hammer guns have become known, adopted similar methods to produce a variety of 'gas seal' revolvers, and realised quite early on that a bottom strap was a very desirable feature indeed. As well as improving the overall rigidity of the frame, they allowed the fitting of ramming levers – either simple plungers or compound levers such as those employed by Colt and the other Americans – which, because they allowed the seating of a somewhat over-sized bullet, also helped to prevent flash-over. Patents covering the gas seal principle were awarded to a number of English gunmakers, including Philip Webley in 1858, and very similar revolvers were

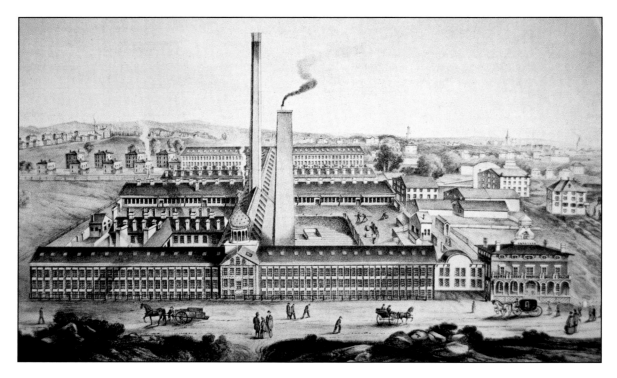

■ABOVE: Colt's Patent Firearms Manufacturing Company at Hartford, in 1862. Nineteenth-century engineering and manufacturing processes made the mass production of firearms possible.

also manufactured in Belgium. Interesting though they are, if largely for negative reasons, the transitional revolvers were little more than a sideline to the history of the handgun, and elsewhere in Britain, gunmakers were already at work on much more effective pistols to rival those Colt was turning out in Hartford. Chief among them was Robert Adams.

COLT'S BRITISH VENTURE

In 1851 Samuel Colt, along with many other industrialists, made it his business to be in London for the Great Exhibition of the Works of Industry of all Nations, housed in Paxton's Crystal Palace, in Hyde Park. This was the most imposing display of manufacturing excellence the world had ever seen, and we can be sure that he lost no opportunity to convince anyone who would listen of the supremacy of American engineering in general, and of his weapons in particular, collecting the usual mixture of acolytes and enemies in the process. On 25 November 1851, Colt presented a paper

entitled *On the Application of Machinery to the manufacture of Rotating Chambered-Breech Fire-Arms and the peculiarities of those arms* to the British Institute of Civil Engineers, but anyone who attended hoping to hear talk of manufacturing methods in the machine age would have been disappointed, for Colt turned his lecture into a sales pitch. In the discussion period which followed, he found himself confronted by a London gunmaker, Robert Adams, who had earlier that year secured, on behalf of his firm, Deane, Adams and Deane, a patent for a five-chambered self-cocking (i.e. double-action) revolver. It seems that Colt had packed the audience, and Adams had little chance to sing the praises of his own gun, but the 'Yankee Adventurer's' aggressive lobbying tactics did not go unnoticed by protectionist journalists, politicians and industrialists alike.

Colt's objective was certainly the wider acceptance of his firearms in the biggest market of the day – the British Army – and to this end he devoted some of his time in London to searching out a possible site for a factory. He eventually located premises near the River Thames, in Bessborough Place, Pimlico, and only a short carriage ride from the Army's headquarters at Horseguard's Parade.

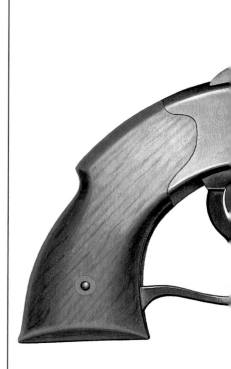

The factory opened its doors in 1853, and while production was initially confined to the assembly of Hartford-made components, a full production line was soon set up. The key personnel were drafted in from Hartford, but the works manager was a Briton, Mr Charles Manby, who, perhaps by coincidence, happened to be the Secretary of the Institute of Civil Engineers. Colt's tactics were rewarded the following year with an order for some 65,000 guns from the British Army, and between 1854 until it closed in 1856, Colt's London Armoury the factory produced some 40,000 Navy Model 1851 pistols in .36 calibre, as well as 10,000 pocket pistols.

ADAMS SELF-COCKING REVOLVER

Meanwhile, Adams and his partners were far from idle. The Adams Self-Cocking Revolver, based on the 1851 patent, went into production in a factory in south London in a variety of calibres, initially in 34 bore or 12.9mm (.507in), and later in 36 bore, 12.7mm (.5in), and 54 bore, 11.2mm (.4in) for service use. There were also 90 bore, 9.1mm (.35in) and 120 bore, 8.1mm (.3in) pocket pistols, though

considering that there was no change in the guns' overall external dimensions from one calibre to another, and that they were 33cm (13in) long and weighed almost 1.36kg (3lb), those last must have been a very full pocketful, while actually providing very little stopping power.

The revolver's action was self-cocking only; that is, there was no provision made for the hammer to be pulled back manually. Indeed, there was no hammer spur to allow this, and the action could only be initiated by steady pressure on the trigger. Thus, the revolver could only be carried in complete safety with the hammer down, its nose resting on the (empty) nipple of the chamber most recently fired. If all five chambers were loaded the hammer would have been resting on a live cap, as that of a fully loaded Colt invariably did. To prevent accidental discharge in this position a rudimentary safety catch was provided on the left-hand side of the frame, behind the cylinder. This was in the form of a simple leaf spring acting at right angles to the revolver's axis, anchored at the lower end and with a small stud at the upper. As the trigger was drawn back,

thumb pressure on the spring forced the stud through a hole drilled in the frame, and when the trigger was released again it engaged the hammer below its nose and held it off by a little more than the depth by which the nipples were recessed into the rear of the cylinder. This 'safety catch' was released by further light pressure on the trigger, which caused the hammer to retract far enough to stop it resting on the stud, allowing the leaf spring to return to its relaxed position. This catch also permitted the cylinder to be rotated by hand so that its chambers could be loaded and the caps replaced.

Two years later, in November 1853, Adams, acknowledging the inherent tendency towards inaccuracy in a double-action only pistol, produced a revised design which has been called a 'hesitation action'. The hammer was brought to full cock in the normal way, but once there, a spring-loaded pawl engaged a notch in the hammer breast and took the pressure off the trigger, which could then be released slightly, allowing fresh aim to be taken. Renewed pressure on the trigger disengaged the pawl and allowed the hammer to fall in the normal way. The

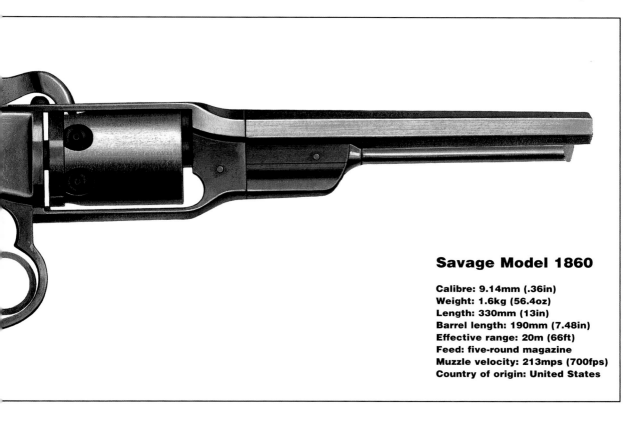

Savage Model 1860

Calibre: 9.14mm (.36in)
Weight: 1.6kg (56.4oz)
Length: 330mm (13in)
Barrel length: 190mm (7.48in)
Effective range: 20m (66ft)
Feed: five-round magazine
Muzzle velocity: 213mps (700fps)
Country of origin: United States

Colt Model 1862

Calibre: 11.2mm (.44in)
Weight: 1.25kg (44oz)
Length: 349mm (13.74in)
Barrel length: 203mm (8in)
Effective range: 12m (40ft)
Feed: six-round magazine
Muzzle velocity: 213mps (700fps)
Country of origin: United States

hesitation action wasn't quite as light as single action, but it was certainly an improvement over regular double-action.

The first Adams revolvers had no rammer, and were loaded by finger pressure alone. To improve the seating of the round in the chamber, a wad was used between projectile and charge, and this was yet another piece of ingenuity. The bullet mould supplied with the pistol deliberately left a small tang on the cast projectile; the wad was fixed over this spike, which was then peened over – a tap or two on the gun's frame would have sufficed – holding wad and bullet together. Later models employed a compound rammer which lay down the left-hand side of the barrel when not in use.

REVOLVER RAMMERS

A number of different types of rammer, all similar in character, were employed, one patented by Brazier, another by Tranter, both of whom were Birmingham gunsmiths who supplied part-finished components to Deane, Adams and Deane,

and who also assembled Adams revolvers themselves. Adams himself later patented a simple rammer which lay alongside the frame above the trigger guard when not in use. His partner in London Armoury, James Kerr, patented another, as did the Webley brothers; one or other style was fitted to every revolver manufactured, and where necessary, a small royalty paid. Advances in even apparently unimportant areas such as this were jealously guarded, and patent infringements were often the cause of lawsuits, so there was every incentive to attempt to come up with different enough modifications to be patentable in its own right.

BEAUMONT-ADAMS REVOLVER

Colt's decision to close his British factory was taken mainly as a result of increasingly effective opposition in the marketplace from gunmakers in London and Birmingham, who were better placed to lobby than the American, though there were good reasons why the British soldiers of the day preferred Adams'

revolvers, to Colt's. Even before the Pimlico plant had closed its doors, Adams abandoned his partners, and with Frederick Beaumont, William Harding and James Kerr formed the London Armoury Company, found premises some streets away, and had begun work on a new model, patented the previous year, the Beaumont-Adams Revolver.

The Beaumont-Adams took the best features of Adams' own pistol, notably its unitary construction, with barrel, frame and top strap being forged out of one piece of iron. It married them to a version of his double-action mechanism as improved by Lieutenant Frederick Beaumont, late of the Royal Engineers, which permitted the gun to operate in either single- or double-action mode. The Beaumont-Adams was the subject of British Army trials without delay, and was adopted as the official Service Revolver in 1855, in time to see service during the Indian Mutiny, though many officers had carried Adams' own revolvers, purchased at their own

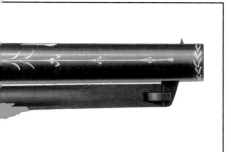

'An officer, who especially prided himself on his pistol-shooting, was attacked by a stalwart mutineer armed with a heavy sword. The officer, unfortunately for himself, carried a Colt's Navy pistol, which, as you may remember, was of small calibre, and fired a sharp-pointed picket bullet of sixty to the pound and a heavy charge of powder, its range being at least 600 yards, as I have frequently proved. This he proceeded to empty into the sepoy as he advanced, but, having done so, he waited just one second too long to see the effect of his shooting, and was cloven to the teeth by his antagonist, who then

subject of the stopping power of different pistol rounds differ greatly. For example, one expert source – the British Army's close-quarters combat specialists, W.E. Fairbairn and E.A. Sykes, in their 1942 book *Shooting to Live with the One-hand Gun* – produced evidence to support the view that the .45 round was not sure to stop a determined man, but that a high-velocity jacketed round, such as the 7.63mm Mauser, would. The subject of calibre and bullet form as they effect a projectile's capability will be discussed at further length later, for the discussion was to have far-reaching consequences for the specification of military sidearms

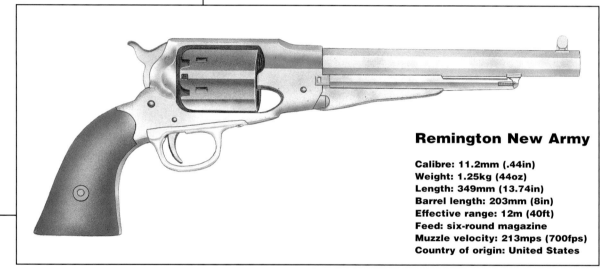

Remington New Army

Calibre: 11.2mm (.44in)
Weight: 1.25kg (44oz)
Length: 349mm (13.74in)
Barrel length: 203mm (8in)
Effective range: 12m (40ft)
Feed: six-round magazine
Muzzle velocity: 213mps (700fps)
Country of origin: United States

expense, during the earlier Crimean War. It was to prove a firm favourite; many maintained that in the mêlée of close combat a single-action revolver couldn't hold its own, and that the speed at which one could get off repeated shots with a double-action pistol in those circumstances more than made up for any loss of accuracy. By its ability to operate equally efficiently in either double- or single-action mode the Beaumont-Adams resolved any remaining argument between these views once and for all. Its heavier calibre also proved its worth time and again, the .50 and .44 rounds proving a sure man-stopper where Colt's higher-velocity but lighter .36 rounds were not. Colonel George Fosbery – who later invented an ingenious semi-automatic self-cocking revolver – related an incident which demonstrated the reality of the situation quite graphically:

dropped down beside him. My informant, who witnessed the affair, told me that five out of the six bullets had struck the sepoy close together in the chest, and had all passed through him and out at his back.'

THE PROLIFERATION OF COPYING

American soldiers (or more accurately, Marines) were to encounter similar problems with .38-calibre rounds in the Philippines during the Moros rebellion, early in the twentieth century. The American Government reacted in exactly the same way as the British, by readopting the .45-calibre pistol – and on that occasion, Colt benefited from the changeover. Somewhat surprisingly, at least on the surface, most of the world's armies soon opted for reduced-calibre handguns once again, most of them even before World War II. Opinions on the

during the twentieth century.

The success of the Adams revolvers of the 1850s can be gauged by the degree to which they were both imitated and produced under licence. The Massachusetts Arms Co. in the United States produced Beaumont-Adams revolvers between 1857 and 1861, and during the Civil War the Union Army purchased over a 1000, most of them in .36 calibre. Some were made in London but many were produced locally. Adams revolvers modified to one degree or another were also produced in Prague, then part of the Austro-Hungarian Empire, and there is some evidence that pistols using Adams' double action were also made in the Prussian state armoury in Suhl. Licences were granted to several gunmakers in Belgium, notably Pirlot Freres and David Herman, while others copied Adams' revolvers more or less directly without any authority at all, though piracy was never quite the problem to Adams that it was to Colt, perhaps because Colt's patents were rather more basic.

WILLIAM TRANTER – GUNMAKER

Around the mid-point of the nineteenth century, patent protection, like copyright, was still somewhat shaky and very definitely patchy, the concept of international protection being still quite unknown. Different countries' laws gave differing degrees of protection. For example, those of the United Kingdom gave 14 years with the possibility of an extension for a like period if the patentee could show that he had not been 'properly reimbursed despite his best efforts' for the expenses incurred in perfecting his invention. American patent law gave 14 years' protection with the possibility of extension for a further seven. The laws of other countries gave protection, usually to natives and foreigners alike, for periods of between one and 20 years, though in some places the protection was not guaranteed, but was still the prerogative of the sovereign, who often held that it did not apply to him or his armed forces. Others – notably Holland and Switzerland – had no system of patent protection until the end of the century.

In order to be eligible for protection from piracy or imitation, an invention or process had to be demonstrably new,

wholly or in substantial part; if a device or a process was already in use, even if not the subject of a patent, then any subsequent application would be turned down. The overall effect was to prompt inventors to apply for patent protection covering every possible variation and eventuality (during the 1860s, an average of some 8000 British patents were granted each year). The result was some very strange objects and methods indeed. Some of them, which clearly did not perform the function intended for them, went on to be startlingly successful in spite of themselves, usually once an essential intermediate step which had been previously overlooked was supplied, or where the process in question could be applied in a different way than had originally been envisaged. An example of this is the case of Rollin White and the bored-through cylinder revolver. The system sometimes forced inventors to go to considerable lengths to circumvent the protection granted to others, but surprisingly often, the addition of a single intermediate step which made the process in question more efficient was enough to render the precursor obsolescent and drive it out of the market, even though its protection remained in force. That was the case with Robert Adams' 'hesitation action' patent of 1853, which was effectively killed off by Beaumont adding a link between the hammer breast and the pawl which

rotated the cylinder. The history of nineteenth century technology can be traced accurately by reference to patent applications alone (though the trail would be a very tortuous one, thanks to all the patents granted for almost unworkable products); the story of the development of the pistol is no exception and so the topic arises fairly frequently.

Among the other English gunmakers, one of those which supplied Robert Adams with semi-finished components, William Tranter, was similarly engaged in trying to perfect a double-action revolver which could also be pre-cocked like a single-action pistol. Tranter could be said to have actually forestalled Frederick Beaumont, though the means of operation he chose seems unnecessarily complicated at first sight, especially since his 1853 design didn't have Beaumont's patent to circumvent.

TRANTER'S REVOLVERS

Tranter's first double-action revolver had what appeared to be two triggers, the conventional one inside the guard and a second, immediately below it, which was actually a cocking lever, though it also served to permit the second finger to steady the pistol and help keep the muzzle down. To pre-cock the action and index the cylinder, one pulled back on this lower trigger alone; a very light pressure on the upper trigger then served to fire the piece. In a tight corner,

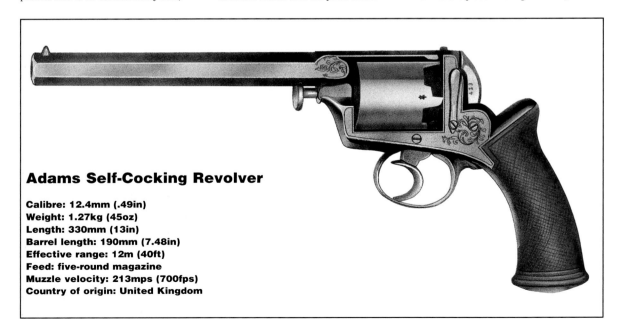

Adams Self-Cocking Revolver

Calibre: 12.4mm (.49in)
Weight: 1.27kg (45oz)
Length: 330mm (13in)
Barrel length: 190mm (7.48in)
Effective range: 12m (40ft)
Feed: five-round magazine
Muzzle velocity: 213mps (700fps)
Country of origin: United Kingdom

however, one could pull back on both triggers simultaneously and achieve normal double-action rapid fire. Tranter employed a combined safety catch and hammer restrainer similar in principle to, but rather better engineered than, that fitted by Adams. There was considerable contemporary criticism of Tranter's system as being unnecessarily complicated, but it proved quite effective in action, to the point where his pistols were second in popularity only to Adams' own. Until 1856, Tranter revolvers, like those of Adams himself, had no hammer spur and could not be cocked by thumbing the hammer back. From that year on, though, Tranter incorporated a link between hammer and pawl very similar to that developed by Beaumont and produced what he called 'triple-action' pistols, with both double triggers and hammer spur. Later still Tranter reverted to a single-trigger double action, but his double-trigger models were sufficiently popular for him to continue to manufacture the two side by side. He continued to produce high-quality pistols until long after the introduction of the bored-through cylinder, and became associated, more so than any other English gunmaker, with the rim-fire cartridge in heavier calibres.

JOHN ADAMS' PATENT

All Tranter's pistols – the early examples of which, like those of Adams, were made not by the mass-production methods Colt was already employing, but rather were hand-finished in the traditional English manner – were outstandingly well made, and enjoyed a high reputation as a result. Unfortunately that didn't prevent the company running into such severe financial difficulties in 1885, that Tranter was forced to sell out to George Kynoch. Kynoch was already at this stage a successful business man who was well on the way to becoming the best-known European manufacturer of ammunition.

More competition for Adams came from within the London Armoury Company (LAC), from his younger brother John and from all the other original subscribers save Frederick Beaumont, as well as from one of Adams' original partners. John Adams left the

company in the mid-1860s to start the Adams Patent Small Arms Company, having already recorded several patents of his own. The most important of these, awarded in 1861, referred to a breech-loading cartridge revolver which could also employ a closed-chamber cylinder equipped with nipples for percussion caps. Indeed, it was for centre-fire cartridge revolvers that John Adams is best known, but first, in 1866, he began producing a front-loaded six-shot pistol whose main components were 'built up': barrel and top strap were forged in one piece and fitted into a slot in the frame.

INVENTION OF THE HAMMER CATCH

This was necessary to circumvent his elder brother's patent on the solid frame revolver, and the method had earlier been adopted by William Harding. The action John Adams devised was similar to that of the Beaumont-Adams but incorporated a

lifter for the hammer not unlike that used by Tranter's original double-trigger design. This method was later widely used in all cartridge revolvers.

Another revolver which bore a marked resemblance to the Beaumont-Adams was that manufactured and marketed by Adams' original partner, John Deane Snr., and developed by LAC subscriber William Harding. In fact the action of the Deane-Harding five-shot pistol, which was based on a patent granted to Harding in mid-1858, was a considerable step forward in the design of the double-action revolver. It dispensed with both the lifter and the secondary sear Beaumont and Tranter had employed, having instead an extension to the back of the trigger which engaged between paired 'bents' on the breast of the hammer. The upper of these was pivoted so that it engaged the trigger extension when the hammer was down but not

■RIGHT: An American Civil War Union soldier with a Colt Dragoon revolver. Note the compound rammer beneath the barrel, used to force bullets into the chambers.

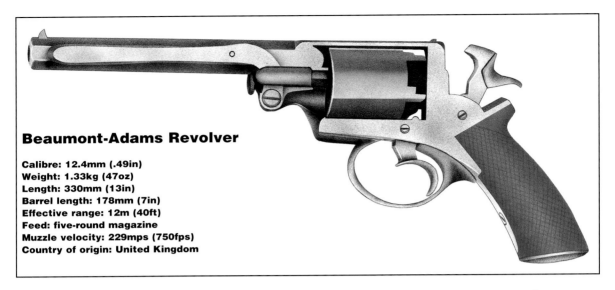

Beaumont-Adams Revolver

Calibre: 12.4mm (.49in)
Weight: 1.33kg (47oz)
Length: 330mm (13in)
Barrel length: 178mm (7in)
Effective range: 12m (40ft)
Feed: five-round magazine
Muzzle velocity: 229mps (750fps)
Country of origin: United Kingdom

when it was cocked manually, when the lower bent acted on it instead to activate both the pawl which indexed the cylinder and the bolt which locked it. This pivoted extension to the hammer, which Harding called a 'rule jointed rod', Colt a 'strut' and Smith & Wesson a 'sear' is also referred to as a hammer catch. It became virtually universal, once Harding's patent protection ran out.

THE DEANE-HARDING REVOLVER
The Deane-Harding revolver, which like John Adams' was forged in two, the top strap and barrel being co-located with the lock frame by means of two pins, one in the standing breech, just before the hammer, the other in the lower frame, below the rammer. The cylinder pin was screwed into the face of the standing breech. It was otherwise undistinguished save for an alarming tendency to fail to function just when it was most needed. Lord Roberts, one of the most elevated soldiers of his day, had a particularly poor opinion of it. 'It is an arm,' he said, 'which could always be depended upon to get out of order at a critical moment.' Certainly it was never adopted as an official service revolver, though at a time when many officers bought their own weapons it did gain some currency. Later experts have suggested that it was poor hand-finishing of the internal components which made it unreliable; perversely, if more examples were available today, doubtless some enthusiast would, with a deal of patience and by meticulous reworking have

managed to produce a sound, reliable pistol from it.

It is known that Adams' defection from Deane, Adams and Deane, just when the company looked set to take off thanks to Adams' own work, caused ill-feeling between them. Certainly, John Deane criticised the Beaumont-Adams revolver at every possilble opportunity as being unnecessarily complicated, holding up the Deane-Harding in its stead, even when his rival was clearly superior. One is tempted to observe that had he devoted more of his time to seeing that his own product was properly engineered on a day to day basis, he would have had less to complain about.

Deane wasn't the only person to criticise the new trend towards over-complication, and neither was he overstating the case. After all, it was one thing to have one's revolver break down somewhere near a competent gunsmith, but quite another if it happened in some far-flung corner of the world where the best one could hope for was the assistance of a blacksmith. James Kerr, another original subscriber to the London Armoury Company, set out to address this problem with a design based on patent applications filed in 1858 and 1859. He produced both single- and double-action five-shot revolvers in 54 bore, 11.2mm (.44in), and 80 bore, 9.8mm (.4in), with simple side locks, their actions mounted on a plate which could be quickly and easily removed to reveal a set of basic components which even a rudimentary blacksmith could repair in many cases.

A handful of other more or less competent English gunsmiths turned their hands to the manufacture of percussion revolvers during the scant three decades of viability the genre enjoyed before the coming of the brass cartridge and the bored-through cylinder. Manufactured in small quantities only, and therefore by methods more suited to a bygone age, the majority were little more than curiosities, even in their own day. The names of their makers – Bailey, Daw, Harvey, Pennel and so on – are known today only to collectors of guns of this type (though the firm of Westley Richards, established since 1812, who also manufactured a double-action revolver during the 1850s and 1860s, became very well known for their excellent shotguns and sporting rifles). What little merit their various patented improvements may have had has not stood the test of time. It is all the more surprising, then, that since the early products of another Birmingham firm, that of the brothers James and Philip Webley, certainly showed no greater promise, they were to come to dominate the market in the United Kingdom for almost a century.

CONSTABULARY MODEL GUNS
Webley revolvers did not really come to the fore until 1867, with the introduction of the much later double-action centre-fire Royal Irish Constabulary models. The firm was established in 1835, when the two brothers, each of whom had served a seven-year apprenticeship in the trade, joined forces and set themselves up

as gun-lock makers in Weaman Street, in Birmingham. Philip married three years later, and in 1845 bought the gun implement manufacturing business of his father-in-law, William Davis. For the next decade the brothers prospered, turning out bullet moulds, wadding punches and sundry small tools, as well as gun and pistol locks. Then, in 1853, they took out patents for a single-action revolver of their own creation.

THE LONGSPUR

The resulting gun, widely known now as the Longspur, from the length of the hammer spur, was rather similar to Colt's first guns of almost two decades earlier. The five-round cylinder turned on an axial pin in an open frame, the barrel secured to the cylinder pin by means of a rectangular steel wedge. In the case of the Webley the frame was also joined to the barrel by means of a hinge at the front of the trigger guard, the subject of Philip Webley's first patent.

This hinge arrangement was later discarded in favour of a thumbscrew (or a cheesehead screw, in the larger-calibre models), passing through the lower part of the barrel extension and into the frame, following the gun's axis. The action itself was simple though perhaps not very robust, and the pistol was made in three models in a variety of calibres, from 48 bore, 11.6mm (.45in) down to 120 bore, 8.1mm (.3in). During that same period, the Webley brothers also offered for sale a series of essentially similar but

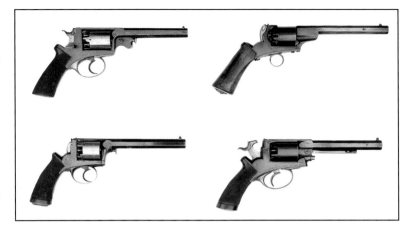

rather better quality double-action revolvers apparently designed by another Birmingham gunsmith, Joseph Bentley, who patented a self-cocking action in 1852. Bentley's pistols had no proper half-cock provision, and in early models he employed a safety-catch-hammer lock very much akin to that found in Robert Adams' pistols. He later refined this arrangement so that, while basically operating in a similar fashion, it was located in the hammer head and took the form of a vertically acting spring-loaded plunger. Bentley's other major contribution, though it proved to be short-lived, was his system of locking the cylinder in line with the barrel. This relied on radial slots machined into the rear of the cylinder and a bolt which

■ABOVE: Examples of nineteenth-century revolvers. The Beaumont-Adams (top left), the Adams Self-Cocking (bottom left), a copy of the Adams (top right) and the Deane-Harding (bottom right).

formed part of the trigger itself, locking the action as the trigger was pulled right to the rear.

Bentley seems to have worked very closely with the Webley brothers, to the point where his pistols are sometimes referred to as Webley-Bentleys, and may very well have been even more closely associated with Philip after James' retirement in 1868. By then the Longspur revolver was long out of date, and production of a series of full-frame, double-action five-shot revolvers was

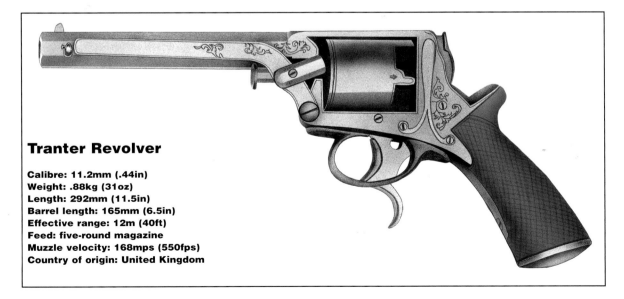

Tranter Revolver

Calibre: 11.2mm (.44in)
Weight: .88kg (31oz)
Length: 292mm (11.5in)
Barrel length: 165mm (6.5in)
Effective range: 12m (40ft)
Feed: five-round magazine
Muzzle velocity: 168mps (550fps)
Country of origin: United Kingdom

under way. These have become known as the Wedge Frame pistols, since their barrel and top strap was retained by the by-now familiar plain wedge passing through the barrel extension and the cylinder pin. Like John Adams, Philip Webley made some of his later pistols in so-called 'dual ignition' form in the early 1860s, the cylinder being interchangeable with one which was bored through and accepted brass cartridges. In this case the rammer, which by that time was usually of the simple pattern patented by Kerr, did double duty as an ejector rod.

PRUSSIA'S NEEDLE-FIRE GUNS

While it is true that many front-loading revolvers were manufactured other than in Britain and the United States of America, very few of them warrant even a cursory examination. European gunmakers were hampered both by their adherence to craft methods and by their own conservatism, while their customers were not much more adventurous. The French Government, for example, did not adopt the revolver as an official arm until

■BELOW: Examples of the revolvers of William Tranter, which incorporated two triggers, the bottom one acting as a cocking lever and the top one for firing.

1856, for the French Navy; and the individual small states which made up what are now Italy and Germany were the same. The most significant advance in firearms technology (as opposed to advances in the field of ammunition) in Europe came from Prussia where Nikolaus von Dreyse developed the needle-fire, breech-loading, single-shot rifle in 1838. He later made some single-shot pistols on the same principle, and the Dreyse Model 1856 pistol in 15.4mm (.6in) calibre was issued to the Prussian cavalry. Some 14 years later a variation on that same system, adapted for a six-shot revolver, was patented in London by George Kufahl.

Kufahl's system was later put into production by Franz, Nikolaus' son, at the Sommerda factory of Waffen und Munitionsfabrik von Dreyse, which was to become Rheinische Metallwaren und Maschinenfabrik in 1901, and employ Louis Schmeisser as a designer. The method was not well-suited to a revolver, though Kufahl's pistol stayed in production until 1880, long after the metal cartridge had been universally accepted. The cylinder of Kufahl's pistol had to be removed for loading, and to simplify this it was mounted on a loose-fitting axial pin, which was removed by turning it through 90 degrees and withdrawing it to the front. The action

was more complicated, since the Dreyse principle required a needle to be driven the length of the propellant charge (which came in a fabric cartridge which also contained the bullet) and strike a percussion cap located in a hollow at the back of the projectile. As in Dreyse's rifles, the needle, together with the spring to propel it forward, was housed within a bolt. It was logical and natural to pull the bolt back to open the breech of the rifle, thereby cocking the spring which would later drive bolt and needle forward, but less so in a revolver pistol, though Kufahl at least engineered his creation so that the needle retracted itself back within the bolt once the trigger was released. The chambers were not bored through, but rather had a small hole drilled in the rear to admit the firing needle.

THE LE MAT PISTOL

Around about the same time that Kufahl was trying to find a manufacturer willing to take his needle revolver on board, a French physician resident in New Orleans, Louisiana, Jean Alexandre Le Mat, was developing a far more serviceable revolver. It had two barrels, the upper, usually of .42 or .36 calibre, was served by a revolving cylinder, while the lower, which formed the axis for that cylinder, was of .63 calibre, smooth-bore

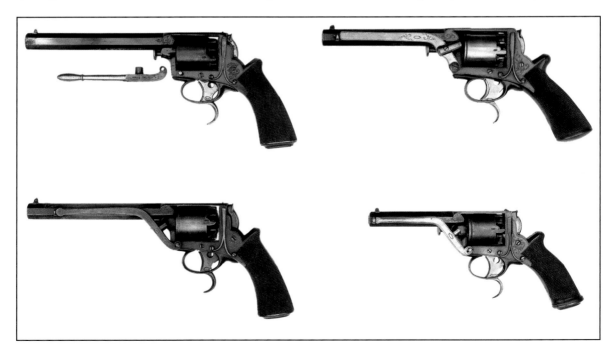

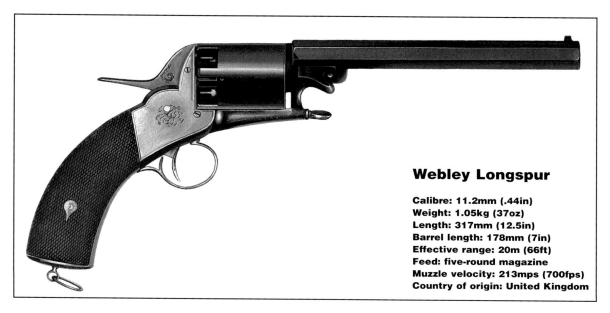

Webley Longspur

Calibre: 11.2mm (.44in)
Weight: 1.05kg (37oz)
Length: 317mm (12.5in)
Barrel length: 178mm (7in)
Effective range: 20m (66ft)
Feed: five-round magazine
Muzzle velocity: 213mps (700fps)
Country of origin: United Kingdom

and was loaded with a single charge of buckshot. Both barrels were fired by the same hammer, by virtue of its having an adjustable nose, and naturally, by the same trigger. Le Mat's pistol enjoyed some very small distribution during the Civil War, perhaps because his partner was Pierre Beauregard, the Confederate General victorious at Bull Run. It was otherwise widely regarded as a curiosity (though no less a luminary figure than J.E.B. Stuart carried one), and had it not been for the Civil War, the pistol would probably never have been heard of again. Le Mat also obtained a British patent, and later extended it to cover a centre-fire version of his hybrid revolver, firing 9mm (.35in) ball and 14mm (.55in) shot cartridges. A pin-fire version is also said to have been made in small quantities, the central smooth-bore barrel still being muzzle-loaded and fired by a percussion cap. The centre-fire and pin-fire versions enjoyed even less success than the original.

Even more unusual were the 10-or 12-shot revolvers manufactured by John Walch of New York in the late 1850s. Walch returned to the long-outmoded practice of superimposing loads, and constructed his pistols with double-length cylinders fitted with two rows of nipples, to accommodate special paper cartridges. Each of these contained two loads and two projectiles separated by a division compounded of ordinary household soap. The revolvers had two hammers, one

with a conventional nose, positioned to strike the rearmost nipple and set off the rearmost charge, the second with an elongated nose, to strike the forward nipple and set off the forward charge. Both hammers were originally controlled by one trigger, and failure to release the trigger promptly after firing the forward charge resulted in the rear charge being detonated immediately afterwards. Later examples had individual triggers, and there was even an improved design which reverted to a single trigger equipped with a safety interlock. Perhaps thankfully, Walch's pistols never acquired much of a following.

A PLETHORA OF PATENTS
Walch was by no means the most eccentric man to have ever designed and manufactured a repeating pistol, however. We should perhaps pay homage in passing to the likes of Jarre's 'harmonica' pistol, with its linear magazine; Iverson, with his radial-cylinder 'turret gun' (in which one chamber – perhaps a loaded chamber – pointed straight back at the firer's head; and the Josselyn pistol, with its endless belt of chambers.

The appearance of unlikely devices such as these, which were the work of optimistic inventors determined to circumvent the process of patent protection, even where the product or process they were trying to supplant was clearly superior to their own invention,

was characteristic of the latter part of the nineteenth century. It was by no means limited to firearms – the libraries of the world's patent offices are full of weird and wonderful attempts to make a better mousetrap in the hope that the world would, in the colourful words of Ralph Waldo Emerson, beat a path to the inventor's door. Generally the protection process worked, but just occasionally, a crack-pot got there first, as was the case with the bored-through cylinder.

BREECH-LOADING DESIGNS
Even by the late 1850s, when the front-loading, percussion cap revolver had evolved into an efficient, reliable firearm, there was still a small coterie of sportsmen (and even the odd military man) who favoured the old system of one chamber per barrel, insisting that such weapons packed more punch, since there was no possibility of the loss of propellant gas between the chamber and the breech end of the barrel. Such guns, and they exist in both double and quadruple barrel versions, are often called 'howdah pistols', having been used, we are solemnly assured, for shooting tigers from the backs of elephants (at least as back-up guns). Curiously, they did not disappear with the coming of the brass centre-fire cartridge, and continued to be employed with both ball and shot loads, the best known examples being those made in considerable numbers by Charles Lancaster and his successor, Henry

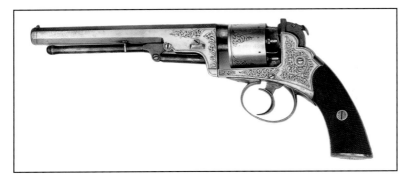

■ABOVE: One of the Bentley revolvers, which first appeared around 1853. The barrel was a separate component from the frame and butt, which were forged from one piece of iron.

Thorn. The four-barrelled 'Martin Mitrailleuse' also deserves a mention, despite its alarming proclivity for sometimes setting off more than one charge at a time.

The next great leap forward in handgun design, that of a reliable breech-loader, depended on a number of key developments coming to fruition. These included the evolution of the unitary brass cartridge containing detonator, charge and projectile, together with the development of new, better types of propellant and the changing characteristics of the bullet.

It has been suggested that the invention of gunpowder – or perhaps, to be more accurate, one should say the discovery that a mixture of saltpetre,

■BELOW: The Webley Longspur, so called because of the length of its hammer spur. The chamber has five chambers with horizontal nipples separated from each other by partitions.

sulphur and charcoal had explosive properties – was extremely unlikely, but that ignores the curiosity of pre-scientific man. What is perhaps more surprising is that gunpowder ever became widely used, given the difficulty of obtaining one of its ingredients. Saltpetre, or potassium nitrate, is the source of the oxygen which combines with carbon to form carbon dioxide, the gas produced so rapidly and in such copious quantities when gunpowder burns. Tests conducted in the late nineteenth century showed that properly packed, the finest gunpowder available produced 290 times its own volume of gas and a pressure of 4000 atmospheres at a temperature of about 3300 degrees Celsius.

Saltpetre occurs in nature as a by-product of the decay of vegetable matter, but not in particularly large quantities. As the demand for it increased an intensive process of nitre farming, as it was known, came into being. Farmyard manure was laid in shallow trenches, kept warm and covered with light soil. It was then raked and stirred regularly, to ensure that the bacteria which released the nitrates had a sufficient supply of air. Then a quantity of wood ash was added, so that the potassium it

contained could replace the hydrogen in the weak nitric acid the bacteria produced, forming potassium nitrate. The admixture of soil, manure and ashes was then washed and allowed to soak, which dissolved the saltpetre, and the resulting solution was evaporated to leave crystalline potassium nitrate.

It was the scarcity of potassium nitrate which had prompted Napoleon Bonaparte to set the eminent chemist Claude Louis Berthollet searching for an alternative, leading to his discovery of the alternative oxygen source, potassium chlorate, in 1786. This work was to lead indirectly to Forsyth's development of the percussion gun (see previous chapter). Gunpowder only became easier to produce after the middle of the nineteenth century, when vast deposits of nitrates were discovered in Chile, albeit in the form of less-reactive sodium nitrate, which still had to be treated to produce saltpetre, and later with the invention of a process to fix nitrogen directly from the air. Ironically, those discoveries almost coincided with the invention of new explosives which soon took over from gunpowder, removing the

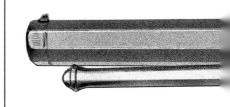

Bentley Revolver

Calibre: 11.2mm (.44in)
Weight: .94kg (33oz)
Length: 305mm (12in)
Barrel length: 178mm (7in)
Effective range: 12m (40ft)
Feed: five-round magazine
Muzzle velocity: 183mps (600fps)
Country of origin: United Kingdom

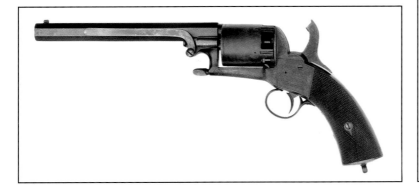

need for potassium nitrate anyway!

The first new explosive was the notoriously unstable nitro-glycerine, invented by an Italian chemist named Sobrero, in 1846. Almost 20 years later, Alfred Nobel solved some of the problems of handling nitro-glycerine when he discovered that an 'infusorial earth' named kieselguhr or diatomite would absorb up to three to four times its own weight of it. Earlier, in 1838, Theophile Pelouze had produced a highly inflammable material by treating cotton with concentrated nitric acid, a process which led eventually to the discovery of nitro-cellulose. Another chemist, Christian Schonbein, continued the work, and introduced sulphuric acid into the process, producing what became known as guncotton.

PRACTICAL PROPELLENTS

Paul Vielle synthesised the first propellant from guncotton when he treated it with a mixture of alcohol and ether to make the smokeless 'Poudre B', but it was left to Nobel, however, to show how the two lines of research could be combined by gelatinising the nitrated

cotton with nitro-glycerine. These compounds which, like gunpowder, are progressive explosives (as distinct from high explosives, in that their rate of combustion can be controlled to some extent), form the basis of all modern smokeless propellants.

Gunpowder itself is an adequate explosive, but it has two distinct drawbacks: in loose form it is difficult to handle, and when burned it produces copious quantities of smoke together with a considerable solid residue which soon renders any gun employing it unusable until it is cleaned. The second problem is inherent in the nature of the material, and there is nothing one can do about it, but the first could be addressed by making it up into convenient discrete charges, wrapped up in paper or fabric, an approach which was adopted as early as the sixteenth century.

EARLY CARTRIDGES

These first cartridges were nothing more elaborate than a means of containing a measured weight of powder; they were opened, and the charge poured into the muzzle of the gun. If they also contained

the projectile, that was then tamped in afterwards, usually on top of the wrapping from the cartridge, which served a useful second purpose as a containing wad. Additionally, the paper itself could be impregnated with grease, usually tallow or animal fat, which served as a lubricant. It was the presence of this tallow, allied to the infantryman's practice of biting off the top of the cartridge to open it, which is said to have sparked off the Indian Mutiny in 1857. A false rumour spread through the Honorable East India Company's largely Hindu Sepoy (native) troops that the tallow in question came from cows. These animals are sacred to Hindus, and the consumption of any part of which was strictly taboo; inevitably, Hindu religious leaders ruled, biting into the cartridge meant ingesting small quantities of tallow, and this was sufficient to contravene the dietary laws.

These first cartridges were something of an improvement over loose powder carried in a horn or flask, but not much. It was not until they began to appear with the wrapping rendered highly inflammable, it having been soaked in a

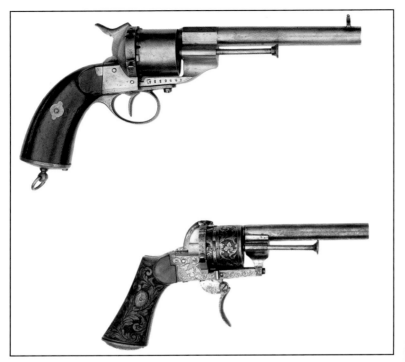

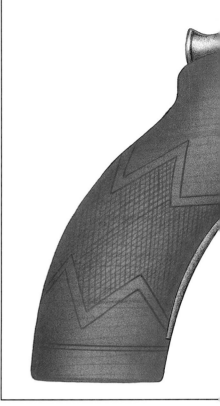

■ABOVE: Two pin-fire revolvers. The Lefaucheux model (top) and the rather cruder example (bottom) are illustrative of this type of revolver.

saltpetre solution in exactly the same way as the slowmatches of a by-gone day, that they really started to make the shooter's life easier. Cartridges of this sort became popular with pistol shooters, who had previously tended to stick to the use of powder flasks and loose balls, after about 1850. As an alternative to being wrapped in nitrated paper, they were sometimes formed entirely of powder which had been made into a thick paste with collodion (a syrupy solution of a nitro-cellulose named pyroxylin in ether or alcohol), moulded and then allowed to dry. The bullet, by now usually cylindro-conoidal or cylindro-ogival rather than spherical (that is, either a short cylinder with a straight-walled, cone-shaped point or a short cylinder with a rounded head), was attached to it by means of either collodion or regular glue. This latter approach produced a cartridge which was waterproof enough, an important consideration, but which was brittle and easily damaged.

SKIN CARTRIDGES

Robert Adams experimented with thin-walled metal tubes, a projectile loosely crimped into one end and the open base sealed with nitrated paper. William Eley and Samuel Colt improved on that in

1855 by wrapping the charge in thin tinfoil, sealing the joint with waterproof cement, and attaching the projectile by means of a spot of glue. Both approaches left metal residue in the chambers, however, which had to be removed before they could be reloaded. The following year a British naval captain, John Hayes, filed a patent application for what became known as the skin cartridge (though that was something of a misnomer, as the skin involved was actually gut). His design used the intestines of small animals in rather the same way that the butcher uses the same product to make sausages, strengthening it by wrapping the cartridge in thread, rather as one whips a rope's end. William Storm improved on Hayes patent in 1861, when he treated the dried gut cartridges with gutta-percha varnish. This rendered the cartridge both completely waterproof and brittle when it dried, so that it fragmented when being forced into the chamber by the rammer.

Imperfect though these cartridges were, they were nonetheless in huge

demand – the Civil War alone saw to that. One of the most impressive statistics to come out of that conflict concerns the colossal number of pistol cartridges it consumed: for the 19 types of handgun it issued to its troops, the Union Army alone bought no less than 68,385,400 rounds.

THE CENTRE-FIRE CARTRIDGE

None of these cartridges contained a detonator, of course, though that idea had been around for almost half a century, thanks to the pioneering work of the Swiss, Samuel Johannes Pauly, in Paris towards the end of the Napoleonic Wars. In fact, Pauly's chief interest was in improving the still very imperfect breech-loader, but in order to do that, he realised he first had to devise a means of containing projectile, charge and detonator in one cartridge. Pauly worked more or less closely with Prélat, the plagiarist who later claimed to have invented the percussion cap, and almost certainly heard of Forsyth's work with loose fulminates as detonators through him.

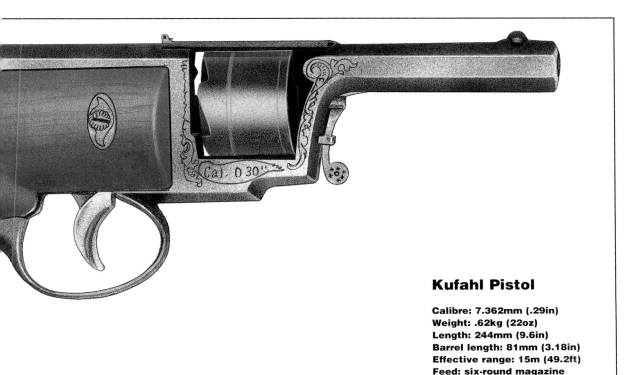

Kufahl Pistol

Calibre: 7.362mm (.29in)
Weight: .62kg (22oz)
Length: 244mm (9.6in)
Barrel length: 81mm (3.18in)
Effective range: 15m (49.2ft)
Feed: six-round magazine
Muzzle velocity: 152mps (500fps)
Country of origin: Germany

This was the missing link that made his notion viable, and in 1810 or 1811 he produced the precursor to the modern centre-fire brass cartridge, with a rimmed base of soft metal which expanded on discharge and formed a seal against escaping gas, thereby curing the most serious problem of the early breech-loader. The body of Pauly's cartridges was either of paper, like shotgun shells were until the 1960s, or of brass, in which case they could be reloaded. The primer was more primitive, for – the percussion cap having not yet been invented – the only method available was to place a small amount of priming powder in an open pan. In order to make sure the priming was contained, Pauly was forced to utilise a flush standing breech, pierced to take a spring-loaded firing pin, and the hammer-like extensions one sees on his guns are in fact just cocks for concealed strikers. Pauly patented his first gun, a breech-loading rifle, in 1812, and also produced pistols. His rifles had tip-up breech blocks, his pistols were generally break-open designs, and his work was

copied, though not widely. Curiously, the fact that his brass cartridge bases expanded to form a gas-tight seal at the breech seems to have gone unremarked for many years.

On arriving in Paris, Pauly employed a young Prussian gun lock maker, Nikolaus von Dreyse; indeed, it was von Dreyse who made the guns Pauly designed. In 1814, when Pauly moved to London, Dreyse returned to his native Sommerda, where, 10 years later, he opened a small factory manufacturing percussion caps. As already noted, he later developed the needle-fire system which proved decisive in two short wars, with Denmark in 1864 and with Austria in 1866, but was soon overtaken by other, more reliable actions. The 'capping breech-loader' earlier developed by Christian Sharps, which enjoyed a long production life thanks to the strength of its falling-block action and its renowned accuracy, was probably the last rifle manufactured in significant numbers which did not use a self-sealing brass cartridge case. When finally the Sharps rifle was modified to take brass

cartridges, in 1877, much of the work was carried out by a young German named Hugo Borchardt, who was later to take a very significant step indeed in the development of the pistol.

THE METALLIC CARTRIDGE

Another alumnus of Pauly's workshop, Clement Pottet, was also to make an important contribution to the evolution of the cartridge when he substituted a percussion cap for the open cup or pan Pauly had used to contain the priming, probably sometime in the 1820s. Meanwhile, elsewhere in Paris, another gunsmith, Casimir Lefaucheux, was at work on a subtly different means of setting off the propellant charge, and in the process produced the first satisfactory self-primed metallic cartridge, though his initial efforts, like Pauly's, involved a paper body on a brass or copper base. Lefaucheux's pin-fire cartridge was first introduced in about 1826. The pin itself was effectively a firing pin; it acted on a central percussion cap, but at an angle of 90 degrees to the axis of the cartridge,

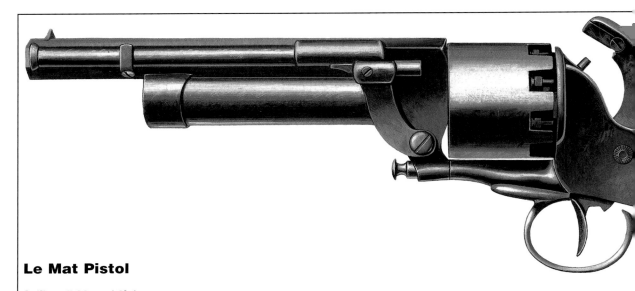

Le Mat Pistol

Calibre: 7.62mm (.3in)
Weight: 1.64kg (58oz)
Length: 337mm (13.26in)
Barrel length: 178mm (7in)
Effective range: 15m (49.2ft)
Feed: nine/one
Muzzle velocity: 183mps (600fps)
Country of origin: France

protruding from the side of the case near its base. It made breech loading a practical proposition, even though it was to a degree fragile and susceptible to accidental discharge. A point in its favour was that the pin made extraction of the spent case somewhat easier, and also provided an easy means of checking, by feel alone if necessary, how many rounds one had fired from one's revolver.

PIN-FIRE VERSUS RIM-FIRE

Over the next 20 years the pin-fire system became quite popular in France and Germany, though it attracted very little attention in Britain. Lefaucheux's basic design was improved on by Hall in London and Houiller in Paris. In 1854, Lefaucheux's son Eugene obtained a British patent for the innovative single-action pin-fire revolver exhibited by his father at the 1851 Great Exhibition. When the French Government accepted the revolver for use by its armed services in 1856, Lefaucheux pin-fire pistols were chosen. In 1858 the Italian Navy, and the armies of Norway, Spain and Sweden followed the French example. Pin-fire

revolvers were still being produced in Europe until late 1939, although many of them were of quite appalling quality.

Another Frenchman, Louis Flobert, is widely credited with inspiring the less important of the two types of metallic cartridge still in everyday use today. The rim-fire cartridge started out as a drawn copper case little bigger than a percussion cap, in which the priming fulminate acted as propellant, shooting a low-mass projectile at low velocity. These cartridges, in 4-9mm calibre, with round and cylindro-conoidal projectiles, or even shot, were used for target practice and vermin control. Flobert also exhibited his wares at the 1851 Great Exhibition, and though his cartridges aroused considerable interest, they never achieved the same popularity in Britain as in France and Belgium.

THE RIM-FIRE'S DRAWBACKS

An American gunsmith, Daniel Wesson, thought enough of Flobert's work to turn his own hand to rim-fire cartridges, concentrating on .22-calibre and increasing the case length somewhat to

accommodate a small (three or four grain) charge of black powder. Wesson had better tooling available to him than Flobert had, and succeeded in forming a true rim to the cartridge where the Frenchman had only managed a slight swelling, placing the fulminate priming there instead of simply depositing a blob of it somewhere in the head of the cartridge. The rim served not only to aid ejection, but also to regulate the headspace – the distance between the breechblock and the struck face of the cartridge. Pauly's cartridge had achieved that, but succeeding designs had not; misfires were common as a result.

The basic defect of the rim-fire cartridge was one of material strength. In order for the strike of the hammer to be able to detonate the primer, the case of the cartridge had to be both thin and soft, but in larger calibres, the charge necessary to propel the projectile often then proved sufficient to split the case. In addition, it was difficult to ensure the even distribution of primer around the cartridge's rim, and this often resulted in misfires. And a relatively high proportion

of primer to propellant frequently caused the rim to split and even to separate from the case proper, which normally rendered the weapon unusable without the attention of an armourer.

These problems were to cause the demise of the rim-fire cartridge in all but .22-calibre, but, initially at least, the genre took over. Rim-fire rifles and pistols chambered for calibres as big as .50 were produced, though the most popular were .32 (and pistols chambered for this round were produced until 1963) and .41, the latter being used in the famous Remington Double Derringer. Some of the most famous rifles of that same era, the Winchester Model 1866, the Henry rifle from which it was developed, and the Spencer, the outstanding repeating rifle of the American Civil War, were also chambered for rim-fire cartridges. Likewise the only single-shot cartridge pistol ever to be adopted by the US Government for general issue (the exceptions were specialist items such as assassination weapons like the 'Liberator' and certain adapted target pistols, a few survival weapons and flare pistols), the Remington Navy Model 1865, with its rolling block action, was chambered for a .50-calibre rim-fire cartridge. Despite the popularity of large-bore rim-fire revolvers

in Britain, notably a whole series produced by William Tranter, and their continuing popularity in France and Belgium, the only European power to adopt a rim-fire weapon officially as a service arm was Switzerland. Here the Chamelot-Delvigne revolver in 10.4mm calibre saw service between 1873 and 1878 before being modified to a centre-fire operation.

BOXER AND BERDAN
A number of men deserve the credit for conceiving the centre-fire cartridge, though little good it did them. These include Pauly and Pottet, Dreyse, and an Englishman named Joseph Needham, who produced a modified version of the Dreyse system and convinced a number of gunmakers, Rigby among them, to utilise it. In the end, there were to be many false starts made and not a few false paths followed before the reloadable, solid brass centre-fire cartridge became a practical reality, even though all the components of a successful design, and all the workshop techniques to realise it, were available as early as 1840.

Worthwhile contributions were made by George Morse, who constructed tubular brass cartridges with wire 'anvils', against which percussion caps could be detonated. The annular gap left

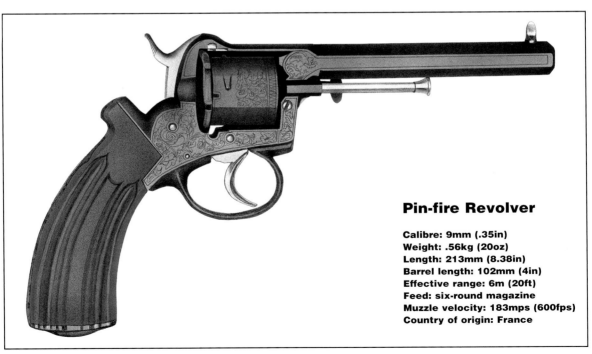

Pin-fire Revolver

Calibre: 9mm (.35in)
Weight: .56kg (20oz)
Length: 213mm (8.38in)
Barrel length: 102mm (4in)
Effective range: 6m (20ft)
Feed: six-round magazine
Muzzle velocity: 183mps (600fps)
Country of origin: France

■ABOVE: Belgian (top) and Spanish (bottom) pin-fire revolvers. The French Navy adopted pin-fires in 1856 for its boarding and landing parties. They were to be used in conjunction with the cutlass. The Italian Navy, suitably impressed with their performance, followed the French example in 1858.

when the cap was fitted was filled with a rubber retaining ring, More significant was the work of two military officers, one British and the other American, Colonel Edward Mounier Boxer, of the Royal Laboratory at Woolwich, and Colonel Hiram Berdan, late of the elite Sharpshooters Regiment of the Union

Army. It was these two, with considerable help from assistant technicians, who designed and produced the first truly workable reloadable centre-fire cartridges with set-in primers, Boxer in 1866, Berdan two years later.

Boxer's cartridges were made up of coiled brass walls, a drawn brass head

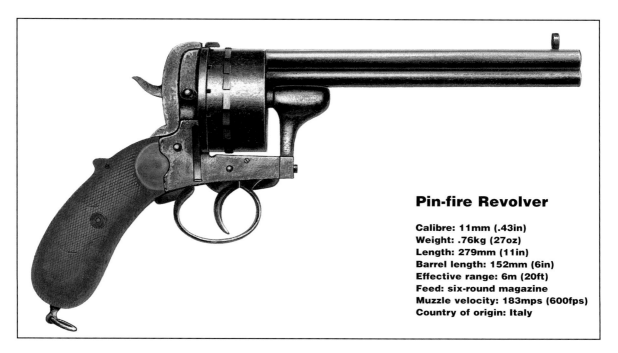

Pin-fire Revolver

Calibre: 11mm (.43in)
Weight: .76kg (27oz)
Length: 279mm (11in)
Barrel length: 152mm (6in)
Effective range: 6m (20ft)
Feed: six-round magazine
Muzzle velocity: 183mps (600fps)
Country of origin: Italy

cup drilled to take the primer and a separate anvil to strike it on, and an iron disk which served as the extraction and seating rim. In practice they proved to be less than perfect under the rigours of active service, particularly when used in rifles such as the Enfield-Snider and the Martini-Henry then issued to the British Army. On firing, the cases often swelled and jammed in the chamber, and the iron rim was all too easily torn off by the extractor claw. They were also assembled by hand, and inevitably, mistakes meant misfires; annoying on the firing range, life-threatening in battle, as the British found out to their cost all too often. Revolver rounds manufactured on the same principle proved less troublesome, but the problem wasn't finally resolved until solid drawn cartridges were issued, for revolvers in 1880 and for rifles five years later.

Berdan's inspiration came primarily from the work of another soldier, Colonel S.V. Benet (despite his name, an American). He was Chief of Ordnance of the US Army at the Frankford Arsenal. Berdan's major contribution was to see that the anvil for the primer could be formed as part of the case itself, and his claim to primacy rests on having used solid drawn cases right from the start, thus avoiding the major problems which beset Boxer's ammunition. Surprisingly,

Berdan didn't take the obvious next step and patent the design for a primer to fit his cartridge cases; that was left to A.C. Hobbs of the Union Metallic Cartridge Co, in 1869.

NEW CARTRIDGES AND BULLETS

At this stage, all cartridges were rimmed or flanged, the rim rather than the form of the cartridge and projectile locating the round in the breech. This continued to be convenient until the advent of guns (both rifles and pistols) with box magazines, when it became a liability. If rimmed rounds are wrongly packed into a box magazine, they won't feed. The answer was the rimless round. In this case the neck of the cartridge case, which is of slightly greater diameter than the projectile it contains, and its overall length, determine its accurate seating within the chamber, with all that entails for headspacing and extraction.

The shape and make-up of the projectile itself also began to change from around this time. The first improvement was the move away from the round ball of the early muzzle-loader to the cylindrical bullets with a more or less rounded nose used in the non-unitary cartridges, a form which carried over into the unitary cartridge. With the advent of self-loading pistols, which in general used less powerful loads than revolvers, there

was a move towards projectiles with greater stopping power for a given velocity. These included bullets which expanded on impact; soft-nose, hollow-point and partially deformable rounds in particular. Fragmenting and exploding bullets have been available since the nineteenth century. Their use was universally condemned – but only against white men, not against the coloured races. This curious but widespread racist sentiment harks back to Pope Innocent II's banning the use of the crossbow against Christians, but permitting its employment against infidels. It is also demonstrated by James Puckle's provision of square bullets for use against Turks in his 'Defender', the rotary-magazine light cannon he made in 1717. More civilised cylindrical projectiles were to be used against fellow Europeans and appropriate barrels were provided. Even in such a barbaric conflict as World War I, where the most horrific expedient weapons such as hatchets and nailed clubs were routinely used in close combat, it was widely held that German troops summarily executed Allied officers found with revolvers loaded with either square-headed ammunition or what were popularly known as 'dum-dums' – regular round-headed rounds with a cross incised in them. The name 'dum-dum' came from that of a British armoury near Calcutta,

■ABOVE: Abraham Lincoln's night at the theatre is about to be irrevocably spoiled by John Wilkes Booth; in April 1865, he used a Colt Deringer No 3 to shoot the president.

in India, where, presumably, the practice originated, probably during the mutiny. The rumours had a basis of fact. In 1898, a new official British service pistol cartridge, the .455-calibre Mark 3 – was issued. It was cylindrical, with a hemispherical cavity in both nose and base. There was an immediate outcry against it, and despite British protestations that it was meant solely for use against 'uncivilised' enemies, its use was outlawed by the Hague Convention. In 1902 they were declared obsolete, and the round-nosed Mark 2 bullet was issued in their place. In 1912 this was replaced by the Mark 4 – a plain lead cylinder with a flat front – and it was the presence of these rounds in captured officer's pistols which gave rise to the outcry and talk of summary execution for contravention of the Hague Convention. As far as one can tell, the threat was never carried out – but in the bestial atmosphere of that particular war, who knows? The Mark 4 rounds were withdrawn – though they were not actually declared obsolete until 1946. They were also commercially available – under the name 'Manstopper' – during much of the interwar period.

The introduction of self-loading pistols, which feed rounds into the chamber from

Chamelot-Delvigne Revolver

Calibre: 10.4mm (.4in)
Weight: 1.13kg (40oz)
Length: 284mm (11.18in)
Barrel length: 159mm (6.25in)
Effective range: 6m (20ft)
Feed: six-round magazine
Muzzle velocity: 190mps (625fps)
Country of origin: France

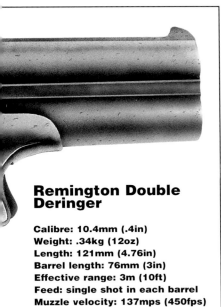

Remington Double Deringer

Calibre: 10.4mm (.4in)
Weight: .34kg (12oz)
Length: 121mm (4.76in)
Barrel length: 76mm (3in)
Effective range: 3m (10ft)
Feed: single shot in each barrel
Muzzle velocity: 137mps (450fps)
Country of origin: United States

a box magazine, saw pure lead projectiles giving way to an alloy of lead with a hardening agent, usually tin or antimony, in an attempt to cut down distortion and resultant misfeeds. The ultimate solution to that problem was the introduction of bullets 'jacketed' with steel or cupro-nickel. In modern times, only .22 rim-fire rounds are generally to be found with pure lead projectiles.

THE UNITARY CARTRIDGE

In one way it could be argued that the coming of the unitary cartridge and the revolver (and the rifle) which fired it was a retrograde step. Now, the empty case had to be extracted before a new cartridge could be inserted in its place, whereas before the chamber was, in theory at least, left empty by the discharge. A great deal of ingenuity went into making the ejection of spent cases as automatic an action as possible, but even at its most time-consuming the real advantages of the unified rear-loading cartridge over front-loading with separate percussion caps were still considerable.

In the early days of the cartridge there was some question as to their general availability, and for that reason, many revolver conversions from 'cap and ball' permitted a speedy return to the old methods by reverting to the original cylinder and rammer. That criticism lost ground rapidly as time went on and the trend toward cartridges became confirmed.

Samuel Colt ushered in the heyday of the front-loading revolver with his 1836 patent, so perhaps it is only fitting that the expiry of that protection in the USA, in 1857 should have just as effectively sounded its death-knell. The revolver is still being developed and improved upon today, yet the legacy of the early inventors is clear. Smith & Wesson, Webley and Remington, names that are synonymous with many legends of the Wild West, relied heavily on Sam Colt's pioneering work. The fact that his firearms are held in such high esteem – almost reverence by collectors, and replicated at the modern Colt factory, is testimony to their importance in the history of gunmaking.

CHAPTER 3
THE CARTRIDGE REVOLVER

The perfecting of the percussion system facilitated the introduction of the self-contained cartridge, which contained primer, propellant and projectile in a single case. These cartridges could be loaded and fired from breech-loading weapons without any preparation.

One of the earliest patented self-contained cartridges was that developed by Walter Hunt of New York. This used a small charge of powder – some six and a half grains – housed inside the hollow base of a .38-calibre lead bullet which itself weighed 100 grains (6.5g), detonating it by means of a percussion cap acting through a hole in the cork plug which closed off the base aperture. Two years later, Hunt took out a US patent for what he called a 'Volitional Repeater', a gun with a tubular magazine using this ammunition, and which had a firing pin activated by a coiled spring, which was some years ahead of its time. Lacking capital, he assigned the patent almost immediately, to a machinist named George Arrowsmith. An employee of Arrowsmith's, Lewis Jennings, worked on the gun design, simplified and strengthened it, and himself obtained an additional patent which he, too, assigned to Arrowsmith. Arrowsmith in turn sold both the Hunt and Jennings patents to Courtland Palmer, who contracted with the firm of Robbins and Lawrence, of Windsor, Vermont, to produce 5000 rifles to this design. Over the next two years, two journeymen-gunsmiths, Horace Smith and Daniel Baird Wesson, refined the design further in their spare time and in 1854 they joined forces, together with Palmer, to manufacture it as both a rifle

■LEFT: 'Hard Pushed', a painting by Charles Schreyvogel. The ubiquitous cowboy on the left is using a Colt Single Action Army Model known as the Peacemaker, a truly great handgun.

and a pistol. The pistol version carried eight to 10 rounds of ammunition in a magazine below the barrel, feeding them to the breech by the forward-and-down action of the trigger guard, which acted as a cocking lever.

The following year, Smith, Wesson and Palmer sold out to the Volcanic Repeating Arms Company, a consortium of some 40 investors from New Haven and New York, one of whom was a shirt manufacturer named Oliver F. Winchester. Volcanic continued to manufacture firearms, the only major change being to the round they fired. Instead of black powder, the base of the bullet was now charged with a fulminate-based percussion powder, which acted as a self-priming propellant and did away with the need for a separate percussion cap. It was Daniel Wesson who had devised this charge; dissatisfied with its performance, he had gone on to develop a true centre-fire cartridge in 1854. The Volcanic Company acquired the rights to this cartridge along with the other assets of Smith, Wesson and Palmer, but never put it into production.

THE RIM-FIRE UNITARY CARTRIDGE
It was the original round's poor performance which eventually spelled disaster for the Volcanic rifle and pistol, and the company went into bankruptcy early in 1857. On 19 March that year, Winchester purchased its assets and assigned them to a new company, the New Haven Arms Co., with himself as president. Knowing nothing whatsoever about firearms, he brought in Benjamin Tyler Henry to run the manufacturing

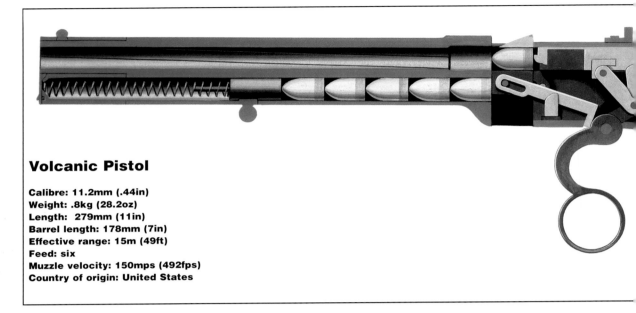

Volcanic Pistol

Calibre: 11.2mm (.44in)
Weight: .8kg (28.2oz)
Length: 279mm (11in)
Barrel length: 178mm (7in)
Effective range: 15m (49ft)
Feed: six
Muzzle velocity: 150mps (492fps)
Country of origin: United States

side of the business, and it was Henry who decided to abandon the pistol and concentrate instead on making essential improvements to the rifle. He also devised the .44-calibre rim-fire unitary cartridge it was to fire, producing one of the most famous lines of rifles ever seen in the process.

SMITH AND WESSON'S CYLINDER
Wesson stayed on as works manager when he and his partners sold out to Volcanic, while Smith retired to run a livery stable with his brother-in-law. They maintained contact, however, and between them worked up the design of a rim-fire revolver to utilise cartridges Wesson had devised as an improvement on Flobert's. This was in 1856, the year before Colt's all-important patents expired, and the two men worked in full expectation of being able to use features of Colt's design, along with elements they had added, to produce a handgun utilising Wesson's unitary cartridges. One of the most important of these elements was the bored-through cylinder, essential to the entire concept. However, the bored-through cylinder was already covered by a dubious patent granted the previous year to Rollin White of New Haven, as part of a design for an impractical revolver conceived to evade other elements of Colt's patent!

The White gun had never been put into production, and there was much speculation at the time as to whether the patent he had obtained was valid. His design was basically flawed, but the patent application included the telling phrase 'extending the chambers through the rear of the cylinder for the purpose of loading them at the breech from behind'. Smith and Wesson had two alternatives: to produce their revolver and challenge the validity of the White patent in the courts, knowing that if they won, the idea would pass automatically into the public domain, and every revolver-maker in the land would have a right to it, or to proceed as if the patent was valid, and try to obtain explotation rights from White.

WHITE'S PATENT EXPIRES
They chose the latter course, and in November 1856 secured White's agreement in return for a royalty of 15 cents on every weapon they sold with a bored-through cylinder. The agreement also provided that White, and not Smith and Wesson, would bear the responsibility (and the cost) of defending his patent against any infringement. White was forced to do this almost as soon as the first Smith & Wesson rim-fire revolver, in .22 calibre, appeared on the market in 1857, for imitators were hard on their tail. The White patent was attacked repeatedly, most of them either attempts to load unitary cartridges by some means other than by sliding them in from the rear, or modifications to the basic form of

the cartridge so that a complete boring-through of the cylinder was not necessary. In each case the courts either upheld White's rights – and by extension Smith & Wesson's – or the gun in question proved unworkable or unsaleable. By this means the pair held on to a virtual monopoly of the cartridge revolver market until White's patent expired in 1869. By then Rollin White had made a considerable sum from an invention which had originally appeared to be worthless and he needed little encouragement from his associates to try to renew the protection for a further seven years. The attempt was scotched by the intervention of the President of the United States, Ulysses S. Grant, who vetoed the appeal, saying, 'justice to the government and to the public forbids this patent from being renewed'.

Their comparative novelty aside, Smith & Wesson's early products actually had little to recommend them. It is said that Union soldiers off to the Civil War frequently bought Smith & Wesson's .22-calibre rim-fire pistols. At $12, plus 75c more for a 100 cartridges, the little seven-shot guns were certainly cheap enough, and at just 17.8cm (7in) long, and weighing 340gm (12oz) loaded, they were easy to conceal. They were just as popular at home, too, and by 1864, Smith & Wesson were quoting two years' delay in filling orders. Even so, this did not deter the pair from putting a new .32-

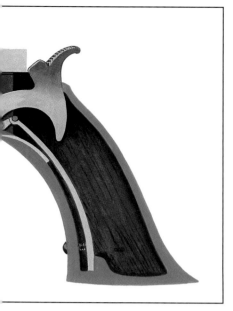

calibre pistol into production, it proved even more popular than its predecessor. The Model No 1 pistol, in three variants which differed only in detail, stayed in production until 1879. The .32 calibre Model No 2, a six-shot revolver, and the awkwardly-named five-shot Model No 11, also underwent detailed changes in the course of a long production life.

THE FIRST SMITH & WESSONS
These first pistols were single-action guns with a simple top-hinged, tip-up frame, retained by means of a catch at the front of the bottom strap. With the barrel out of the way, the cylinder was removable, the spent cases being ejected one at a time by passing a suitable pin, mounted below the barrel, through the chambers. This straightforward arrangement continued until 1869 when, with their patent protection now expired, the company came out for the first time with what might be called a service revolver. This was chambered for a new cartridge, the centre-fire .44-calibre round which later became known as the .44 S&W American. It was named thus to avoid confusion with rounds of a similar calibre but a different case length, for which a revolver Smith & Wesson later furnished to Russia in huge numbers was chambered. The revolver which fired the new cartridge was known as the Model No 3 or the American Model. It was a much larger pistol, 292mm (11.5in) long

and weighing 1.13kg (2.5lb). It was a bottom-hinged, break-open design with the locking catch on the top of the standing breech, just in front of the hammer, and the chamber mounted on a pin fixed into the barrel extension. It had an integral ejector which automatically acted on all six chambers at once, whenever the gun was broken open. Smith & Wesson had acquired the rights to this from its inventors, W.C. Dodge and C.A. King (Dodge's patent covered the break-open action; King's concerned itself with the simultaneous ejection of spent cases). The extractor itself was in the form of a star, each truncated point being located in the gap between one chamber and the next. Actuation was by means of a partial cog-wheel or pinion which was part of the hinge, which acted on a rack cut into a sleeve around the cylinder pin. This system was to become widely adopted in break-open revolvers the world over, but was usually actuated by a much simpler device involving a cam or spur.

In 1870, Wesson struck a deal with the Imperial Russian Government to supply 20,000 Model No 3 revolvers to a slightly modified design, the most obvious new features being a slight hump (or prawl) on the back strap, designed to stop the

ABOVE: The Dodge City Peace Commission. This gang of frontier 'peace officers', led by Wyatt Earp (front row second from left), were armed with Colt long-barrelled Single Action Army pistols donated by an enterprising journalist, including Neal Brown, (front row, extreme right), Charly Bassett (front row, extreme left) and Bat Masterson, (back row, extreme right).

revolver slipping down through the hand as it recoils. There was also a spur for the second finger on the trigger guard. More important was the new cartridge, the .44 S&W Russian, the most powerful and accurate pistol cartridge of its day in that calibre. It had a slightly longer case and a very slightly smaller projectile than the original round.

Wesson was also selling the original Model No 3 at home, though with no conspicuous success. The US Army, after initially turning it down flat, eventually took just 1000 guns and refused to order more, saying they were too fragile for everyday use by soldiers. In 1871, Smith & Wesson produced an improved Model No 3 for the home market, incorporating a larger cylinder pin and what we would today call an interlock: a notch or groove in the hammer which overlapped a

■LEFT: A Belgian copy of the Smith & Wesson No 3 revolver. It has a round barrel with a top rib and a round, brass foresight. The backsight is a notch cut in the front of the barrel catch.

projection on the barrel catch, ensuring that the pistol would not fire if the barrel and top strap were not latched properly with the standing breech. A variant of this latch became the first improvement to the pistol devised by the man who was to become its main promoter: Colonel George Wheeler Schofield.

IMPROVING THE S&W N0 3

Schofield, an officer in the US 10th Cavalry and a Civil War veteran, probably first came into contact with the Model No 3 when a board of officers under the command of his brother tested it for possible acceptance by the US Army in 1871. They turned it down, but Schofield was still impressed, and became an agent for Smith & Wesson in Kansas and Colorado and began to work out ways of improving the pistol. The most significant of those was a change to .45 calibre, but Schofield also increased the length of the barrel, from 150mm (6in) to 178mm(7in), and replaced the fragile and expensive rack-and-pinion ejector actuator with a simpler cam. He also modified the barrel latching system so that the catch itself was a part of the standing breech, rather than being fixed to the top strap. Even then the latching system was not entirely effective, and it remained a source of concern to Smith & Wesson for some years; eventually the company switched over to swing-out cylinders instead.

Despite Schofield's best efforts, the Schofield-Smith & Wesson, as the modified pistol was officially known, still only sold in limited numbers to the best of its potential customers, the US Army. Between 1873 and 1879 the Government bought just 8285 altogether, though there was also a steady sale to private individuals, and both Wells, Fargo and

Company and the American Express Company equipped their guards with them. One of the most notorious outlaws, Jesse James, carried a Schofield-Smith & Wesson, though his brother Frank preferred a Remington New Model Army. Not surprisingly, perhaps, when Colonel Schofield – who had always suffered from depression – took his own life at Fort Apache in December 1882, it was one of the revolvers which bore his own name that he chose.

THE BABY RUSSIAN

Horace Smith retired in 1873, selling his shares in the company to Daniel Wesson, who continued to use his ex-partner's

name. Wesson re-worked the Model No 3 in a variety of different calibres: .450 British, .44 Russian, .44/40 Winchester and .38 and .32 in two different loadings. It was also used with considerable success as a match target pistol, the first revolver to consistently beat purpose-built single-shot pistols. The practice of building small-calibre pistols with heavy frames, which continues to this day, dates from this time. In 1876, at the Philadelphia Centennial Exposition, the company introduced a lighter .38-calibre pistol, called the .38 Model No 2 in official literature but colloquially the 'Baby Russian', to avoid confusion with the earlier Model No 2 in .32 calibre. Perhaps the most interesting thing about this pistol was the ammunition for which it was chambered: the centre-fire .38 S&W, which became the de facto standard cartridge for American pocket pistols and was widely used throughout the world. In 1877 a new Model No 11 appeared, this time chambered for a .32 calibre centre-fire cartridge, and with that, the rim-fire cartridge virtually disappeared from the mainstream. Three years later the first Smith & Wesson

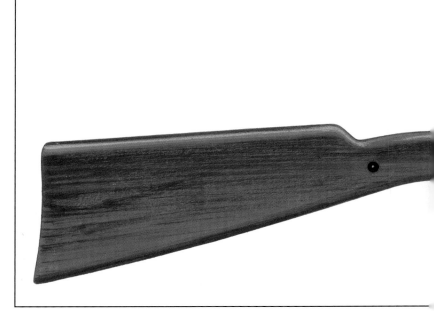

double-action pistols appeared, in .32 and .38 calibre and in five different models, the first pocket pistols the company produced with a trigger guard instead of a sheathed trigger. They were among the most successful pistols ever sold, were copied all over the globe and confirmed Smith & Wesson as America's (and therefore the world's) number one manufacturer of handguns, just 25 years after the two partners had set up in business together. But what of their biggest rival, Samuel Colt?

THE COLTS SOLDIER ON

There must have been great gnashing of teeth in Hartford, Connecticut, when the Smith & Wesson pistol first appeared, particularly as, Rollin White had offered Colt the rights to the bored-through cylinder in 1855 and been turned down. There is even speculation that White's original attempt to circumvent Colt's patents had been made with the sole aim of blackmailing Samuel Colt into paying him to go away. Colt having been in an unassailable position for 21 years, thanks to the protection of the original patent, now found the boot on the other foot. He was unable to challenge Smith & Wesson's protection and was thus forced to continue manufacturing and selling guns which were technically obsolescent. In fact, the bulk of Colt's pistols were aimed at a different type of consumer,

one who would very likely have been caught dead had he had to rely on a small-calibre rim-fire pistol. Sales of the .44 and .36 Army, Navy and Police Models of 1860-62 were barely affected by the Smith & Wesson pocket pistols, which opened up a new market segment rather than encroaching on Colt's preserves. If anything, Colt had more important competition from Remington, Starr and Savage than he did from Smith & Wesson.

There was little doubt that the unitary cartridge was here to stay, and as it gathered adherents, many Colt owners converted their cap-and-ball pistols to accept metallic cartridges. These guns continued to give sterling service, often for decades to come. Then, with the expiry of Rollin White's patent, in 1869, Colt was free to exploit the breech-loading principle, and eventually produced what was to become arguably the most famous pistol of all time. Samuel Colt did not live to see it, since he died in 1862.

Colt's first attempts at producing cartridge revolvers were not great successes. The four-shot, open frame .41 calibre rim-fire House Pistol of 1871, with its distinctive clover-leaf cylinder, is remembered only because it was Colt's first breech-loading pistol. It was designed by Charles Richards, Assistant Factory Superintendent at Hartford, who was responsible for the method Colt used

to convert percussion cap revolvers to accept brass cartridges. The House Pistol was later modified to accept a five-round cylinder, and was joined by a seven-shot .22-calibre Pocket Model, also with an open frame – the last such pistol Colt produced. They were superseded in 1873 by a range of New Line Pocket Revolvers in no less than eight versions, from .22 to .41 calibre, in both rim- and centre-fire, which were joined by the New Line Police and House series, in four barrel lengths, from 64mm (2.5in) to 150mm (6in). This was a seemingly bewildering plethora of products until one remembers the doctrine of interchangeability of components for which Colt was justly famous. The entire range was made up of three frames (the only difference between those of the New Model Police and House pistols was the shape of the butt), with different cylinders and screw-in barrels for each calibre and chambering, and a different profile hammer nose for rim- or centre-fire ammunition.

In addition to this range of pocket and handbag pistols, in 1872 Colt launched a new belt pistol. This was a heavy frame, .44-calibre rim-fire revolver which was little more than an updated version of the Model 1860 Army percussion revolver. It was, however, the direct ancestor of the .45-calibre centre-fire Colt Single Action Army (SAA) pistol of 1873, the 'Peace-maker' of legendary fame.

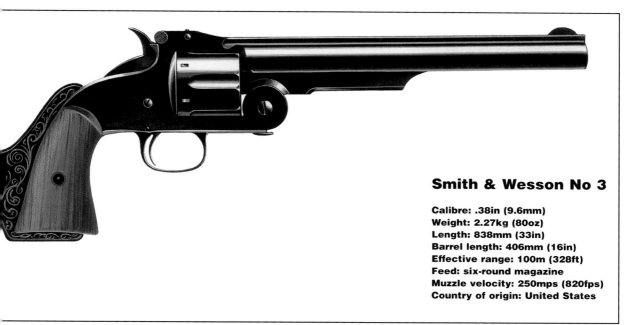

Smith & Wesson No 3

Calibre: .38in (9.6mm)
Weight: 2.27kg (80oz)
Length: 838mm (33in)
Barrel length: 406mm (16in)
Effective range: 100m (328ft)
Feed: six-round magazine
Muzzle velocity: 250mps (820fps)
Country of origin: United States

The Model P, as the Colt Company originally designated the 1873 pistol, was a six-shot single-action revolver. It used a spring-loaded ejection rod which extracted cartridges one at a time from the 'three o'clock' chamber via a hinged gate in the recoil shield, new loads being introduced the same way. It could be quickly dismantled down to the last component with only rudimentary tools, and the accuracy with which every part was machined meant that new components could be fitted without using an armourer. It could be made to fire, after a fashion,

even if some of the parts were missing or broken. It was available with a range of barrels from 76mm (3in) to 190mm (7.5in) and was eventually made in over a dozen calibres, from .22 rim-fire to .476 Eley centre-fire. These included the .45 Colt and the .44/40 WCF (Winchester Center-Fire) versions, which were produced to appeal to 'Frontiersmen' who carried a Winchester rifle, and wanted a pistol which shared its ammunition. As well as everyday working pistols, Colt produced two 'tuned' versions for target shooters: the 'flat top' Single Action Target Model

(the 'top' in question was the top strap) and the Bisley. The Bisley Model was a superior pistol with an improved action, broader, knurled hammer spur and trigger, deeper rear frame, higher back strap and enlarged grips and trigger guard, as well as greatly improved rear and foresights. Both models were blued throughout as standard (regular models had their frames left in the original case-hardening, with cylinder and barrel blued) but all models were available either nickel or silver-plated, with a choice of plain finish or three levels of engraving. There was a choice of grips, too: black composition was standard, but walnut, ivory and mother-of-pearl were all available as factory options.

COLT'S LONG-BARRELLED FOLLY
Perhaps the most unusual – and certainly the least useful – of the Colt SAA variants was the so-called 'Buntline

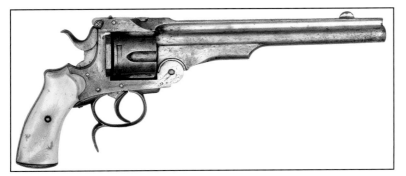

■LEFT: A Belgian copy of Smith & Wesson's Russian, of poor overall quality, the standard of workmanship and finish is crude – this gun would be dangerous to fire!

Smith & Wesson Russian Model

Calibre: .44in (11.2mm)
Weight: 1.02kg (36oz)
Length: 317mm (12.5in)
Barrel length: 203mm (8in)
Effective range: 20m (66ft)
Feed: six-round magazine
Muzzle velocity: 214mps (700fps)
Country of origin: United States

Special'. Available with 254mm (10in) and 406mm (16in) barrels, this version came with a nickel-plated cast brass skeleton shoulder stock. In 1876, the company produced what it called 'Colt's pistol with carbine barrel and attachable stock', which it put on display at the Centennial Exposition. The gun drew some attention from the general public, particularly that of one Edward Judson, a writer of western fiction, 'journalist' and promoter ('Buffalo Bill' Cody was one of his products; Annie Oakley was another) who used the pen-name Ned Buntline. Judson bought five of the long-barrelled pistols for $26 each and presented them amid much ado to five famous frontier 'peace officers': Wyatt Earp, Neal Brown, Charly Bassett, Bat Masterson and Bill Tilghman, in a ceremony in Dodge City, Kansas, at Christmas that year, putting it about that he himself was responsible for the gun's design. In fact, the long barrel made the gun extremely unwieldy, and there is no conclusive evidence that four of the five recipients did other than keep their presentation guns as curios. However, Earp is said to have favoured his, though he didn't use it in the face of

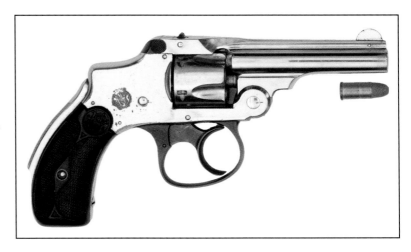

real trouble. In his most celebrated battle, near Tombstone, Arizona's OK Corral, he relied on a Schofield-Smith & Wesson. In all, the Colt Company made 30 such pistols between 1876 and 1884, and not a few remained unsold, though it re-launched the guns in 1958 when public demand for the original SAA had reached new highs, and sold them in a variety of calibres and barrel lengths.

THE COLT SAA
The US Army readily adopted the Colt SAA in 1873 to replace its single-shot rolling-block Remingtons, and it stayed in limited service use until finally super-seded by the double-action New Service Revolver in 1907. Even then, it still had its adherents. Lieutenant George S. Patton bought a pair of Single Action Army pistols, fully engraved and silver plated, with carved ivory grips, before setting out with 'Black Jack' Pershing on the expedition in pursuit of Pancho Villa in 1916. He later wore them through two World Wars. It was an almost identical gun to Patton's, a present from his cousin Frank, which Robert Ford used to shoot Jesse James in the back of the head in April 1882.

WILD BILL HICKOK
The popularity of the revolver helped to create the myth of the Western gunfighter, whose image of a heroic, independent individual with fantastic shooting skills has endured to this day.
The Colt Frontier DA pistol in .44 calibre is said by one of his numerous biographers to have been the favourite weapon of a man many hail as the Western gunfighter to beat them all –

■**ABOVE: The Smith & Wesson .32 Safety Revolver, one of a number of break-open, self-extracting pocket revolvers that were made by the firm in the 1880s.**

James Butler Hickok. Hickok (better known by the popular nickname of Wild Bill) actually died by being shot in the back of the head by Jack McCall in the course of a poker game that got out of hand on 2 August 1876. This was in fact two years before the Colt Frontier DA pistol was put on sale, so it is safe to say that this biographer erred, at least regarding the weapon that was used.
It is the preponderance of basic errors of fact in many similar studies which have long cast doubt on the real abilities of men such as Hickok and his contemporaries – the likes of Ben Thompson, Wyatt Earp, Bill Tilghman, Charlie Bassett, Luke Short, Clay Allison and Jim Curry. Nonetheless, a catalogue of Wild Bill Hickok's skill with a handgun, no matter what its make or model, still makes fascinating reading, and if some of the exploits seem incredible, who has the right now to say that he could not actually perform as witnesses from his era say he did? According to Wyatt Earp, for example, Hickok once demonstrated, his ability to put 10 rounds, five from each of his pistols, into the 'O' of a sign on a saloon wall, about 90m (300ft) away from where he stood, firing from the hip. Earp averred that a man 'of Hickok's skill' could make a six-gun 'which he knew' effective at up to 370m (1200ft), with the aid of a measure of luck – an amazing feat of skill.

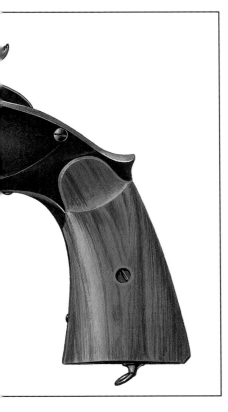

■RIGHT: The Colt Single Action Army pistol adorned a plethora of cheap prints, trashy novels and lurid posters during the last quarter of the nineteenth century.

Another, later report of Hickok's prowess as a pistoleer was written by a noted hunter and gun collector, Robert Kane. While he was working as the chief editor of the popular magazine *Outdoor Life*, Kane watched a demonstration Wild Bill gave at a fairground in Milwaukee, as part of 'Buffalo Bill' Cody's first Wild West Show (organised, directed and written by Ned Buntline, and featuring him, too, when he wasn't too hopelessly drunk).

'Mr Hickok treated us with great courtesy', wrote Kane, 'showed us his weapons and offered to do a little shooting for us if it could be arranged for outside the city limits. Accordingly the early hours of the afternoon found us on our way to the outskirts of the city. Mr Hickok's weapons were a pair of beautifully silver-plated SA .44 Colt revolvers. Both had pearl handles and were tastefully engraved. He also had a pair of Remington revolvers in the same calibre. The more showy pair of Colts were used in his stage performance. On reaching a place suitable for our purpose, Mr Hickok proceeded to entertain us with some of the best pistol work which it has ever been my good fortune to witness.

'Standing on a railroad track, in a

deep cut, his pistols cracking with the regularity and cadence of an old house clock, he struck and dislodged the bleaching pebbles sticking in the face of the bank, at a distance of about 15 yards.

'Standing about 30 feet from the shooter, one of the party tossed a quart can in the air to the height of about 30 feet. This was perforated three times before it reached the ground, twice with the right and once with the left hand.'

Kane went on to add, at a later date, that he was 'prepared to believe any story of his [Hickok's] skill or prowess that

does not conflict with the laws of gravitation and physics.' And whether one agrees with his opinions or not is a matter of personal choice.

THE JAMES GANG

But gunfighter mythology also embraced that of the outlaw, preying on vulnerable communities and transport links; hardened killers who often still managed to draw admiring press for their exploits. The James Gang were a remarkably successful group of outlaws. Jesse and Frank James and Cole, Jim and Bob Younger were its core members, but they were joined by a variety of others over the years. If their leader didn't quite invent the bank hold-up (as he certainly did the train robbery), they were by far its most successful early perpetrators. Their reign lasted from 14 February 1866, the day that they relieved the Clay County Savings and Loan Association, of Liberty, Missouri, of $15,000 in gold and $45,000 in bonds, plus an unknown amount of silver and paper currency, until 7 September 1876, when bad luck and poor intelligence brought them to the First National Bank of Northfield, Minnesota. Their final disastrous raid was sparked off by gang member Bill Chadwell, a native of the region and one of the few of their number not to have ridden with William Quantrill during the American Civil War, who claimed that the target was the richest country bank in the state.

Colt Single Action Army 'Peacemaker'

Calibre: .44in (11.2mm)
Weight: 1.08kg (38oz)
Length: 330mm (13in)
Barrel length: 190mm (7.5in)
Effective range: 20m (66ft)
Feed: six-round magazine
Muzzle velocity: 198mps (650fps)
Country of origin: United States

After 10 years, the gang was still employing the same basic stratagem which Jesse James had devised at the outset of his criminal career. A group of gang members would 'hurrah' the town, riding through shouting, hollering and firing their guns in the air, with the objective of driving its citizens indoors. At the same time two or three would enter the bank and rob it at gunpoint, whereupon all would flee in the confusion. They were still employing the same modus operandi because it had worked like a charm 10 times in a row, and no-one saw any reason to change a winning way.

The five cousins were joined by Chadwell, Charlie Pitts and Clell Miller. The eight journeyed north from their home state of Missouri to Minnesota by train, bought there the best horses they could find, and made their way toward Northfield, travelling in groups of two and three, posing as either cattle buyers looking for choice stock or surveyors. All of the riders wore long linen dustcoats, which both offered a measure of protection from the inclement elements and concealed the weapons they wore.

THE NORTHFIELD RAID

The gang arrived in the vicinity of Northfield on the morning of 7 September. As the lunch hour approached, three – Jesse James, Charlie Pitts and Bob Younger – rode into the town, hitched their horses outside Jeft's Restaurant, and there ate a leisurely meal, topped off by a cigar. Mounting their horses once more, they rode slowly toward the Scriver Block, composed of offices above, reached by an outside iron staircase, and mostly stores on the street level, including Lee & Hitchcock's and Scriver's itself. At the rear of the block, facing east, was the First National Bank, its back door opening onto an alley which separated the Scriver Block from the next, which

■ABOVE: Buffalo Bill Cody, one of the legendary marksmen and showmen of the late nineteenth century. His Wild West show included other famous personalities such as Wild Bill Hickok.

contained two hardware stores, those of J.A. Allen and A.E. Manning. Facing them across the street were more business premises, including Wheeler & Blackman's Drugstore, and a small hotel, the Dampier House. As Jesse and his companions reached the intersection, the whole town seemed asleep in the autumn sunshine. They dismounted from their horses and stood talking quietly.

DISASTER AT THE FIRST NATIONAL

Suddenly, the peace was shattered by shouting, shooting and the hammering of horses' hooves as five men, dressed very similarly to the three strangers conversing outside the bank, came charging into the square from two different directions, 'hurrahing' the town in no uncertain fashion. The three men walked swiftly into the First National, which was empty of customers, and vaulted across the counter, at this time unprotected by the bars and grilles which were later to become standard protective equipment. There, with pistols in their hands, and a cry of 'This is a robbery. Open the safe!' they encountered the cashier, J.L. Heywood, and two tellers,

■BELOW: US Cavalry battle with Plains Indians in this Charles Schreyvogel painting. As ever, the 'good guys' are armed with Colt Single Action Army models.

Frank Wilcox and A.E. Bunker. Heywood stood forward, and with a shake of his head declined to capitulate; Jesse James, seeing that the outer door to the vault was ajar, took matters into his own hands. He stepped inside and went to try the inner door. But before he could reach it, Heywood bounded forward to slam the outer door and imprison the outlaw inside. Charlie Pitts was quicker; he struck the cashier over the head with the barrel of his revolver, knocking him to the floor where he lay, bleeding profusely from the wound to his scalp. Jesse stepped out of the vault without trying the inner door, which being unlocked, would have opened to his touch.

Meanwhile, Pitts had drawn a Bowie knife with his other hand, and knelt over the unfortunate Heywood with it held at his throat. Even thus menaced, Heywood still refused to open the safe, and was probably saved from further injury – at least for the moment – by the actions of A.E. Bunker, who suddenly made a dash for the back door, bursting it open with his shoulder and tumbling down the steps into the alley beyond with shots from Charlie Pitts' revolver resounding around him harmlessly. He ran for his life down the alley, but fast as he was, Bob Younger's pistol was, inevitably, faster. The outlaw fired, just once, and took Bunker in the shoulder, the force of

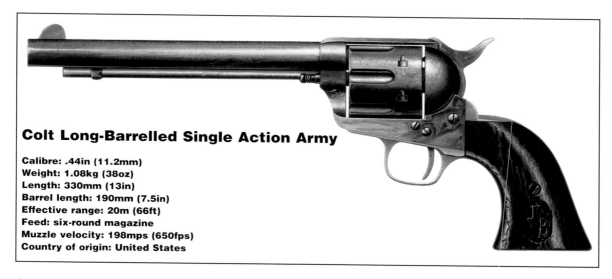

Colt Long-Barrelled Single Action Army

Calibre: .44in (11.2mm)
Weight: 1.08kg (38oz)
Length: 330mm (13in)
Barrel length: 190mm (7.5in)
Effective range: 20m (66ft)
Feed: six-round magazine
Muzzle velocity: 198mps (650fps)
Country of origin: United States

the bullet at close range almost knocking him off his feet. He stumbled, recovered, and then found the shelter of a doorway.

THE MINNESOTANS FIGHT BACK

Outside, in front of the building, the diversionary party was riding back and forth, still hollering and shooting their pistols. Bob Younger returned to the bank, and he, Jesse and Charlie Pitts, apparently convinced that the safe was locked, scooped up what money they could find and ran towards the door, Jesse bringing up the rear. Just as he reached the door, he glanced back, and saw Heywood, who had struggled to his feet, reach into a drawer. Reasoning that he would come up with a gun he fired one round from his Schofield-Smith & Wesson, hitting the cashier in the head and killing him virtually instantaneously. Alone of the bank staff, Frank Wheeler had stayed quite still, and escaped unscathed as a result.

In the street the 'hurrahing' tactics had not had quite the desired effect; most people had slammed their doors, certainly, but some of the Minnesotans proved to be made of sterner stuff – and the sound of gunshots from the bank told them that this was no mere razzing. Instead, the bank containing their savings was being robbed! More than one man made a dive for his gun, while the proprietors of the two hardware stores, Allen and Manning, both threw open their gun cabinets and began furiously loading weapons, shouting for unarmed men to come and get them. Young Henry Wheeler, a 19-year-old medical student at

home on vacation, was just leaving the drugstore in which his father was a partner when he heard the shouts of alarm. His own hunting rifle was at home, he knew, and much too far away to be of any use at all – but he remembered that next door, in the Dampier House, there was to be found a breech-loading carbine, a relic of the war between the states. He dashed to the hotel, secured both it and a handful of cartridges, and made his way upstairs to a bedroom overlooking the street. He was just in time to see a Norwegian immigrant, a man named Nicholas Gustavson, felled by a bullet to the head from the gun of one of the mounted outlaws. With trembling hands, Wheeler open the breech of the Model 1859 Sharps' and pushed a .50-calibre bullet home.

THE BATTLE HOTS UP

He wasn't the first townsman to fire, though; Elias Stacey grabbed the first gun thrust at him by one of the hardware merchants, along with a box of ammunition and dashed to the second floor of the Scriver Block, where he quickly loosed off at the first outlaw to cross his sights. Unfortunately his gun was a shotgun and his ammunition birdshot. He hit Clell Miller full in the face, doing little real damage but provoking a great deal of blood and the rage of the Missourian, who turned toward the window from which the shot had been fired and levelled his revolver. The next moment, and before he could attempt to extract revenge, he was thrown from the saddle by the heavy

round fired by Henry Wheeler from Room 8 in the Dampier House. He was as good as dead before he hit the ground, the first member of the James gang to die in the action. Stacey went on firing though knowing that the light loads which were all he had were of nuisance value only; by the time the gang were driven out of town, almost all of all them carried a sizeable load of birdshot somewhere about their person.

Wheeler's next round hit Cole Younger's hat, and the next moment, the veteran outlaw was hit in the shoulder by another carbine round, this one fired by the storekeeper Manning, who had stepped out into the street to get a clear view of his potential targets. He almost paid for his bravery with his life, when a round from Bob Younger – who had emerged from the bank to see his horse shot down before his eyes – narrowly missed him. Then it was Younger's turn, however, for in shooting at Manning he had attracted Wheeler's attention. The heavy slug took him in the right elbow, and though he switched his revolver to his other hand, he was now much less effective than before. Manning recovered soon enough. Bill Chadwell, half blinded by a charge of shot from Stacey's gun, was riding slowly down the street when the merchant's carbine spoke again, hitting him directly in the heart and killing him instantly.

It was time, the James Gang realised, to get out of the sleepy town which had turned into a deathtrap before their eyes. As one man they turned and made a break down the street – all except for

■**ABOVE: An idealised painting of a gunfight in the Wild West. In fact, many gunfighters died after being shot in the back in the dark – a code of honour did not exist between gunfighters.**

Miller and Chadwell, dead or dying, and Bob Younger, wounded and afoot. Younger's anguished cry – 'My God, boys, you're not deserting me? I'm shot!' – attracted his brother Cole's attention,

and wounded though he was himself, he gallantly turned back into what was by now a hail of bullets, scooped Bob up, and crouching low over his horse's neck, dashed after the others.

For the people of Northfield, Minnesota, the battle which had been suddenly thrust upon them was over, with two of their number dead and a third with a serious, but survivable, bullet wound in his shoulder. They had

two other bodies to bury, of course, namely those of Clell Miller and Bill Chadwell, the newcomer to the gang who had sung the praises of this sleepy little northern town in the first place. Bury them they did, though in Miller's case, only temporarily. In later years, Doctor Henry Wheeler, now practising as a physician in the town, would sometimes invite guests to view the carefully articulated skeleton he kept suspended in a cupboard in his consulting room. It was that of the man he had killed in front of the Dampier House, that fateful September day in 1876.

COLT'S SOUVENIR MODELS
The Colt Single Action Army stayed in production until America's entry into World War II in 1941, when it was discontinued in favour of more modern weapons. But no sooner was the war over than specialist gunmakers started making copies to satisfy public demand, and Colt finally bowed to the inevitable and reintroduced it themselves in the late 1950s. They made it in a variety of calibres and chamberings including .357 Magnum, the high-power cartridge introduced in 1935 by Smith & Wesson, and in 1959 produced a version in .22 rim-fire as the Colt Frontier Scout.

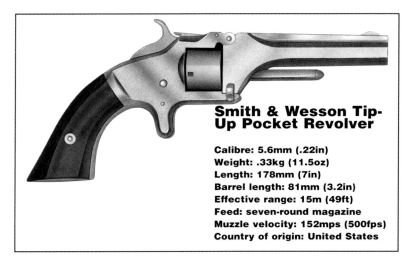

Smith & Wesson Tip-Up Pocket Revolver

Calibre: 5.6mm (.22in)
Weight: .33kg (11.5oz)
Length: 178mm (7in)
Barrel length: 81mm (3.2in)
Effective range: 15m (49ft)
Feed: seven-round magazine
Muzzle velocity: 152mps (500fps)
Country of origin: United States

During the 1960s, Colt began producing special 'commemorative models' of the reduced-calibre version of the famous gun. For example, 1000 gold-plated 'Pony Express Frontier Scouts' were made to mark the centenary of the mail-carrying service which operated between St Joseph, Missouri and Sacramento, California until the coming of the railway. Another souvenir model was released in 1962, to mark the 50th anniversary of the birth of the state of New Mexico, and yet another two years later for the centenary of the state of Nevada. By 1970 the SAA was being produced in nine variants, and perhaps the most distinctive 'commemorative model' of them all was issued to mark the gun's own centenary in 1973. By the time of its 125th birthday, reproduction SAA pistols were still available from at least three respected US gunmakers (and many others elsewhere) in calibres ranging from .22 rim-fire to .45 centre-fire as well as in both .357 and .44 Magnum loadings.

Despite the popularity of the Single Action Army model, Colt was well aware that many Europeans, in particular, preferred a double-action pistol, and actually had one on the market ahead of arch-rivals Smith & Wesson. The .38-calibre Lightning and the .41-calibre Thunderer were launched in 1877 and were followed by a heavier model, the Frontier Double Action, available in a variety of calibres, including .45 Colt, .44/40 Winchester and .455 and .476

British, the following year. They were adopted by the US Army, largely at the behest of the cavalry, who had long been crying out for a gun which operated faster in a mêlée. The guns stayed in service until they were replaced in 1892 by the Army version of the swing-out cylinder model of 1889, but they were hastily recalled in 1902 to arm troops fighting in the Philippines. The Thunderer was said to be the preferred gun of the psychopathic William Bonney, better known as Billy the Kid, until he was shot down at the age of 21 by erstwhile drinking companion-turned-lawman Pat Garrett in Fort Sumner, New Mexico, on 4 July 1881.

ELIPHALET REMINGTON

The man responsible for the first DA colts was William Mason, Factory Manager at Hartford from 1866 until 1882. Mason then left Colt to go to Winchester, and once there, designed a single-action pistol which could well have made serious inroads into Colt's pre-eminent position in the heavy service revolver market. It may not be entirely coincidental that at that very time, Colt was busy trying to sell an under-lever action rifle, the Colt-Burgess, which had a remarkably similar specification to the Winchester Model 73. In any event, and whether as a result of intimidation or as part of a more or less friendly deal, Colt quickly shelved the rifle project, while for its part Winchester Arms never put its promising single-action pistol on the market. The Mason-

designed pistol Winchester didn't quite put into production in 1883 wasn't the company's first essay into the handgun business, however.

In 1876, Hugo Borchardt, a German who had emigrated to the USA in the 1860s, and who had been with Winchester since 1870, produced a design for a single-action six-shot pistol. His design initially had a swing-out cylinder and simultaneous ejection; a later one used a side gate and rear-mounted lever extractor. Like Mason's work after him, Borchardt's designs were shelved, and he left the company for the Sharps Rifle Company where he was responsible for bringing the excellent Sharps rifle into the brass cartridge era. He returned to his native Germany in 1880, and went to work for Ludwig Loewe where he was to produce the first really effective self-loading pistol.

Winchester was not alone in seeking to challenge the control of Colt and Smith & Wesson over the American pistol market. Eliphalet Remington produced a version of his Army Model front-loader adapted for metallic cartridges in 1875, and a re-vamped version in 1891, both heavy, solid-frame six-shot revolvers in .44 calibre. He also made the 'New Line' sheath-trigger, five-shot single-action

■BELOW: This is the first Remington cartridge revolver, which appeared in 1875. It differed very little from the firm's earlier percussion pistol, the Remington Army Model 1863.

revolver in three lighter calibres, .30 and .32 rim-fire and .38 centre-fire, but his efforts were both too little and too late, and he never made any significant inroads into the big two's dominance. Remington quit the pistol business in 1894, save for a brief foray into the field of self-loading pistols in 1919, and returned to making rifles.

SMALL-CALIBRE POCKET PISTOLS

There was business to be done at the lower end of the market, producing cheap pocket pistols in the smaller calibres. Companies such as Iver Johnson, Harrington and Richardson, Forehand Arms and its predecessors, Allen and Wheelock and Forehand and Wadsworth (and that list is by no means exhaustive), all made .32- and .38-calibre revolvers. Some of them were quite decent, reliable guns but many more were of mediocre quality, both in terms of design and especially of execution and finish. Among the better manufacturers of inexpensive handguns were Iver Johnson and Harrington and Richardson, both of them, coincidentally, founded originally in 1871.

The eponymous Iver Johnson went into partnership with Martin Bye in Worcester, Massachusetts, that year, manufacturing not only both front- and breech-loading pistols but also leg-irons and handcuffs. In 1883 the partnership was dissolved, and Johnson continued in the same line of business under his own name, moving to Fitchburg in 1891. His first revolver was the 'Favourite', a break-open-single-action rim-fire pocket pistol in .22, .32, .38 and .44 calibres, which was quickly followed by similar models bearing such names as 'Defender', 'Encore', 'Smoker' and 'Tycoon'. Johnson made a curious swing-out cylinder revolver in 1879, which was interesting in that the cylinder pin was pivoted on a vertical pin below the barrel, allowing the cylinder to exit the frame in a horizontal arc. He returned to break-open action for future guns. The quality of his product steadily improving, Johnson launched the Safety Automatic Double Action revolver in 1892 and followed that, in 1894, the year before his death, with a hammerless

■BELOW: One of Iver Johnson's six-round break-open revolvers. When the revolver was opened the extractor at the rear of the cylinder was forced out. It was a very reliable pistol.

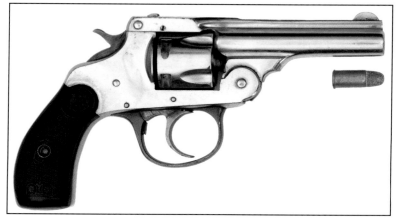

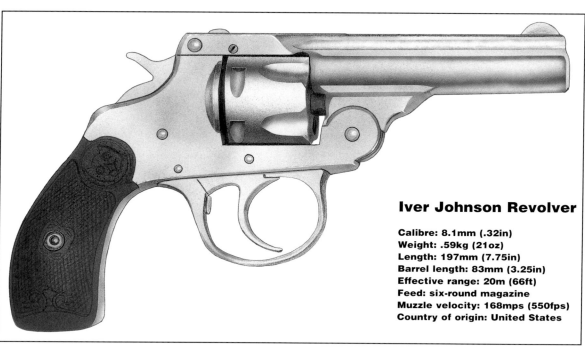

Iver Johnson Revolver

Calibre: 8.1mm (.32in)
Weight: .59kg (21oz)
Length: 197mm (7.75in)
Barrel length: 83mm (3.25in)
Effective range: 20m (66ft)
Feed: six-round magazine
Muzzle velocity: 168mps (550fps)
Country of origin: United States

version, essentially similar to a pistol Smith & Wesson had brought out in 1887. In fact, these 'hammerless' pistols were no such thing; rather, their hammers, which were spurless, operated inside a built-up shroud, the purpose being to lessen the chances of the pistol catching on clothing. Johnson's Safety Revolvers, whether with the hammer concealed or not, incorporated the 'famous safety lifter' – a false sear which lifted the hammer away from the firing pin and allowed its nose to rest clear of it when the gun was not in use. This safety device was also known as the 'Hammer the Hammer' feature. The pistol also incorporated a coiled mainspring acting on the hammer via a plunger, which made tension adjustment a simple matter. The company survived Johnson's death, and indeed, was still active a century later.

THE USRA MODEL

Harrington and Richardson started life as Wesson and Harrington, Daniel B. Wesson's brother Franklin having gone into partnership with his sister's son, Gilbert Harrington. The two took on William Richardson as their factory manager, and in 1874, nephew bought out uncle and then set up Harrington and Richardson. The pair made single-action pocket pistols for four years, and then launched a series of five-, six- and seven-shot double-action models in .22 rim-fire and .32 and .38 centre-fire chamberings. Perhaps their most famous pistol was far simpler, however – a single-shot target pistol known as the USRA Model. Like similar pistols from Smith & Wesson (the Model 1891 target pistol) and Colt (the Camp Perry model), the H&R USRA was based on the frame of a heavy revolver, a

'make-weight' barrel extension occupying the space normally taken up by the cylinder. Indeed, some pistols of this type were actually equipped with the hardware necessary to index a cylinder and lock it; by simple substitution of the barrel 'group', by releasing the pivotal pin at the front of the frame, a single-shot pistol could become a revolver.

LEFAUCHEUX'S CARTRIDGES

For a variety of legal reasons, Rollin White's patent, as licensed exclusively to Smith & Wesson, had no standing outside the USA. As a result, there was no artificial barrier in Europe to the exploitation of the breech-loadable metallic cartridge in the way there was on the far side of the Atlantic. In England, especially, gunmakers set to converting their existing percussion cap pistols to accept unitary cartridges, as well as drawing up new models. While on the Continent gunmakers began to manufacture revolver pistols in earnest, having largely neglected them for so long. In Liège in Belgium, for example, then and since a centre of the armaments industry, a large number of manufacturers turning out pistols of all styles and qualities could be found. Those which abandoned Lefaucheux's pin-fire cartridge (and some did not, for many decades to come) usually went directly to centre-fire for heavier calibres and produced only miniature calibres using rim-fire ammunition. Many copies of English designs, chiefly those of Adams, Tranter and later Webley, were produced in Belgium, and many were quite as good as the originals (though some, inevitably, were simply dreadful; more of a danger to anyone tempted to fire them than to any potential target). Home-grown Belgian

and French designs frequently lack the aesthetic quality associated with Colt's and Remington's guns, though the same could be said of Webley's, Tranter's and Adams' pistols. European weapons often seem very old-fashioned when seen alongside American pistols of the same vintage, ornament apparently taking pride of place over cleanliness of line and functionalism. The Parisian gunmaker Lagrasse, for example, was making very ornate and complex revolvers as late as 1866, as was Perrin. In the same city, Devisme, who had produced a successful double-action revolver as early as 1830, and had also been an early proponent of the centre-fire cartridge, was already producing a workable break-open revolver, hinged at the base of the standing breech in front of the (set back) trigger guard. Devisme's pistol lacked any form of simultaneous extractor, each spent round being ejected by a rod, one at a time, though loading would have been faster than with the side-gate system.

EUROPEAN PISTOLS

Tip-up (top-hinged break-open) pistols were popular in both Belgium and France; in Liège, both Spirlet and Fagus produced many to that design, while Henrion, Dassy and Heuschen produced one in 6mm (.24in) centre-fire calibre with double over-and-under barrels and no less than 24 chambers in two concentric rings in the cylinder. Other Belgian (and French) manufacturers produced twin side-by-side barrelled revolvers in similar miniature calibres (usually 6mm or .22), often designing them so that both barrels fired simultaneously. More conventional six-, seven- or eight-shot miniature revolvers were still more common.

Much more important among the ranks of Belgian pistol makers were the Nagant brothers and Charles Francois Galand. The Nagant brothers gained renown primarily, though not solely, because revolvers of their design became the most common side-arm used in Russia before the Revolution and in the Soviet Union afterwards. They served through two world wars as well as during the troubled period between them, when much of the country was riven by civil war. Even after the appearance of Soviet

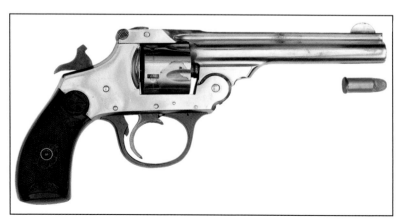

■LEFT: An Iver Johnson revolver incorporating the Safety Automatic Double Action lock mechanism, developed by Johnson and others in the 1890s.

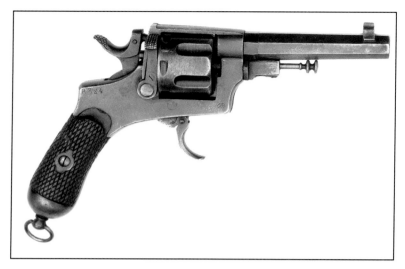

ABOVE: The Italian Bodeo Revolver, a simple and robust weapon, albeit not particularly inspiring or attractive, which by 1891 had become Italy's standard service model.

self-loading pistols such as the Tokarev, the Stechkin and the later Makarov, Nagant revolvers were still popular.

THE NAGANT PISTOL

The first Nagant model to enjoy wide acclaim was patented in Britain in 1879, though it had already been adopted the previous year as the official Belgian service revolver in 9mm (.35in) calibre. It was a simple solid-frame, rod ejector, six-shot double-action pistol with an interesting feature: the trigger guard could be hinged down, by the simple expedient of removing a set-screw at the front, which had the function of taking the tension off the mainspring if the pistol was not to be used for any length of time. The armed forces of Norway and Sweden also adopted this pistol, the latter in 7.5mm (.29in) calibre and the former in both 9mm (.35in) and 7.5mm (.29in). In 1894, the younger Nagant brother, Leon, obtained a patent for a revolver basically very similar to the one Emile had produced, but with one additional feature: a means of shifting the cylinder forwards just prior to the moment of discharge to effect a gas seal between the chamber and the breech end of the barrel. This function was assisted by the 7.62mm (.30in) rounds for which the pistol was chambered being of rather unusual construction, in that the

cartridge case extended forwards beyond the nose of the bullet and abutted the barrel when the trigger was pressed.

Galand's pistols of the same period are best known for their patented simultaneous extraction system, credited to the Belgian and an English associate, a Birmingham gunmaker named Somerville. The basic principle involved an elongated cylinder pin, along which the cylinder and barrel assembly could be withdrawn, leaving the expended cartridges held by their rims by a circular pierced plate or a star. The cylinder and barrel assembly were attached to a compound double-link lever not unlike Colt's original ramming lever in appearance, though it worked in the opposite sense. Another variant has the locking-cum-extractor lever brought right back to form the trigger guard. The main drawback to the system was an innate weakness of the frame due to the lack of a top strap, as well as the complication of the extraction and loading system, as compared to that of the break-open pistols. Nonetheless, the design had its imitators, and Galand-Somerville system revolvers were widely sold in Europe. Some examples are to be found with an integral, folding all-metal shoulder stock, though of such flimsy execution and materials that it serves its purpose but poorly.

BELGIUM'S VELO-DOG

Galand also produced (as did others) a range of small-calibre pocket pistols, aimed, we are led to believe, at a growing market among cyclists who were troubled by fierce dogs while out riding in the

countryside. The Velo-Dog pistols, as they were called, were made in large quantities not just in Belgium, but in France, Germany, Italy and Spain. They were generally no larger than the palm of a man's hand, with a barrel often only barely 25mm (1in) long, usually with a solid-frame, completely enclosed hammer and folding trigger. Early versions were chambered for 5.5mm or .22 cartridges, but later models are found in much more powerful 6.35mm (.25in) and 7.65mm (.30in) calibres. We are told that special cartridges, loaded with salt, pepper or dust shot, were also available. Velo-Dog pistols were still in production in small numbers well after World War I.

FRENCH CHAUVINISM

In 1867, Paris hosted an international exhibition which should have been quite as influential as the Great Exhibition in London, 16 years earlier, but was not. Despite the presence of the world's most important arms manufacturers, all of them with important new weapons to show and sell, the French (particularly their officer class) showed nothing but disdain for new-fangled mechanical weapons of all types. For example, they were offered the Gatling gun, and despite it being demonstrated conclusively, turned it down in favour of the already obsolescent Martigny *Mitrailleuse*, a volley firing gun which was a whole generation out of date.

Three years later, borne on a tide of quite baseless national pride, and incapable of gauging the strength and readiness of their adversary-to-be, they went to war with Prussia, and got the bloodiest nose imaginable. One of the effects of the stunning defeat, which led to the occupation of much of France and bloody revolution in Paris, was a very rapid re-evaluation of the merits of modern weaponry, among which the pistol came in for its share of attention.

THE MODEL 1874 REVOLVER

The French Navy had long since accepted the Lefaucheux pin-fire revolver, and in 1870 replaced it with a new model from the same designer, a six-shot double-action, centre-fire revolver with a solid-frame and rod ejector. One commentator has described it as 'sturdy, well-made but somewhat clumsy'. Certainly, when the chastened French Army came in 1873 to examine the revolver its sister service had adopted, it rejected it, and turned instead to a Chamelot-Delvigne design, as slightly modified by a board of officers. This practice of submitting designs to selection boards was to have far-reaching ramifications for the French, who produced a series of mediocre weapons (and at least one downright dreadful one, the Chauchat light machine gun) as a consequence. Other military establishments followed the same practice, but with occasionally more reliable results. In the case of what was to become the Model 1873 revolver, the selection board actually chose the best alternative, rejecting not only the Lefaucheux but also a decidedly unwieldy design submitted by Galand. Together with a slightly lighter version, styled the Model 1874, the pistol proved to be serviceable and hard-wearing. Ostensibly replaced in 1892 by a swing-out cylinder pistol, many examples found their way into the trenches during World War I, and from there into the affections of many French soldiers. Originally, however, the cartridge specified for the first French 'regulation revolver' (*revolver reglementaire*) was a derisory thing, producing a muzzle velocity of just 130 metres per second (426 feet per second) and just 10kg per metre (73 foot/pounds) kinetic energy. Not only was it not a man-

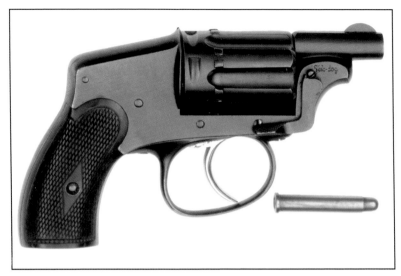

stopper, it was barely a man-slower, as French colonial troops like those guarding the surveying party for the trans-Saharan railway found out. When they were set upon and massacred by their Tuareg Arab guides, even revolver fire at point-blank range proved ineffective. Eventually, more powerful

■ABOVE: The Galand Velo-Dog, one of a number of cheap pocket revolvers wich were made in considerable numbers at the end of the nineteenth century. They were apparently designed to be used by cyclists who wanted to defend themselves against the attacks of vicious dogs.

Nagant 1895

Calibre: 7.62mm (.3in)
Weight: .79kg (28oz)
Length: 229mm (9in)
Barrel length: 110mm (4.33in)
Effective range: 20m (66ft)
Feed: seven-round magazine
Muzzle velocity: 178mps (584fps)
Country of origin: Belgium

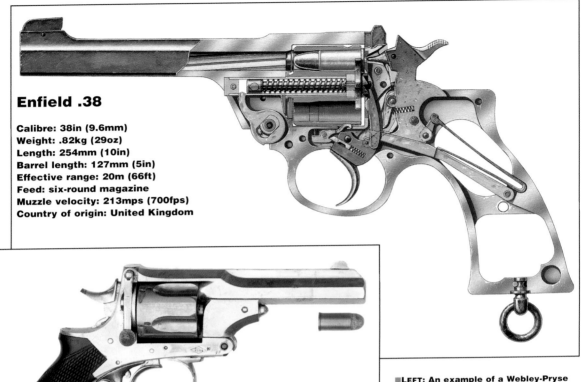

Enfield .38

Calibre: 38in (9.6mm)
Weight: .82kg (29oz)
Length: 254mm (10in)
Barrel length: 127mm (5in)
Effective range: 20m (66ft)
Feed: six-round magazine
Muzzle velocity: 213mps (700fps)
Country of origin: United Kingdom

■LEFT: An example of a Webley-Pryse revolver. Their characteristic feature was a star-shaped ejector at the rear of the cylinder. These revolvers were also fitted with a rebounding hammer which prevented accidental discharge.

cartridges were developed and issued as the 1873/90, their muzzle velocity up by 50 per cent and their energy doubled, and although that still didn't approach the power of the same calibre .45 Colt rounds, the new ammunition proved effective enough.

LEBEL'S SMOKELESS CARTRIDGE
The modified Chamelot-Delvigne eventually gave way to a revolver which became known officially as the *Modele d'Ordonance* 1892, but more commonly after the man who chaired the commission responsible for selecting it, Colonel Nicholas Lebel. Lebel was better known for the rifle he championed which was swiftly adopted by the French Army

as the *Fusil d'Infanterie Modele 1886*. The 8mm (.32in) round for which it was chambered was the first 'smallbore' military rifle cartridge' and employed smokeless powder, two attributes which were to have very important and far-reaching consequences on the battlefield. The revolver used this same calibre, though the cartridge was much shorter and the loading much lighter. Lack of power was a common fault in smaller-calibre pistol ammunition of the period; in the case of the Lebel revolver, this was to be its major defect.

Lebel is frequently credited with actually having designed both the rifle and the pistol, however there is no real evidence to support that contention.

The Lebel revolver, a conventional solid-frame, six-shot double-action pistol, had a swing-out cylinder which emerged to the right – a very odd choice indeed, since four-fifths of the population is right-handed. The reason for this lies in the original conception of the pistol as a cavalry weapon, and thus one which was to be used in the left hand, the right being occupied, of course, by the cavalryman's real weapon: the sword. More useful, perhaps, was the ease with which the left sideplate could be removed to allow access to the entire action for cleaning and stripping. Even though the entire cylinder swung out, and was fitted with a hand-operated star extractor, there was still provision made for the loading (though not the ejection) of single cartridges via a loading gate on the right-hand side; a completely useless adjunct to a pistol with a swing-out cylinder.

Similar Chamelot-Delvigne revolvers to those issued in France were adopted by the Swiss Army in 10.4mm (.41in) calibre rim-fire as the Model 1873. It was later modified to accept centre-fire cartridges of the same calibre, as the Model 1878. This modification to the original design was carried out by an Army officer, Major Rudolf Schmidt, and the pistols in question are sometimes known, perhaps unjustifiably for the changes were minor, as the Schmidt-Delvigne. They were superseded in 1882 by a 7.5mm (.29in) revolver of essentially similar character but with a lock similar to that designed by Nagant.

NEW LOADING PROCESSES

It also sported an important modification by Abadie, which allowed the hammer nose to be held off and the hammer disconnected from the trigger itself automatically when the loading gate was opened, thus permitting the cylinder to be rotated by pressing the trigger. The loading and unloading process was speeded up considerably as a result. This same system was adopted by the French for the Model 1892 pistol, by the Austrian, Leopold Gasser for his Model 1898 pistol, and by the Italian Army, too, for later 10.4mm (.41in) versions of the same basic Chamelot-Delvigne design. The Dutch adopted the same pistol for their army, gendarmerie and customs services (and subsequently modified it considerably) as did the Swedes, the former in 9.4mm (.37in) centre-fire, the latter in 11mm (.43in) centre-fire chambering. The Chamelot-Delvigne revolver in Italian

Chamelot-Delvigne 1874

Calibre: .45in (11.4mm)
Weight: 1.08kg (38oz)
Length: 230mm (9in)
Effective range: 20m (66ft)
Feed: six-round magazine
Muzzle velocity: 183mps (600fps)
Country of origin: France

service was superseded in 1889 by a somewhat lighter, but basically similar, design known as the Bodeo Revolver, once again, like the Lebel, named after the man who chaired the Commission which accepted it.

THE BODEO REVOLVER

The Bodeo, a six-shot double-action, side gate/rod extractor design (with the Abadie modification) in 10.4mm (.41in) calibre, was made in two distinct versions, one with a rounded barrel and a trigger guard, the other with an octagonal barrel

and a folding trigger. Manufactured in a number of different locations in Italy, the pistols were sturdy and robust and some of them had a very long service life indeed – at least 50 years in some cases.

After having been a considerable force in the development of firearms in general, Germany fell behind Britain and the United States especially during the eighteenth and early nineteenth centuries. The success of Prussia in her wars against Denmark, Austria and France and then the final unification of the states into Germany as we have come to know it, led to a rise in militarism. That, plus the now established benefits of mass production and new workshop practices, caused a sudden resurgence of interest in gunmaking. Among the independents, Dreyse of Sommerda was still the most important by the mid-1870s, though the state arsenals, of which the most significant was at Erfurt, were already growing in stature. However, Dreyse was about to be completely overshadowed by newcomers such as Peter Paul Mauser and Ferdinand Ritter von Mannlicher. While all three were best known for their rifles, the latter two were to have a profound effect on the development of the pistol. But Mauser's first attempt was

■LEFT: The French Chamelot-Delvigne revolver. It had a strong and reliable double-action lock, making it particularly suitable for military service.

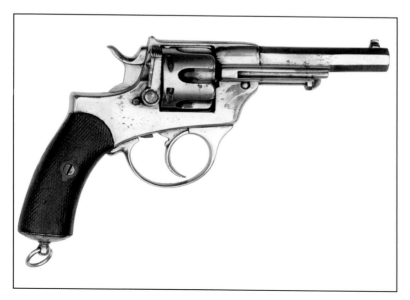

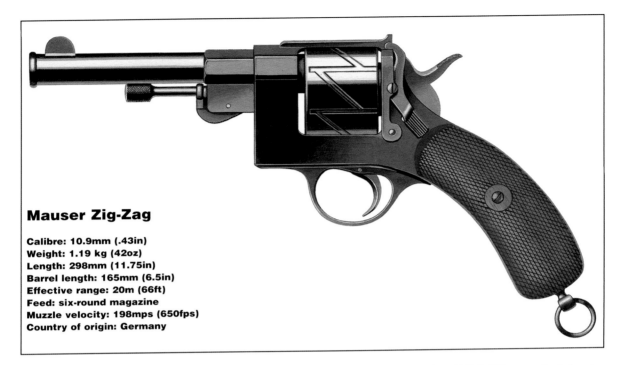

Mauser Zig-Zag

Calibre: 10.9mm (.43in)
Weight: 1.19 kg (42oz)
Length: 298mm (11.75in)
Barrel length: 165mm (6.5in)
Effective range: 20m (66ft)
Feed: six-round magazine
Muzzle velocity: 198mps (650fps)
Country of origin: Germany

inauspicious, and he failed, quite signally, to get his first handgun accepted by the German Government despite it being superior in every way to the revolver accepted by the Spandau Military Commission. Mauser produced a variety of designs, both in single and in double action, in both solid-frame and hinged frame versions. The most significant features of his revolvers was the use of coiled mainsprings lying parallel with and beneath the cylinder, in place of the more usual flat spring found in the butt. He also adopted an alternative to the ratchet-and-pawl normally used to index the cylinder, consisting of a system of two sets of parallel grooves, one axial and the other helical, machined into the outer surface of the cylinder, together with a stud on the mainspring carrier which located in it. As the hammer was brought back, either by the thumb, in the single-action version, or by taking up the pressure on the trigger, in the more complicated double-action pistol, the mainspring, which was coiled around a rod in the lower part of the frame, was brought into tension. At the same time the mainspring carrier, and the stud mounted on it, moved forward, the stud travelling in a helical groove and turning the cylinder by one-sixth of a revolution in the process. By the time the hammer

came to full cock the stud rested at the head of an axial groove, and when the mainspring was released, travelled back down it, keeping the cylinder in battery in the process. A similar process had been thought out, though not fully developed, by Samuel Colt, who had obtained a British patent in 1853, not entirely dissimilar to the one that was granted to Mauser in 1878. Colonel Fosbery used a basically similar system for the automatic revolver he designed and which Webley put into production in 1901. Later hinged-frame models of Mauser's Zig-Zag pistol incorporated a simultaneous extraction system, and most were double action. In .32 calibre, they proved popular with civilians.

DREYSE'S UNINSPIRED PISTOLS
Mauser's revolvers were extremely well made, and as a result were both reliable and expensive. The Spandau Commission liked the former attribute, but not the latter, and decided on a simple single-action 10.6mm (.42in) six-shot revolver to be manufactured by Dreyse (and later in the Erfurt Armoury). Known as the Model 1879, the year of its adoption by the German cavalry, it had little to distinguish it. A later model, that of 1883, was issued to infantry and artillery units, its barrel reduced from 178mm (7in) to

117mm (4.6in). Officers received almost identical pistols, save that they were double action. Curiously, there was no provision for the ejection or extraction of spent cartridges, though a hinged loading gate was provided and the cylinder was quite easily removed. Reloading under fire must have been a very nerve-wracking business indeed.

GASSER'S PISTOLS
Born in 1836, Leopold Gasser served his apprenticeship as a gunmaker, and by the time he reached his mid-twenties was already producing copies of Robert Adams' percussion revolvers. In 1870 he received a patent for a revolver to his own design, though with its open frame it was actually quite similar in general to the heavy Colt pistols of almost a quarter-century earlier. It was chambered for an 11mm (.43in) cartridge originally developed for a carbine, and though the pistol cartridge was less heavily loaded, the outward similarity of the two was to result in many an accident. At almost 380mm (15in) long and weighing in excess of 1.36kg (3lb), it was easily the biggest, heaviest general service revolver of its day.

Leopold Gasser died young, the year after his original revolver went into production, and was succeeded by his younger brother, Johann. He developed

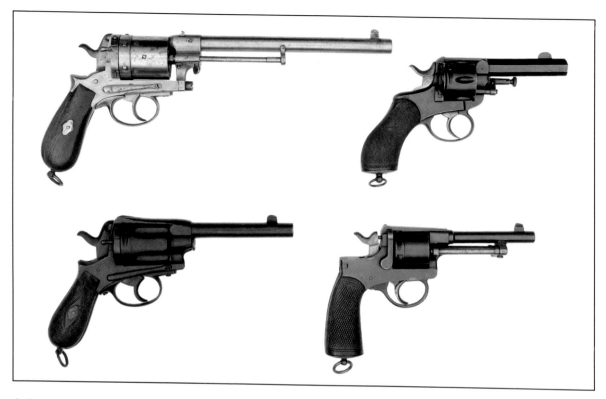

■ABOVE: Pistols produced by the Austrian firm Gasser. The Model 1870 (top left), a copy of the RIC Revolver (top right), the Montenegrin (bottom left) and the Rast and Gasser Model 1898 (bottom right).

the business until it was the largest producer of pistols in the Austro-Hungarian Empire, providing its service revolvers and supplying an active civilian market there and throughout the Balkans. In 1878, together with the Inspector-General of the Austro-Hungarian Army, Alfred Kropatschek, Gasser produced a 9mm (.35in) six-shot revolver which was adopted as the official service revolver of the Austrian infantry as the Gasser-Kropatschek *Infanterie-Offiziersrevolver*. It was also issued to the gendarmerie. The large stocks of the earlier Model 1870 were sold off, mostly in the Balkans, and became known as the 'Montenegrin' revolver, as a result.

There is an apocryphal story which suggests that the King of Montenegro, Nicholas, had a large financial interest in Gasser's firm, and issued a proclamation that every one of his adult male subjects should purchase a revolver, making sure that the only such gun widely available was the army surplus Gasser. Top strapless Gasser pistols were widely copied elsewhere, particularly in Belgium, but also in Germany, Greece and Italy. Many of them were modified to break-open designs with simultaneous extracting

systems, and these too found a ready market in the Balkans, where the Gasser name was the only one widely associated with handguns. The younger Gasser was also responsible for the last Austro-Hungarian service revolver, this time in conjuction with designer August Rast. The Rast und Gasser Model 1898 was an eight-shot double-action pistol in 8mm (.32in) calibre, and had what was widely held to be insufficient stopping power for a service arm as a result. The gun was somewhat ahead of its time, though it was not unique, in that its firing pin was a spring-loaded plunger contained in the frame, rather than forming a part of the hammer's nose. In common with most of Gasser's own pistols (and indeed, with most service revolvers of the period the world over), the Model 1898 had a loading gate and a simple rod ejector, though in this case, the ejector was actually a slotted hollow tube retained by a central rod.

THE SIDE GATE SYSTEM
The problems of extracting spent cartridge cases and introducing fresh rounds had come in for considerable attention as soon as the bored-through

cylinder revolver became a viable proposition, and many and varied were the means developed to make the process simpler and faster. The world's armed services, in general, stuck to the side gate/ejector rod system because it was both cheap to manufacture and virtually foolproof. With the addition of Abadie's interlock the side gate also became a rather cumbersome form of safety catch. Cheapness and simplicity had not been the reason for Colt adopting the side gate system for the SAA revolver of 1873, though. In Colt's opinion the strength imparted to the design by a solid frame with a fixed top strap was much more important, and the side gate was the simplest way to load the pistol while retaining that feature. Even after Smith & Wesson adopted C.A. King's patent simultaneous extraction system for the Model No 3 pistol, and indeed proved in the process that the bottom-hinged,

Webley & Scott Mark VI

Calibre: .455in (11.55mm)
Weight: 1.05kg (37oz)
Length: 279mm (11in)
Barrel length: 152mm (6in)
Effective range: 20m (66ft)
Feed: six-round magazine
Muzzle velocity: 198mps (650fps)
Country of origin: United Kingdom

break-open design was both practical and strong enough for a heavy calibre pistol, there were still those who clung to the outdated notion that a service pistol needed to be a solid-body design with a rigid top strap.

NEW EXTRACTION METHODS

The only effective way to incorporate a simultaneous extraction system into such a revolver is by means of a swing-out cylinder, but the development of a satisfactory design was still some way in the future. In 1869, Birmingham gunmakers Tipping and Lawden tried another method when they took up a patent awarded to J. Thomas, also of Birmingham, in 1869. Thomas' patent revolver had its barrel as a push-fit into the frame, where it was locked into position, its breech end being permanently secured to a static plate fixed to the cylinder rod. In order to clear the chambers, the barrel was twisted through 180 degrees (a knob was fitted for the purpose) round its axis and then pulled forward. This action pulled the cylinder forward into a space in the frame the length of a spent cartridge case, the empty cases being held by their rims in a star extractor fixed to the standing part of the breech. They would fall free of their own weight with a flick of the wrist or as the cylinder, now free of

any locking mechanism, was spun. The barrel and cylinder were then returned to the normal position, and fresh rounds were loaded through a sidegate. It is perhaps worth quoting from Tipping and Lawden's advertisement for the Thomas pistol to examine what the discerning pistoleer of the day was thought to want from his weapon. The pistol was, the manufacturers said:

'A Double Action Revolver, simultaneously extracting the exploded cases – therefore can be loaded on horseback, in the dark or while moving about in any way. The usual revolver, requiring a rod to extract each exploded case, is useless after being discharged until the operator can remain quite still to re-load it.

'It revolves on an axis perfectly shielded from the effects of the powder, therefore is not liable to clog and have its action stopped, even though fired day after day without cleaning.

'It can be reloaded in less time than the exploded cases of others can be ejected.

'It has a SOLID FRAME, forming an integral part of the body enclosing the cylinder, without which no revolver can be depended upon for many successive discharges.'

An ostensibly somewhat similar design was sold in the United States by the

Brooklyn gunmakers Merwin and Hulbert, the significant difference being that the frame was not solid. The top strap was integral with the barrel, and was retained at the top of the standing breech on a dovetail cut in an arc, while a similar dovetail was cut into the front lower frame. The barrel and top strap could be rotated through somewhere between 60 and 90 degrees, which action unlocked the barrel group from the frame and allowed it to move forward, taking the cylinder with it, the expended cartridges being retained by the extractor fixed to the standing breech.

ENFIELD'S BREAK-OPEN DESIGN

A partial combination of those two systems was employed in the .476-calibre Enfield Mark I revolver, adopted by the British Army to replace the .450 Adams in 1880. Devised by an American inventor named Owen Jones, who obtained a British patent for it in 1878, the Enfield was a bottom-hinged, break-open design like Smith & Wesson's Model No 3. The cylinder, which was attached to the barrel extension by a pivot, could slide forwards and back along its fixed pin, being free to move forward as the barrel was tipped down thanks to an angled cut-out in the lower front portion of the frame. Once again, the spent cases were retained by a star extractor and then shaken free, and reloading was by means of a side gate with the barrel returned to the closed position.

The procurement of arms and equipment during the latter third of the nineteenth century was a fickle business, largely as a result of the wholesale changes that industry in general, and metallurgy and pyrotechnics in particular, were undergoing. This can be demonstrated by the British example. By the mid-point of the century, the army was armed with muzzle-loading Beaumont-Adams revolvers. Robert Adams' brother John began converting those revolvers to accept centre-fire cartridges and had the result accepted by the British Army in 1868, before producing the first purpose-built centre-fire service revolver, probably that same year. Like the converted percussion cap pistols, which were styled Government Model Mark I, his Mark II and Mark III pistols were fitted with a simple side gate/ejector rod system of extraction, the actuation of the rod varying from model to model. They were six-shot capacity,

however, rather than five like the Beaumont-Adams. They stayed in service until they were superseded by the Enfield Mark I 14 years later, though in the meantime Adams had to shake off competition from the two other major players in the British pistol market, Tranter and Webley.

WILLIAM TRANTER'S PISTOLS

Though simple rod ejectors were essentially foolproof, they had one drawback. Lacking any form of mechanical advantage, they often failed to shift a stubborn case, whereupon the shooter had no recourse but to either remove the cylinder and drive the case out with anything which came to hand, or try to apply force to the ejector rod end – a practice which often resulted in a bent or broken rod. William Tranter, for one, overcame this by sticking to the compound lever he'd previously used as a rammer. It is not entirely clear whether this was a conscious decision or whether he found it expedient on his first cartridge revolver – the rim-fire Model

1863, which was a very simple development of the percussion cap Third Model revolver of 1856 – and was happy enough with its operation to continue with it in subsequent models.

Tranter made a wide variety of pistols: his factory in Aston (later the Hercules Bicycle Company's works) was the biggest in Birmingham at a time when Birmingham and Liège were the biggest small arms manufacturing centres in Europe. Having started off by manufacturing rim-fire pistols, he later switched over to centre-fire cartridges. Little of the design of the revolvers changed, save for a switch from the firing pin being fabricated as part of the hammer nose to the use of a spring-loaded, frame-mounted plunger which was struck by the hammer and struck the cartridge's primer in turn. He turned out service revolvers, usually in .450 or

■BELOW: The British attack on Spion Kop in January 1900 during the Second Boer War. Note the British officer firing a Webley revolver.

Webley Bulldog

Calibre: .32in (8.1mm)
Weight: .31kg (11oz)
Length: 140mm (5.5in)
Barrel length: 53mm (2.1in)
Effective range: 15m (49ft)
Feed: five-round magazine
Muzzle velocity: 190mps (625fps)
Country of origin:
United Kingdom

.455 calibre, in five- and six-shot versions. He also made pocket pistols in smaller calibres, often single-action rim-fire models with sheath triggers, but also double-action models chambered for .32 and .38 centre-fire cartridges. Latterly, as cartridge construction became more reliable, and ejection problems due to excessively swollen cartridges began to disappear, he changed to straightforward spring-loaded ejector rods.

Tranter's final attempt to interest the British Army in adopting one of his revolvers as an official service arm was as forlorn as all his others. It was centred on a bottom-hinged, break-open design

with a simultaneous extractor system, very similar in nature to that of the Schofield-Smith & Wesson, but actuated by a spur on the frame pivot, rather than a cam as in the American pistol. Its double-action lock was of a more conventional design than that he had employed in his percussion pistols, with but a single trigger. It was a sturdy, well made gun, as were most of Tranter's products, but unfortunately it wasn't quite enough to keep him in business. In 1885, he sold out to the cartridge maker, George Kynoch, and died five years later.

Kynoch continued to make pistols at what he now called the Kynoch Gun

Factory, the operation being under the day-to-day control of one Harry A. Schlund. He was a busy man, and his fellow directors of George Kynoch Limited complained that he spent too much of his time on other activities, and not enough running the main enterprise. He compounded this by also being a Member of Parliament and president of Aston Villa football (soccer) club. After only three years, however, the cumulative pressure from all these projects became too much, and Kynoch retired. He died three years later, and at that time Schlund acquired control of the old Tranter business, changing its name to the Aston Gun Factory in the process. Schlund himself only lasted in the arms industry (as far as is known) until 1900, but during his 15 years as a maker of pistols – six for Kynoch, and nine on his own account – he produced some interesting revolvers.

KYNOCH'S EXPERIMENTS
Kynoch may have been the money behind the new firm, but it is clear that much of the technical inspiration came from Schlund. No sooner was he established as Kynoch's manager than he began work on a service-calibre revolver using Tranter's 'old-fashioned' double-action/double-trigger lock with a completely enclosed hammer, which gave the pistol an unusual humped-back appearance. What appeared to be an extension of the hammer spur protruding through the shroud was in fact the barrel latch, and de-cocking, should it be necessary, was achieved by manipulating the two triggers. A six-shot, break-open design with a simultaneous extractor, and once again, closely mirroring a pistol of Tranter's, the revolver was chambered for the .455 Kynoch cartridge. It was clearly intended to be a contender to supplant the already unpopular Enfield Mark I and Mark II pistols that were in Army service at that time. In that venture it was unsuccessful, and neither did it achieve much in the way of commercial success, even after Schlund made extensive modifications to the unwieldy trigger mechanism.

Kynoch was a man of catholic interests, and extraordinarily well

◼LEFT: The Webley Royal Irish Constabulary (RIC) Revolver No 2. The newly formed civilian police force in Ireland adopted this revolver as a side-arm, hence its name.

■RIGHT: The Webley RIC Revolver No 1. The RICs were widely used throughout the British Empire, and were copied in Europe. They were, like most Webleys, rugged and reliable revolvers.

travelled for his day. One out-of-the-way country he had visited extensively was Roumania, where he had been well received, and even decorated by the King. While there, he met a young Captain of Artillery named Haralamb Dimancea, who had produced a design for a revolver quite unlike any seen before, and which he had convinced his government to put into limited production, on a trial basis. It appears that Kynoch won the contract to manufacture 1000 examples of the revolver in question, which became known as the Kynoch-Dimancea revolver or Revolverul Dimancea, and either at Kynoch's invitation, or at his government's request, the Roumanian went to Birmingham to oversee the work.

KYNOCH'S 'RATCHET LOCK'

In appearance, the revolver was not dissimilar to the Kynoch, with, for example, what appeared to be a hammer shroud building up the rear of the frame to a considerable height. Once again, the extension to the hammer spur was actually the barrel latch, but this time, instead of breaking forwards in the usual way, the barrel and cylinder tipped to the side, pivoted on a pin running parallel to the cylinder pin and below it. The second, and more revolutionary, aspect to the design was its 'ratchet lock', a spring-loaded star-wheel which both replaced the hammer (acting directly on the firing pin) and indexed the cylinder. Thirdly, the lanyard ring at the base of the butt was also the head of a long set-screw which passed the length of the butt and secured it to the frame; removing it exposed the entire action for inspection and cleaning. Sadly for Kynoch, his optimism for the new design proved ill-founded. When the factory actually tried to put the pistol into series production, they found its design to be simply too demanding to be viable, and had to cry off the contract.

While Kynoch and Schlund were trying unsuccessfully to break into the lucrative market for military small arms, another Birmingham firm – which had already begun to enjoy some success in supplying handguns for home defence and to one regional British police force – was homing in on the same objective. In

the early 1860s P. Webley and Sons were still very junior rivals to John Adams, but by the time 20 years had gone by, they had gone from strength to strength and were ready, willing and able to take up a dominant position.

WEBLEY STALWARTS

The history of Webley revolvers developed from about 1875 is a fairly complex one, if only because of the number of partners the firm continued to take on in order to secure access to their designs. Charles Pryse and Michael Kaufmann were the most significant of them, though Scott, with whom Philip Webley's sons, Thomas and Henry, went into partnership proper, in 1897, was probably more important. One thing, though, is common to the revolvers which resulted: they were all, regardless of calibre and of detailed differences, break-open designs with simultaneous 'automatic' extraction systems.

It says much for the Webley pistols in general that once they were adopted as the British Government service revolver in 1887, taking over from the unpopular Enfield, they were never superseded. Even when manufacture of British service pistols went back to the government's own Enfield smallarms factory in 1927, it was actually Webley & Scott Ltd which furnished the design for what became the 'Pistol, Revolver .38 No 2'. This weapon actually stayed in service until replaced by the Browning 9mm (.35in) self-loading pistol in 1957, completing 70 years of unbroken reliance

on Webley revolvers. Webley's rise began during the early years of the bored-through revolver, with the so-called Royal Irish Constabulary, British Bulldog and Army Express side gate/rod extractor pistols of the 1860s and 1870s, together with the No 1, the first centre-fire revolver Webley made.

Chambered for the massive .577-calibre Boxer cartridge, this latter gun was said to be the most powerful revolver ever made, with the exception of the modern-day heavy Magnums. Charged with 2gm (31 grains) of black powder, and firing a soft lead bullet weighing 19 gm (.6oz), the .577 round could be relied upon to stop even the most aggressive tribesmen, and was extremely popular with the more active imperialists as a result. The Webley .577 revolver was perhaps punching a little above its weight, however; more reliable, though bulkier, were the two-and four-barrel pistols made in similar calibre by George Lancaster and his imitators. In particular, there was a problem with the cartridge caused by its sheer power: it tended to push the primer cap back on discharge, causing it to stand proud of the head of the case. In a revolver, there was always the danger that this would interfere with the rotation of the cylinder, and so to combat this, Webley fitted the No 1 Revolver with a detachable backplate between the standing breech and the cylinder, and which rotated with it. It was pierced with appropriate holes, both to accommodate the firing pin on the hammer nose and to permit the primer to bulge backwards, if necessary, without fouling the mechanism. The innovation worked, but it meant that reloading was an extremely slow process, for the cylinder pin and the cylinder itself had to be withdrawn, the backplate removed, the spent cases ejected (using the cylinder pin as an extractor) and then the whole pistol re-assembled.

Police forces raised from the civilian population, as opposed to gendarmeries, which were military bodies, were unknown in most of Europe before the middle of the nineteenth century. For example, London's Metropolitan Police, founded in 1829, were the first such organization in the United Kingdom. Where they were raised, they rapidly achieved notable results, but some areas were more prone to violent crime and civil disorder than others, and the police in these places had to be fully armed.

WEBLEY'S RIC REVOLVER

Within the United Kingdom, Ireland, which had never been at ease under the conqueror's heel, was the most troublesome of all. A police force was created in Ireland in 1868, known as the Royal Irish Constabulary (RIC). The first gun that the new body adopted was a double-action, solid-frame, six-shot pistol manufactured by Philip Webley and Sons, originally in .442 calibre centre-fire chambering. This became known as the RIC Revolver and was key in establishing Webley's reputation as a maker of sturdy, reliable pistols. A second 1880 model had recessed cylinder locking grooves toward the rear of the cylinder (those of the first model had been towards the front). It also had the swivel ejector originally developed by John Adams and now out of patent, in which the ejector rod proper was housed within the hollow cylinder pin when not in use. Retained by a simple spring, this was withdrawn forwards and turned around its axis through 60 degrees when required. An 'improved' model with a fluted cylinder appeared in 1883. As well as the original .442 chambering, versions were made in a variety of 'British' calibres from .430 to .476, as well as in .44 Winchester and .45 Colt.

THE BULLDOG

The RIC Revolver was the basis for two more solid-frame Webley pistols, namely the Army Express Models which appeared first in the late 1870s, and which were made in both single-and

double-action versions, and the class known as Bulldogs. These were hugely popular five-shot pocket pistols and as a consequence were probably the most widely copied pistol there has ever been. The first version of the Bulldog revolver appeared in 1878, in .442 calibre centre-fire, and other chamberings, up to .45 and down to .32, soon followed. It was a no-nonsense, no-frills gun, usually with a

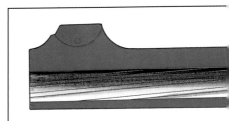

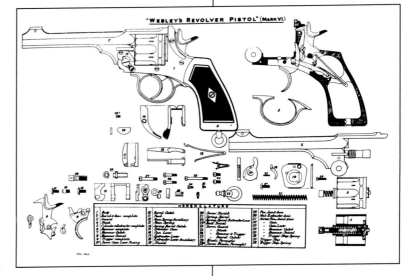

■ABOVE: The constituent parts of the Webley Mark VI, which officially entered service in 1915. It performed well in the mud and water of the Western Front during World War I.

50mm (2in) barrel, being just 140mm (5.5in) long overall and weighing a modest 312gm (11oz). Even a true Webley Bulldog cost just a few pounds in 1910, when a break-open automatic ejector model cost less than £4. Copies could be had for much less, down to around 10 shillings (two dollars and 50 cents at that time) in some cases, which perhaps gives some indication of their quality. Webley kept the Bulldog in production up until 1914, but copies were still being manufactured up until World War II.

PRYSE'S DOUBLE-ACTION LOCK

Break-open revolvers with simultaneous automatic extraction were not new when Webley first produced such a weapon, based on a design patented by Charles Pryse in 1876. Webley was not alone in producing Pryse revolvers; other gunmakers did too, notably Bland,

Bonehill and Horsley, but only in limited quantities. The Webley-Pryse was a conventional six-shot, double-action pistol, hinged at the lower front of the frame with the top strap latched to the upper part of the standing breech by means of two laterally acting bolts or studs passing through the frame and into it. The bolts were withdrawn by two spring-loaded rocking levers, the free ends of which terminated in small milled discs, one on each side of the frame, between hammer and trigger, where they were easily accessible to thumb and forefinger. In fact, there is no mention made of this latch in Pryse's original patent application, and it does not appear on the drawings; it is thought to have been the invention of a Continental gunmaker, and to have been simply 'borrowed' by Webley. Pryse's own innovation was an improvement to the

Webley & Scott Mark VI
(For specifications see page 84)

actuation of the cylinder bolt. The double-action lock was a rebounding type, which is to say that on being fired, the hammer returned to the half-cock position, from when it could be released only by pressure on the trigger or by manually bringing it to full cock. It was impervious to accidental forward pressure, while at the same time, the firing pin on the hammer's nose was automatically protected when the revolver was broken open. It is quite possible that Pryse's revolvers were the first made in the United Kingdom with this particular feature, the invention of a lockmaker named Stanton.

Webley produced Webley-Pryse pistols from 1877 in a variety of 'service' calibres – chiefly .442, .45 and .476, while Bland, for one, went so far as to produce it in .577 Boxer chambering. The main fault of the Pryse revolvers seems to have been the ease with which the barrel and cylinder could be unlatched accidentally from the frame, and it was this defect which Michael Kaufmann sought to rectify in his period of association with the company, from 1878-81. Kaufmann first produced a design for an improvement to the double-action lock then in use, and later developed a device similar to Abadie's modification which allowed free rotation of the cylinder of a solid-frame revolver during loading and unloading, which was used on later versions of Webley's Army Express Model pistols.

THE KAUFMANN LATCH
In between, however, he produced a new method of bolting the top frame of a break-open revolver to the standing breech. This was a complicated arrangement involving a spring-loaded bolt in one side of the frame acting on another bolt installed in the top strap, which in turn acted on a second spring-loaded bolt in the other half of the frame, all the bolts in question having their mating ends machined at matching angles. The Kaufmann latch appears to have been put into production alongside that originally used on the Pryse pistols, and both are found on the earliest examples of the third series of Webley break-open pistols, the 'WG' series. The initials stand either for Webley-Green (though there seems to be no record of who Green actually was) or Webley-Government. It was this pistol, recognisable by its distinctive 'church steeple' cylinder fluting (as it was known in Birmingham), which won Webley the coveted government contract, so the latter root is certainly believable. It was on the first model WG series pistol that

Webley-Fosbery Automatic Revolver

Calibre: .455in (11.55mm)
Weight: 1.08kg (38oz)
Length: 292mm (11.5in)
Barrel length: 190mm (7.5in)
Feed: six-round magazine
Muzzle velocity: 198mps (650fps)
Country of origin: United Kingdom

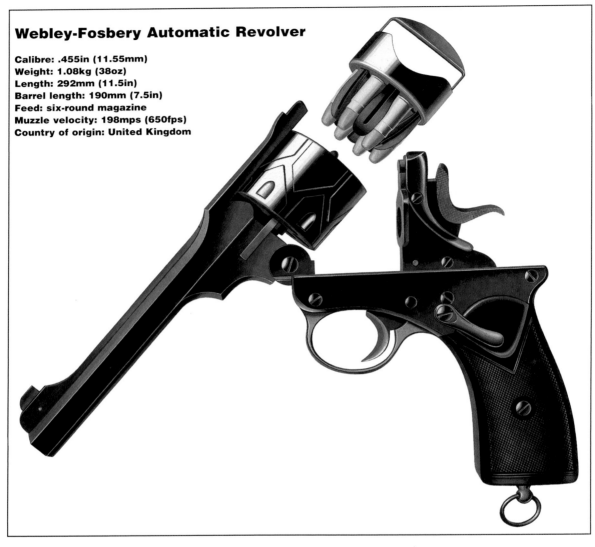

the 'stirrup' or 'bridle' latching system, which was to be employed on every future British service revolver, first appeared in 1885.

The bridle catch seems to have come about in two distinct phases. Firstly, Henry Webley modified Kaufmann's design in 1883 so that the latching bolt was activated by the fore-and-aft movement of a spring-loaded lever acting on an appropriately machined bolt head, rather than by a side-to-side movement. This modification reduced still further any possibility of the top strap coming unlatched due to accidental pressure. Then, two years later, he realised that the complicated arrangement of three

interactive bolts was entirely unnecessary, and that a simple over-strap stirrup was quite sufficient. This stirrup bore on an extension of the top strap which fitted over the upper part of the standing breech, and was actuated by the fore-and-aft motion of the lever. Indeed, it was actually safer, for positioned as it was, if the stirrup was not fully home when the hammer fell, only two things could happen – either the fall of the hammer would drive it home, in which case the revolver would discharge as normal, or the nose of the hammer would be held off and prevented from reaching the primer. The next model in the series, the 1892, incorporated a modified form

releasing the cylinder from its axial pin, while the Model 1893 introduced a spring-loaded striker firing pin and a flat-nosed hammer, a feature soon discarded, though it reappeared as an option in the Mark II 'Police and Military' .38-calibre revolvers of 1896). It also had more conventional grooving to the cylinder in place of the earlier flutes. In addition to standard models, specially set-up target pistols were also available, with 190mm (7.5in) barrels replacing the normal 150mm (6in). They also had rectangular blade/rectangular notch sights, as developed by the American pistol champion, E.E. Patridge. These pistols, in somewhat modified form, were available right up until 1939, and regularly equalled the performance of similar Colt and Smith & Wesson revolvers.

THE WEBLEY MARKS

The pistol Webley produced to fulfil the 1887 contract to supply side-arms to the British Army and Navy was the British Government Model, Mark I, sometimes known as the Mark I Service Revolver. It was a WG series I pistol with a modified 'bird's beak' butt, conventional cylinder fluting and horizontal, triangular holster guides fitted to the barrel extension in front of the cylinder on each side. It was available with both 100mm (4in) and 150mm (6in) barrels, and chambered for .45, .455 and .476 ammunition.

The Mark I pistol was followed by five variants, the first of which to given extensive active use was the Mark IV or Boer War model, which came into service, in 1899. It was superseded by the short-lived Mark V in December 1913, but only 20,000 examples were made before that model gave way in turn to the Mark VI in 1915. The six variants differed only in detail and only the Mark VI, with its squared-off butt in place of the bird-beak type which graced all five earlier models, is identifiable by the layman. Webley's contract for the latter ran to 2500 pistols per week for the rest of the war, and a total of half a million were manufactured before it was retired in favour of the Enfield No 2 Mark I revolver in 1932. During the course of World War I the Mark VI acquired accessories at both ends. A detachable shoulder stock was available, as was a bayonet, though neither was widely used. It proved to be a near-perfect close-quarter weapon in the confused and confusing environment of trench warfare, immune to all but the grossest mistreatment, and firing a heavy round which was almost sure to incapacitate an adversary. It was also available in .22 rim-fire chambering, as a training aid. Parker-Hale also produced a conversion kit, consisting of a barrel sleeve, cylinder and bridging sleeve, which allowed the service-calibre revolver to fire the miniature rounds.

WEBLEY'S POLICE MODELS

The Webley & Scott Government Model Mark VI was the last revolver the firm supplied to the British armed services, though the .38 Enfield pistol which replaced it was developed by them and closely resembles its predecessors. With

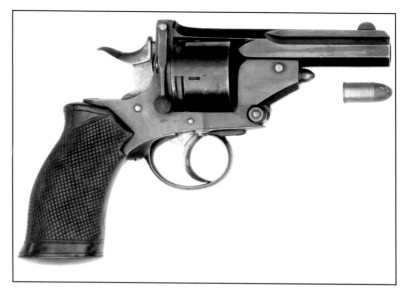

■ABOVE: This Webley-Pryse revolver has a star-shaped ejector which is forced from the rear end of the cylinder when the barrel is pushed down, throwing out the empty cases with force.

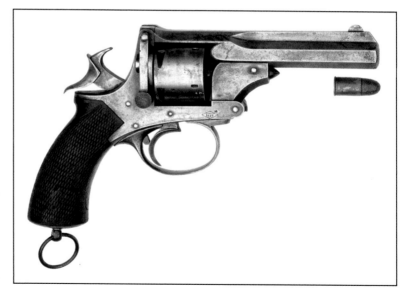

■BELOW: A Webley-Pryse revolver. A special feature of these models was a rebounding hammer, which prevented an accidental discharge caused by a blow on the hammer.

the loss of the military contract, the company went into a decline. But even the huge government contracts had not occupied the whole of the Webley production line, and right from the outset the various Government Models had been available to the public. They were better-finished, and usually with chequered

walnut grips to replace those of rubber composition found on the contract models. Many of these were sold through the Wilkinson Sword Company, and bore their name.

In 1896 Webley introduced the Mark II and Mark III Police and Military Models, the only marked difference between the two being the reintroduction of the flat-nosed hammer and plunger firing pin in the Mark II. The two were available simultaneously, but again, the firing pin version proved unpopular, and was soon dropped by the company, whereas the Mark III, originally available only in .38 S&W calibre, was soon also offered in .32 calibre, and with a choice of 76mm (3in), 10cm (4in) or 127mm (5in) barrels.

There were several different butt styles to chose from, and a gold- or silver-plated Presentation Model, with or without engraving, with mother-of-pearl or ivory grips, was available to order, with a price tag to match its appearance. The Mark III, by now styled the Pocket Pistol, was joined in 1927 by the essentially-similar Mark IV, available in a wider range of calibres.

THE WEBLEY-FOSBERY

Two years after the introduction of the first Police and Military models, they were joined by the Webley Pocket Revolvers, firstly in a version with a shrouded hammer, and in 1901, in a conventional version. Both were available in .320 or .32 S&W chamberings, and with either the familiar thumb lever-operated stirrup latch or with similar latch bereft of the lever. This second type was operated by pulling back the top of the stirrup, which was serrated for the purpose, with the thumb. The 'hammerless' model was provided with a sliding safety catch.

Roughly contemporaneously with the Pocket Revolvers, Webley' engaged on a development programme which led to one of the most unusual revolvers of them all, the Webley-Fosbery Automatic Revolver. Colonel G. Vincent Fosbery, an authentic hero who won a Victoria Cross on the Northwest Frontier (of India), retired from the army in 1877, and devoted himself, to no great effect, to the design of a machine gun. Eventually, Fosbery turned his attention to the subject of self-loading revolvers, Hiram Maxim having effectively sewn up the development of the machine gun for the foreseeable future. In 1895 he obtained a British patent for a revolver which, having once been cocked, was re-cocked after firing by the action of its recoil. The indexing principle he used was not at all unlike that employed by Paul Mauser's Zig-Zag revolver, save that instead of the mainspring carrier and its stud moving backwards and forwards in slots in the cylinder, the entire barrel, cylinder, standing breech and hammer, together with most of its associated mechanism, were free to slide back against a spring in a grooved guide in the lower part of the frame. The trigger and butt remained stationary, the motion being used to cock the action and index the cylinder.

BAD BATTLEFIELD PERFORMANCE

Fosbery's patent drawing was based on a Colt SAA, but naturally enough, when the Webley & Scott Revolver and Arms Co. Ltd took up his idea in 1900, the resulting .455-calibre, six-shot pistol was made up, as far as possible, from standard Government Model parts, as was an eight-shot version, chambered for the .38 Colt cartridge. Both were break-open designs with the standard star simultaneous extractor. The pistol went into production in both calibres in 1901, but development did not cease there, and thus the few true first-series Webley-Fosbery pistols exhibit a confusing variety of detailed specification changes. An improved model appeared the following year, and stayed in limited production for over a decade. It proved to be thoroughly successful on the range. On one particular occasion, Walter Winans, probably the best pistol shot of his generation, put six rounds into a 50mm (2in) bull at 11m (36ft) in a mere seven seconds, a remarkable feat of marksmanship. It was less effective on the battlefield, being prone to jamming in the dirt and mud. An interesting accessory for the pistol was a forerunner of the modern quick-load clip; two versions were produced, one, designed by Webley themselves, the other – Prideaux's Patent Instantaneous Revolver Magazine – independently.

Despite its partial success, the Webley-Fosbery Automatic Revolver was an anomaly; for even before Fosbery had been able to put his theories into practice, both Hugo Borchardt and Paul Mauser had shown where the way forward lay, and had produced viable self-loading pistols that didn't have the innate drawbacks of Fosbery's concept.

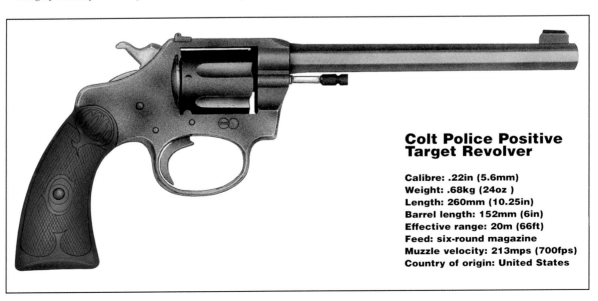

Colt Police Positive Target Revolver

Calibre: .22in (5.6mm)
Weight: .68kg (24oz)
Length: 260mm (10.25in)
Barrel length: 152mm (6in)
Effective range: 20m (66ft)
Feed: six-round magazine
Muzzle velocity: 213mps (700fps)
Country of origin: United States

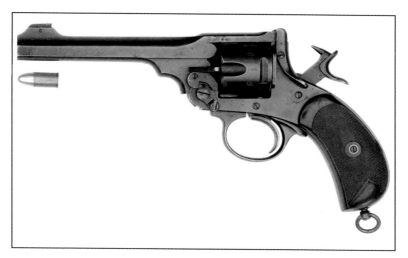

■LEFT: The Webley & Scott Mark V. Only 20,000 were made before it was superseded in 1915 by the Mark VI. Thus it is the rarest of all the Webley government series.

■LEFT: The Webley & Scott Mark V. Only 20,000 were made before it was superseded in 1915 by the Mark VI. Thus it is the rarest of all the Webley government series.

police customers overseas. It stayed in production when war broke out in 1939, and eventually, with the production of regulation pistols falling far short of requirements, the British Government keenly accepted it into service alongside the similar Enfield revolver.

JAPAN'S MEIJI 26

Another significant pre-World War I revolver was the product of a nation to which the industrial revolution came very late: Japan. Following unsatisfactory relations with the Portugese and Dutch merchant adventurers of the sixteenth and seventeenth centuries, Japan shut her doors on the Western world until she was jolted out of her isolation by the Americans in the 1850s, largely in the person of Commodore Matthew Perry. As a result, industrial manufacturing methods were completely alien to the Japanese, who set about catching up with

THE MARK IV WEBLEY

With the transfer of the contract for British service pistols to the government's own factory at Enfield, and despite the fact that much of the actual production of the Enfield No 2 pistol, especially during World War II, was actually undertaken by outside contractors, the commercial production of pistols in Britain started to grind to a halt. Webley themselves began production of a .38-calibre revolver in 1923, styled rather confusingly the Mark IV, and incorporating all the desirable features of the Government Model Mark VI. They sold it widely to military and

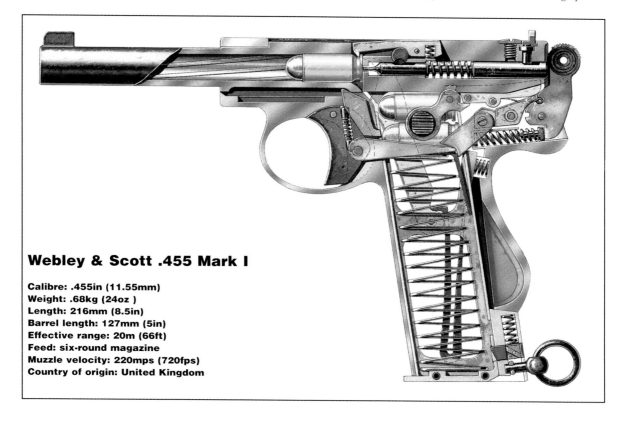

Webley & Scott .455 Mark I

Calibre: .455in (11.55mm)
Weight: .68kg (24oz)
Length: 216mm (8.5in)
Barrel length: 127mm (5in)
Effective range: 20m (66ft)
Feed: six-round magazine
Muzzle velocity: 220mps (720fps)
Country of origin: United Kingdom

■LEFT: A copy of the RIC Revolver. The RIC is probably the most popular revolver ever made by Webley. This example is based on the Webley No I New Model of 1833.

a rush. During the 1870s, the Japanese Navy purchased a quantity of Smith & Wesson No 3 pistols, the first such official procurement. In 1893, the 26th year of the Meiji Era, a home-produced pistol became available, and set what was to become a custom among Japanese arms manufacturers by taking as its 'name', the year of its introduction. The Meiji 26 Nen Shiki Kenju was a basic 9mm (.35in) six-shot double-action, break-open revolver with an automatic ejector. Unusually, it could be cocked by means of the trigger only; there was no spur to its hammer. Much of its design was a straight copy of the Smith & Wesson, but its action and frame seem to have been lifted from the Austrian arms manufacturer Gasser, and it had a hinged side plate reminiscent of a old Nagant design. One well respected expert source says of the Meiji: 'one can but suppose that patriotism held a greater attraction than efficiency. It can charitably be described as serviceable, but little more'.

If revolver production during the twentieth century went into a progressive decline in Britain – and by and large throughout the rest of Europe too – the same was most definitely not the case in the United States, where the production of small arms rose dramatically.

■RIGHT: The Webley Bulldog. They were designed primarily for civilian use and were simple, robust and reliable. They were first sold in 1878, this particular model in 1880.

COLT VERSUS SMITH & WESSON
By the 1880s, the two main contestants, Colt and Smith & Wesson, were trying to solve the reloading problem – not that either would have agreed that such a problem existed. Smith & Wesson was still having trouble with the latching system on their break-open revolvers. Colt was doing its best to exalt the superior strength of the solid frame while playing down the time it took to eject spent cartridges and reload, one cylinder at a time, via the side gate. The solution to both their problems was the swing-out cylinder, the original axial pin now

carried on a 'crane' or yoke, rather than being secured into the forepart of the frame itself. This was a short bar, fixed to a second pin located in the lower part of the frame, just above the bottom strap. The shooter unlocked a latch at the rear of the cylinder, the catch of which was normally located on the left-hand side of the frame where it was conveniently placed for the right-handed user's thumb. The cylinder and crane could then both pivot on the lower pin and emerge from the frame, ideally to the left, leaving the cylinder free to revolve on its axial pin, which also served as the carrier for a manually operated star extractor. This solution was not an entirely new one (Captain A. Albini patented just such a design in Britain in 1869, for example) but it worked, and it was in the public domain. First Colt and then Smith & Wesson fastened on to it eagerly. The final problem besetting the solid-frame revolver was thus solved, once and for all.

Colt put a six-shot double-action revolver with just such a cylinder system into production in 1888 as the Double Action New Navy Revolver, Model 1889, and sold 5000 to the US Navy. An automatic extractor, which had been the work of William Mason before he defected to Winchester, was deleted from the production models in favour of a

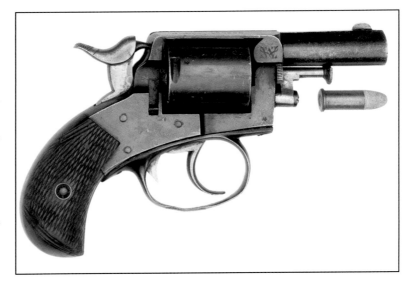

manually operated push-rod fairly early on. The following year the US Army, having decided that it too needed to update its side-arms, also contracted with Colt, on condition that a separate cylinder bolt be incorporated into the design. The pistol in question was accepted as the New Army Revolver, Model of 1892. These revolvers were both supplied to the government in .38 calibre long Colt chamberings, the general feeling being that the new propellants and projectile profiles had improved the smaller round's stopping power to the point of adequate reliability; this was to prove not to have been the case. The Model 1889 was also available in .38 short and in .41 long and short, and with 89mm (3.5in) and 114mm (4.5in) to supplement the Government-issue 15cm (6in) barrel version. For the Model 1892, two additional calibres, .32 WCF and .38 Special, were also offered.

ANTI-CLOCKWISE CYLINDERS
US Navy 'experts' had decreed that the new pistols should have their cylinders rotating to the left, or anti-clockwise, unlike all the previous Colts. On the surface, perhaps, this was simply a matter of taste, and in a side gate/rod ejector revolver, it would not have mattered. In this case it caused a major problem, in that the rotation of the cylinder now threw the cylinder against its locking catch and out of the frame, causing wear which occasionally resulted in the cylinder falling out of alignment with the barrel. This potentially grave

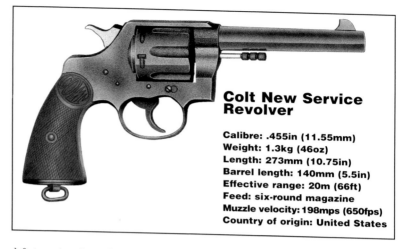

Colt New Service Revolver

Calibre: .455in (11.55mm)
Weight: 1.3kg (46oz)
Length: 273mm (10.75in)
Barrel length: 140mm (5.5in)
Effective range: 20m (66ft)
Feed: six-round magazine
Muzzle velocity: 198mps (650fps)
Country of origin: United States

defect went unchanged in subsequent Colt Government pistols until the Model 1909 New Service Revolver, when Colt were permitted to revert to their previous practice. In Smith & Wesson pistols, whose cylinders had always rotated that way, it was never altered.

These Colt double-action revolvers were progressively improved up to 1905, though the modifications made were minor. The most important functional change was the addition of a safety lock to ensure that the pistol could not be discharged until the cylinder was closed and locked into place. This modification first appeared on the Model 1894, and all earlier models in government service were subsequently retro-fitted with a similar device.

The New Army and New Navy pistols were joined on the production lines at Hartford in 1897 by an apparently similar heavy frame revolver. Suitable for the 'old' service calibres, .45 and .455 in particular, it became known as the New Service Revolver. Certain simple improvements to an already sound basic concept led to an improved model of 1905 and it was adopted by the US Army and Navy in 1909. It was fitted with a rebounding lock similar to that found in the earlier Webley-Pryse revolvers, but with an additional safety feature which Colt called the 'Colt Positive Lock'. Though it was to remain in full government service for only two years, the pistol proved very popular in the civilian market for many years thereafter, and formed the basis for Colt's entire new range of revolvers.

THE NEW SERVICE REVOLVER
The reversion to .45-calibre ammunition for US service side-arms came as a result of complaints from soldiers and Marines fighting Moros rebels in the Philippines during the war of insurrection which followed the United States' first attempt at imperialism. Just as the British had discovered 50 years earlier, the American fighting men found that relatively high-velocity rounds of small calibre (that is, .38) were likely to pass through the body of an aggressive adversary without checking his progress. They clamoured for a return to the slower, heavier projectiles they had used so much more effectively against another equally determined enemy, the Plains Indian. The first .45-calibre pistols to be issued to US troops serving in the Philippines were

Meiji Pistol

Calibre: 9mm (.35in)
Weight: .91kg (32oz)
Length: 235mm (9.25in)
Barrel length: 119mm (4.7in)
Effective range: 20m (66ft)
Feed: six-round magazine
Muzzle velocity: 183mps (600fps)
Country of origin: Japan

Colt New Service 1917

Calibre: .455in (11.55mm)
Weight: 1.13kg (40oz)
Length: 273mm (10.75in)
Barrel length: 140mm (5.5in)
Effective range: 20m (66ft)
Feed: six-round magazine
Muzzle velocity: 198mps (650fps)
Country of origin: United States

hastily procured Colt Model 1878 Frontier Double Action revolvers, 4500 of which were purchased in 1902. They were superseded by New Service Revolvers in 1909.

COLT'S MODEL 1917
A revamped New Service revolver was issued in 1917, just as the United States was entering the war against Germany in Europe, as a stop-gap measure when supplies of the self-loading M1911 pistol fell short of requirements. In total some 150,000 were produced. In appearance the Model 1917 differs from the earlier versions in having a pronouncedly tapered barrel, but the real change lay in its ammunition. The pistol was chambered for the rimless .45 ammunition developed for the M1911,

known as the .45 ACP (Automatic Colt Pistol) round, the first time a completely rimless cartridge had been used in a production revolver. Smith & Wesson produced a very similar pistol, also in large numbers (153,000 in all were procured) chambered for the same cartridge and also known as the M1917. These were the last revolvers selected by the US Government that were designated for general service issue.

RIMLESS AMMUNITION
In other weapons – in bolt-action rifles, for example, and in self-loading weapons of all types – rimless cartridges offer one obvious, distinct advantage over rimmed rounds. In order to chamber a rimmed round, the bolt or carrier which strips the new round out of the magazine (or belt)

has to extract it on its rearwards 'stroke' and continue to travel backwards by the full length of the round before it can change direction and begin to ram it into the breech. Chambering a rimless round, on the other hand, only requires the bolt or carrier to retire to the rearmost extremity of the incoming round and then reverse its direction and ram it home. Location of the round in the chamber, and hence control of the headspace between firing pin and primer, is accomplished by the profile of the cartridge case itself, and particularly by the difference in diameter between it and the projectile it contains. Extraction of the spent rimless case is simple, as a spring-loaded claw which locates into the groove machined around the head of the cartridge is incorporated into the bolt

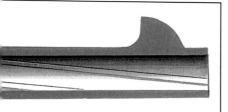

In order to make the ACP (or any other rimless) cartridge function satisfactorily in a revolver, the rounds have to be carried in a clip of some sort, so that the simultaneous extractor has something to act on. Otherwise, while individual rounds may be fired, they can only be ejected manually, one at a time, from the front. In the case of the Colt New Service Model 1917, the ammunition was presented in three-round semi-circular clips which also speeded up the operation of loading the pistol, though that was very much a secondary benefit. It is also essential that the chamber's profile retains them and places them accurately: the Smith & Wesson M1917 revolver's did; early versions of the Colt pistol, the chambers of which were

■BELOW: An advertisement for the Colt Double Action Army Revolver. It first appeared in 1877 but proved to be badly balanced and unreliable – attributes not expected in a Colt pistol.

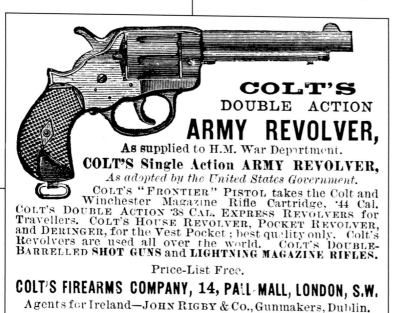

the .45 ACP. The .455 Webley Mark 2 round which the British Army was using at the time produced a velocity of only 177 metres per second (580 feet per second), even though its charge was 10 per cent greater. Different projectile weights, the ACP was the lightest at 14.9gm (230 grains) and the Webley the heaviest at 17.2gm (265 grains), didn't entirely account for the difference in performance, though that did, of course, tend to even out the stopping power.

COLT POCKET POSITIVE RANGE

After the end of World War I 'war surplus' stocks were quickly sold off to eager customers. The two M1917 pistols disappeared from the US Government inventory but stayed in the catalogue of their respective makers. Colt had always made selected, 'tuned' pistols with adjustable sights and a variety of other refinements available as match pistols, and continued the practice with the New Service Target Model. It was supplemented with the Shooting Master in 1932 in a wide choice of calibres, .38 Special, .44 Special, .45 ACP and .45 Colt, and eventually a .357 Magnum version after Smith & Wesson and Winchester developed that round in 1935.

The heavy frame revolvers were joined by very similar, lighter models on a slimmed-down frame as early as 1895, when Colt introduced a new range of pocket revolvers. When the 'improved model' New Service revolver was introduced in 1905, the smaller pistols, too, got the Colt Positive Lock, their name being changed to Colt Pocket Positive. The Pocket Positive was available in no less than five different chamberings, all in .32 calibre, and with 63mm (2.5in), 89mm (3.5in) and 150mm (6in) barrels. They stayed in production until mid-way through World War II.

COLT'S MODEL Ds

A year after the introduction of the new Pocket model, the old New Line Police and House Pistols were superseded by the New Police Model on the same frame as the Pocket Pistols and in the same range of .32 calibre chamberings. In 1905, that gun, too, got the Colt Positive Lock and became the Police Positive revolver, the range of calibres available being stretched to include two .22 chamberings as well as two types of heavier ammunition, .38 S&W and .38 Colt. A version with a 50mm (2in) barrel, known as the Banker's Special, became

face. Clearly, the use of a rimless cartridge both permits faster operation and allows the physical size of the weapon to be reduced. None of these factors apply to a revolver, where the ammunition is contained at the breech to begin with; indeed, here the lack of a rim to the cartridge case constitutes not a solution, but an additional problem.

straight-bored, did not. The difference in the performance certainly merited the lengths Colt had to go to in order to utilise the ACP cartridge. The M1909 .45 Colt cartridge it superseded was almost 1cm (.5in) longer, yet its muzzle velocity was 225 metres per second (738 feet per second) as against the 262 metres per second (860 feet per second) achieved by available in the two .38 calibres in 1928, and was joined by a model in .22 rim-fire in 1933.

Colt's answer to criticism that the Police Positive lacked stopping power was the introduction, in 1907, of a version chambered for the .38 S&W Special cartridge, its cylinder 6mm (.25in) longer and its frame lengthened to accommodate it. The Police Positive Special was later available in three .32 calibre chamberings (for Winchester Centre-Fire, Colt and S&W cartridges) and with 100mm (4in), 127mm (5in) and 150mm (6in) barrels. In 1926 it became available in a 50mm (2in) barrel version, which later went into the catalogue as the Detective Special. Weighing just 0.6kg (21oz), and under 178mm (7in) long overall, the Detective Special was a worthy successor to the Bulldog pistols of half a century earlier. During the mid-1930s a detachable hammer shroud, which could be factory fitted to new guns or supplied as a kit for installation by gunsmiths, became available, not just for the Detective Special, but for all the other versions of the light-frame revolver. By the 1950s, these by-now venerable pistols were not just still in production, but the range of them was even increased. To ease the understandable confusion, Colt Firearms, as the company became, redesignated the various sub-types, the Detective Special becoming the

■BELOW: The Colt New Service Revolver. It was made in six barrel lengths and was used as an American service arm from 1907 onwards until superseded by semi-automatics.

Model D.1, the Police Positive Special the Model D.2, the super-lightweight Cobra (a version of the Detective Special which made extensive use of light alloy) the Model D.3 and the Special Agent (a further cut-down version) the Model D.4.

As if the D.4s weren't light enough, during the Korean War Colt went even further. At the request of the US Air Force they made 1000 of these pistols in aluminium, except for the barrel, for issue to aircrew in place of the cumbersome .45-calibre M1911A1 auto-loader. Smith & Wesson made a similar number of Chief's Specials and Military and Police Models.

In 1960, the remainder of these pistols were recalled after it had been discovered that it was possible to chamber a .357 Magnum round in the Chief's Specials – and blow up the gun as soon as it was discharged. Later efforts to produce ultra-lightweight pistols stuck to the use of steel for their cylinders, even though frames are routinely made from aluminium alloys.

PYTHONS AND COBRAS

As if the Colt range wasn't confusing enough already, in 1908 the company launched a new line of medium-frame pistols to fill the gap between the heavy frame New Service models and the Pocket and Police Positives: the Official Police Model. Originally this pistol was aimed at a US Government contract, and was known as the Army Special, but the armed services became more interested in the heavier revolver and, eventually, in the self-loading M1911. Still, Colt kept the medium-frame pistols on their books,

and was rewarded, in 1926, with a large order from the New York City Police Department for 100mm (4in) inch barrel models chambered for the .38 Special cartridge. Further orders followed, and in 1928 the name of the pistol was changed to the Official Police Model in recognition of its new-found status. It later became the Model E.3, and over the years, non-standard match pistols have been offered under this designation, notably the various Officer's Models.

It was this Official Police Model which was to form the basis for a new range of higher-powered pistols chambered for the .357 (and later the .44) Magnum cartridges to replace the heavy New Service .357 Magnum variant. Known as the Trooper, it was an Officer's Model with adjustable rear sights and a ramp foresight, and was also available in .38 calibre. This, the first of the Model E pistols in the long chambering was soon joined, if only briefly, by the Colt 357. A short-lived design, this was supplanted by an updated pistol with an integral ventilated barrel rib and an ejector shroud which extends to the end of the barrel – the Colt Python, a pistol which set a new standard in handgun performance. The Python was later joined by an updated version of the Cobra, the King Cobra, also in .357 Magnum calibre, and by the Anaconda, in .44 Magnum chambering. All are available in stainless steel, and with the long target barrel this makes for a very heavy gun. The 200mm (8in) barrelled Anaconda, for example, weighs over 1.47kg (3.25lb).

EXTERNAL CHANGES

After the barrel rib and the full-length ejector shroud, the other obvious difference in the make-up of these 'new age' Colt pistols over their predecessors lies in their grips. Whether made of rubber or walnut, they are ergonomically designed to sit more comfortably in the hand. The result is a pistol markedly different in appearance to the 'improved' New Service Model of 1905, but when one looks inside, it is a different story. The mechanical components of the pistol have scarcely changed – a fitting comment on the quality of the original design. The increased availability of stainless steel from the 1970s onwards has also helped to alter the appearance of side arms, though the traditional blued steel finish is still more common. As recently as 1970, the only Smith & Wesson pistol available in stainless steel was the Model

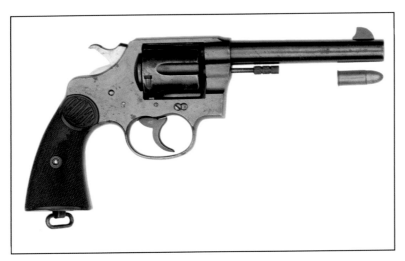

60 Chief's Special; after 20 years it was an option in most models, at a supplement of about 10 per cent on the basic price. All three Colt revolvers and 10 of the company's 11 self-loaders (the exception has a moulded plastic frame) were also available in that material.

SMITH & WESSON'S CHALLENGE

Throughout the twentieth century, just as through the preceding 40 years, Colt Firearms had only one serious rival as a manufacturer of handguns: Smith & Wesson. Like Colt, Smith & Wesson has offered pistols in three basic frame weights ever since introducing the swing-out cylinder with its Model I Hand Ejector pistol of 1896. Naturally enough, there are small differences between the two leading types of US-produced revolver, but despite that, the list of their similarities is much longer.

CLOCKWISE, ANTI-CLOCKWISE

To the shooter, the main difference between Colt and Smith & Wesson revolvers is in the direction of rotation of the cylinder. The Colt's revolves clockwise while the Smith & Wesson's revolves to the left. This produces a characteristic

difference in operational 'feel', as the Colt tends to pull to the right under the pressure of the trigger to cock the hammer and the Smith & Wesson tends to pull the other way. The second major difference lies in the method of locking the cylinder into place in line with the barrel. Colt employs a single latch at the rear of the cylinder, which is released by pulling the catch back; almost all Smith & Wesson revolvers since 1902 (and the exceptions are hardly worth cataloguing) have employed two, the second being located at the forward end of the ejector rod. The latter's latches are released by forward pressure on the catch, which is also located on the left-hand side of the frame, between hammer spur and trigger guard. The third main difference lies in the pistols' capacities: Colt revolvers of twentieth century vintage always hold six rounds; Smith & Wesson's centre-fire revolvers, however, hold either six or five, the latter being a straightforward means of chambering light-frame pistols for larger-calibre ammunition, while early rim-fire models in .22 calibre held seven.

To attempt to enumerate all the various swing-out cylinder revolvers produced by either Colt or Smith &

Wesson would try the patience and abilities of the most avid archivist. If the truncated catalogue of Colt's twentieth-century revolvers as outlined above seems overlong, that of Smith & Wesson – which has always, in modern times, featured more models than Colt – is more bemusing. By the start of the 1970s, between them the two companies had well over 100 different models of handgun in series production, not including the various limited edition commemorative and memorial models each produced from time to time. Even though a considerable rationalisation took place in the decades which followed (particularly in Colt's catalogue), as the end of the millennium approached there was still a plethora of choice available to the revolver shooter, in calibres ranging from .22 rim-fire to .44 centre-fire Magnum. A mid-90's edition of the authoritative *Guns Digest* listed 86 handguns from Smith & Wesson in 77

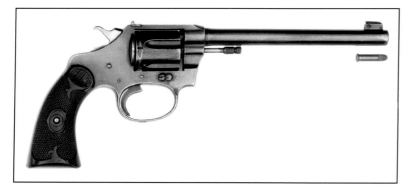

■LEFT: The Colt Police Positive Target Revolver. It went into production in 1910. It was accurate and comfortable to fire, though large-handed firers had to have their little finger off the end of the grip.

different models – and that takes no account of the choice of calibres and chamberings available in many of them! Nonetheless, even though sheer weight of numbers precludes a comprehensive study of all Smith & Wesson's swing-out cylinder models, no book could call itself a history of the world's great handguns without paying attention to the progress made by the pre-eminent producer of handguns in the twentieth century.

SMITH & WESSON'S DESIGNS
Smith & Wesson originally adopted the break-open design because of the ease with which all the spent cartridge cases could be extracted at once, but were plagued thereafter with the American shooting public's wariness of the ultimate strength of such a pistol. In 1895 the company switched over to the construction of solid-frame revolvers with a swing-out cylinder/hand ejector system virtually identical in principle to the one Colt put into production for the New Model Navy. Like its rivals, the company produced such pistols in three basic frame sizes, one for the .32 and similar calibres (the I series), one for the .38 (the K Series) and one for the .44, which Smith & Wesson preferred over the .45 as a 'service' calibre. Perhaps the most famous of the early guns in the K Series was the 1st Model Military and Police revolver of 1899, developed at the request of the US Army and Navy Ordnance Boards. Also known as the Army and Navy Model, it was accepted in small numbers by the US Navy in 1902. In the same year the company began production of a light-frame seven-shot revolver in .22 calibre, the Model M, which became known as the Ladysmith. British customers were perhaps bemused, and wondered why an American gunmaker should have chosen so belatedly to commemorate the relief of

a small town in South Africa from a siege by the Boer rebels, but clearly the name was too good to pass up. There is an intriguing rumour that the Ladysmith pistol was discontinued due to its popularity among whores and other ladies of 'easy virtue', but this can probably be discounted.

Five years on, the Military and Police Model was partially redesigned to take a new, more powerful cartridge based on the old .44 S&W Russian and known as the .44 S&W Special. This cartridge then evolved into the .44 Magnum. In the process, a third cylinder yoke locking device was introduced – a bolt housed in the suitably-modified ejector casing.

TRIPLE LOCK MODEL
The pistol in question became known as the Triple Lock Model, though the alternative name New Century was more evocative. It was this pistol, further modified to accept .45 ACP rimless ammunition, which became the Smith & Wesson M1917, procured alongside the Colt pistol with the same designation during World War I. Combat experience with the pistol showed that the third cylinder lock and the ejector casing which housed it were too prone to become packed with mud and prevent the cylinder from closing, so these additional features were removed.

The popularity of the New Century frame was to be long-lasting In 1930 it was used to produce a .38-calibre pistol, the Outdoorsman, which initially chambered a higher-powered round specially developed by Remington, the .38/44. Three years later a second, similar, pistol – the .38/44 Heavy Duty – was introduced. It immediately found a market among Police Departments in need of a 'hot' load to combat the increasing use of body armour and

reinforced automobile bodies among the criminal fraternity. This line of development led to the .357 Magnum round, produced by Winchester in cooperation with Smith & Wesson in 1935, and the introduction of the Smith & Wesson .357 Magnum revolver that same year. The first of these was presented to the FBI Director, J. Edgar Hoover. The pistol was first produced to special order only, in barrel lengths which varied between 90mm (3.5in) and 220mm (8.66in), but soon became a part of the standard catalogue. Police and Law Enforcement Agencies bought them in quantity, as did individuals for whom the .38 Special round was not powerful enough.

K SERIES MODIFICATIONS
Meanwhile, the K Series revolvers from which the heavyweights had sprung had themselves gone on evolving, the most important modification being the introduction, in 1915, of an intercepting safety device simpler than – though essentially similar to – Colt's positive lock. It was this revolver which saved Smith & Wesson from insolvency in later years, after the company became involved in a disastrous project to develop a semi-automatic rifle for the British Army.

After the fall of France in 1940, Britain and her remaining allies were dangerously short of arms and equipment, much of the existing stocks having been left behind at Dunkirk. They turned to the USA, in particular to Smith & Wesson, to supply side-arms, and the company responded by producing huge numbers (some 900,000 eventually) of what became known as the Model K-200. This was the Model K chambered for the 200 grain .38 round originally introduced in 1876 as the .38 S&W, and to a generation of British and Commonwealth servicemen became known as the 'Pistol, Revolver, .38in, Smith & Wesson Number 2'. It was inevitably compared by those servicemen to the contemporary Enfield No 2, and was judged superior.

Smith & Wesson's total World War II output was huge, some 1,310,000 revolvers, or about 250,000 a year, and this at a time when the standard US military side arm was a self-loading pistol. The war over, Smith & Wesson moved from its 100-year-old factory in

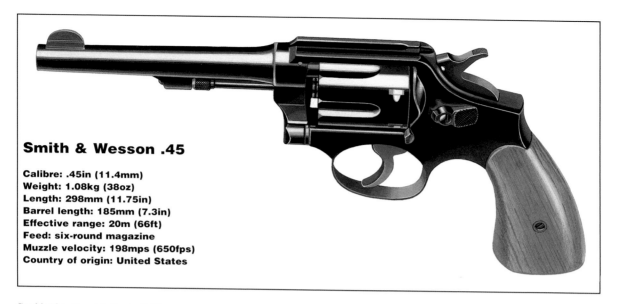

Smith & Wesson .45

Calibre: .45in (11.4mm)
Weight: 1.08kg (38oz)
Length: 298mm (11.75in)
Barrel length: 185mm (7.3in)
Effective range: 20m (66ft)
Feed: six-round magazine
Muzzle velocity: 198mps (650fps)
Country of origin: United States

Stockbridge Street in Springfield, replacing much antiquated machinery in the process (some of the more basic equipment dated from before the Civil War). They started producing their normal range of pistols again, now modified to a new 'short action' which reduced the hammer fall. The early 1950s saw a number of lightweight models including the Centennial, produced to celebrate the hundredth anniversary of Horace Smith and Daniel Wesson's partnership. The Centennial was essentially a 'hammerless' version of the Chief's Special to replace the 'New Departure' hammerless pistol which had been manufactured since the 1890s. It was joined by an ultra-lightweight version known as the 'Airweight', which weighed just 0.3kg (10.58oz), as opposed to the 0.54kg (19oz) of the standard Chief's Special.

MIGHTY MAGNUMS
In 1956, Smith & Wesson had 20 years' experience with the .357 Magnum cartridge developed in conjunction with Winchester. They now went one better – or at least, one more powerful – and collaborated with Remington to produce the .44 Magnum, judged to be twice as potent as the smaller Magnum round and three times as powerful as the .45 Colt cartridge. The revolver to accommodate this cartridge, known as the Model 29, was a six-shot double-action pistol based on the heavy .44 Special frame but strengthened further, with a heavy ribbed barrel, oversize grips and wider trigger

and hammer spur. It was the most powerful pistol in the world at the time, a distinction it held until the introduction of still heavier pistol cartridges such as the .50-calibre Action Express, in the 1980s. The .357 and .44 Magnum rounds were joined in 1964 by an intermediate, the .41 Magnum, and Smith & Wesson were first with a pistol for that, too – the Model 57, which was otherwise very similar to the Model 29.

By that time, Smith & Wesson were manufacturing 10 heavy frame pistols in .357 Magnum, .38 Special, .41 Magnum, .45 ACP and .44 Magnum chamberings; three K-series pistols in .38 Special and three more in .22, all of them purpose-built match guns, and on the light I-Series frame, three .22 calibre pistols, two more in .32 and five, including the Regulation Police pistol, the Chief's Special, the Bodyguard and the Centennial, chambered for the .38 Special round. Like Colt, Smith & Wesson later switched over to ergonomically designed grips, particularly for the heavier pistols, and some models acquired full-length ejector shrouds.

Throughout their long history, Smith & Wesson pistols have probably seen more imitations than any other, particularly from Spain. Some Spanish pistol makers who perhaps started out that way, notably Astra, Unceta y Cia of Vizcaya and Gabilondo y Cia of Eigoibar, now produce excellent revolvers to their own design, the former as Astra, the latter as Llama, though both are better

known for their self-loading pistols. During the last quarter of the twentieth century, in particular, there has been a resurgence of interest in revolvers in the United States, by far the world's biggest market due to its relaxed laws on gun ownership. This has spread to Europe to some degree, with old-established firms, such as Erma in Germany, and new-comers Korth, producing high-quality revolvers for the first time. Best known of all the newcomers, however, and slightly longer-established, having been set up in America in 1949, is Sturm, Ruger.

THE RUGER PISTOL
The first Ruger pistol was a .22 automatic chambered for the long rifle round, and aroused great interest in the target-shooting fraternity. Within five years it was joined by a six-shot single-action revolver in the same calibre, the Single Six, which clearly owed much to the Colt SAA. This later became available chambered for the much more powerful .22 WMR (Winchester Magnum Rim-fire) cartridge in 1959.

In 1955, Ruger produced its first heavyweight revolver, the .357 Magnum Blackhawk, which showed the same similarity to the 1873 Colt design. A .44 Magnum Blackhawk followed in 1956 – the first such pistol after Smith & Wesson's – and in 1959 this was the first model to benefit from an improved and strengthened frame. Other, more modern-looking, models, such as the GP-100 and SP-101 followed, were chambered for a wide range of rounds from .22 LR to .357 Magnum, via 9mm (.35in) Parabellum and .38 Special. They were supplemented by the Hawkeye, a fearsome single-shot pistol on the revolver frame and chambered for the Winchester .256 Magnum cartridge, a round more commonly associated with rifles or carbines. Sturm, Ruger also diversified into rifle and shotgun production, becoming one of the best known and successful producers of small arms in the United States in the process.

By their continued existence as a strong force in the marketplace, by the technical excellence of their products and by the diversity of their appeal, Colt and Smith & Wesson – along with newcomers such as Sturm, Ruger – did much to encourage the continued use of the revolver as a functional side-arm even after the self-loading pistol had been developed into a reliable and popular weapon. Not that Colt and Smith & Wesson had neglected to hedge their bets. Colt were early entrants into the field of the 'automatic' pistol, with a design ready to go into production as early as 1900.

MULTI-BARRELLED PISTOLS

Multi-barrelled pistols continued to have a role to play after the advent of the revolver for two different motives: ease of concealment, on the one hand, and an ability to handle very heavy loads of propellant on the other. A first-generation American of German origin gave his name, albeit unknowingly, to the 'vest-pocket pistol', a gun so small that it could literally fit in a watch-pocket or under a garter and yet be capable of dealing a killing blow at close quarters. Henry Deringer was born in Easton, Pennsylvania, in 1786 and served his apprenticeship to a gunmaker in Philadelphia. At the age of 20 he set up in business for himself, eventually becoming a contractor to the US Army, producing a range of handguns and long arms, firstly flintlock and later percussion. The pocket pistol for which he is best known was only a very small part of his line of guns, and had it not been for the unfortunate fact that John Wilkes Booth chose to use one to assassinate President Abraham Lincoln, in Ford's Theater in Washington on the evening of 14 April 1865, his name would probably have sunk into almost total obscurity.

Under this impetus, however, Deringer became one of that select few whose names have become generic terms, even if

it was deliberately misspelled in the process, and any small pocket pistol was liable, from then on, to be known as a 'derringer'. It took the unitary cartridge to give the little guns any real measure of widespread popularity, though as early as 1849 Christian Sharps (who was much better known for his high-powered large-calibre rifles) patented a four-barrelled muzzle-loading, percussion cap pistol with a rotating striker on the hammer nose which filled the bill admirably. Ten years later he went one better, and patented a similar gun utilising rim-fire cartridges, making it in .22, .30 and .32 calibres.

The chances are that the entire genre would have had but limited appeal had it not been for an oversight on the part of both Rollin White and his licensees, Smith & Wesson. Their White patent of 1855 did not cover barrels bored through to the breech, but only separate chambers for cartridges. Eliphalet Remington was quick to catch on to the oversight, and began producing six-shot pistols which were really no more than 'modernised' single-action pepperbox pistols. These were less than 127mm (5in) long overall, firstly in .22 calibre and later in .32, and used a method of indexing the barrels copied from one of Colt's, which also formed the basis for Paul Mauser's Zig-Zig revolvers.

DERRINGER MANUFACTURE

Later Remington joined forces with William Elliot, who held an essential patent, to produce the most famous of his derringers, the tip-up 'Over and Under' or Double Derringer in .41 rim-fire calibre, in 1866. Almost unbelievably, the gun in question remained in production until 1935, and in the years immediately following World War II, a variety of imitations in calibres ranging from .22 to .45 Colt, by way of .38 Special and .357

Magnum, came onto the market.

Colt made derringers, too, having bought out a specialist New York gunmaker, Daniel Moore, who did little else. In fact, Moore actually beat Remington to it, having been granted a patent of his own in 1861 and produced pistols, first under his own name and later as the National Arms Co., until his acquisition by Colt in 1870. Colt perhaps acquired the National Arms Co. to suppress a competitor (though it kept Moore's pistols in limited production for a while), for that same year it produced a design of its own, featuring a single barrel which swung to the side, engaging an ejector in the process.

MINIATURE REVOLVERS

As recently as 1960, Colt produced a new miniature pistol using the same action, in .22 calibre instead of the original .41. More recently the American Derringer Corporation was set up to manufacture a large range of double-barrelled miniature pistols, its basic model being available in virtually every known pistol calibre from .22 LR up to .44 Magnum, as well as for .410 shot shells. The company also makes a range of diminutive auto-loaders. Well known target pistol maker High Standard also manufactures a derringer, as do at least two other American gunmakers.

In European circles, miniature revolvers were more popular than derringer types, and multi-barrelled pistols were often to be found right at the other end of the size scale, chambered for anything up to and including the huge .577 Boxer cartridge. Versions were also

■BELOW: Colt's New Service Target Revolver. The gun has a hand-finished lock which works very smoothly, and a chequered trigger to stop the finger from slipping.

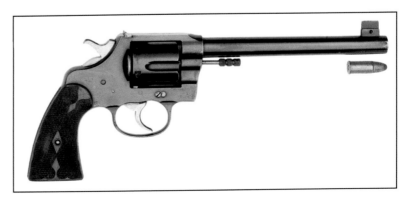

made for shot cartridges in up to 10 bore and were still occasionally loaded with a single ball of that calibre.

LANCASTER'S PISTOLS

These pistols, normally either in twin- or four-barrelled form, were intended to fulfil two distinct purposes. They were used as 'back-up' guns by big-game hunters, particularly in India, where they were known as 'Howdah' pistols. They were also used in combat, especially against enemies known to be aggressive in their determination to kill would-be imperialists, and who merited the sort of ammunition load which would literally stop them dead in their tracks. Best-known amongst the makers of such pistols was George Lancaster who, together with his successor, Henry Thorn, produced guns in the best tradition of the English craftsman-gunmakers until the end of the nineteenth century. The virtue of these multi-barrelled pistols, their supporters maintained, was the greater power they obtained from their charge by being totally gas-tight from breech to muzzle. In this they had a valid point, even if the cartridges they used were so powerful that a little wastage probably didn't matter as their moving parts were concerned, as much attention was paid to the barrel latch as far as to the lock, since it had to withstand enormous pressure. Four-barrelled pistols had star-like cartridge extractors operated by a simple

lever when the breech was opened, while the twins made do with the sort of half-moon extractors found today in shotguns.

Multi-barrel, large-calibre pistols fell out of favour by the turn of the nineteenth century and have never come back into fashion. The closest thing available is one of a range of single-shot pistols like the Magnum Research SSP-91, chambered for anything from .22 LR up to .44 Magnum, or the more traditional-looking Maximum Single Shot, available in a similar range of chamberings including some for rifle ammunition. Remington also returned to handgun manufacture with a range of single-shot pistols, and one auto-loader. The former, which incorporated rifle-type actions and were often chambered for cartridges usually used in long arms, were successful but the latter was not.

The widespread introduction of rifled barrels did more than improve the accuracy of both long arms and pistols alike – it also made each such arm uniquely identifiable from the marks left on the projectile it fired.

FORENSIC EVIDENCE

Since the 1920s, it has become increasingly common for forensic investigations of crimes involving guns to establish from the examination of bullets, first of all the type of gun used, and later the identity of the actual gun itself, when it has been available for comparison. The

pioneering work in this area was carried out almost simultaneously, and with little initial interaction between the interested parties, in the USA and Great Britain. Major Calvin Goddard was the most active and effective researcher in the USA, and the pathologist Sir Sydney Smith and gunmaker-cum-firearms expert Robert Churchill, ably assisted by the polymath Hugh Pollard, lead the way in the UK. Goddard explained the principle succinctly in an article he wrote for the Journal of Criminal Law and Criminology in 1926:

'Every pistol barrel, even when fresh from the factory – and much more so after undergoing wear and tear – contains minute irregularities which are peculiar to it alone, and which will never be reproduced in any other. These irregularities leave their marks, the same ones each time, in the form of fine and coarse linear striations parallel to the deep incisures cut by the groove edges [the rifling grooves], on every bullet fired from this barrel, and they constitute, to all intents and purposes, a fingerprint of that particular barrel.'

This statement of Goddard's wasn't original; two years earlier Pollard – who was editor of a popular science magazine *Discovery* – had published a monograph entitled *What the Bullet Tells*, which had said virtually the same thing. But a detailed examination of forensic science is not within this book's scope.

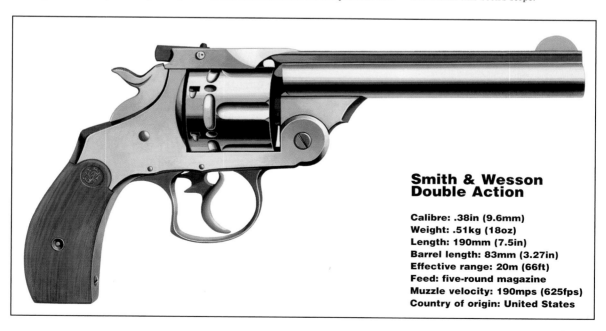

Smith & Wesson Double Action

Calibre: .38in (9.6mm)
Weight: .51kg (18oz)
Length: 190mm (7.5in)
Barrel length: 83mm (3.27in)
Effective range: 20m (66ft)
Feed: five-round magazine
Muzzle velocity: 190mps (625fps)
Country of origin: United States

CHAPTER 4
THE SELF-LOADING PISTOL

The revolver's roots may be almost buried in the past, but the self-loading magazine pistol is a comparatively recent addition to the world's armouries. There are not the same problems of deciding who originated what and who made which improvements, if only because its birth and formative years are well catalogued and recorded.

Hiram Stevens Maxim arrived in Europe in 1881, a rich man at the age of 41 as a result of inventions he had made in electric lighting and power generators. He faced the prospect of years' enforced idleness, having accepted a 'salary' of $20,000 per annum over that period from supporters of rival inventor Thomas Alva Edison, on the condition that he made no further research into electricity. But Maxim, even if he was not particularly avaricious, was not a man to be idle. He turned his attention to small arms instead, after a chance conversation with an acquaintance in Vienna.

MAXIM'S MACHINE GUN
By 1884, now established in London, he invented a gun which, once the first round was loaded into its breech, would continue firing as long as fresh supplies of ammunition were present and the operator kept his finger on the trigger. Once military tacticians got their hands on this gun – and their minds around the possibilities it offered – it would change the nature of warfare to an extent previously unimagined.

Having had the basic idea, Maxim took out patents to cover every possible means and method he could imagine by which

■LEFT: US troops fight Filipino insurgents at the Battle of Bagsak Mountain in June 1913. Note the American officer armed with a Colt Model 1911 – a legendary handgun.

an automatic gun could be made to cycle, and assiduously maintained and defended them all. Even if he himself did not wish to exploit that particular approach, he was well aware indeed of the benefits accruing to a monopoly.

THE SHORT-RECOIL PRINCIPLE
The method Maxim favoured for his machine guns was what we now call the short-recoil principle. The gun's barrel and breech-block were locked together and propelled back over a short distance by the discharge of the first round fired, by which time the projectile had left the barrel and the residual pressure had dropped to a safe level. The two were then unlocked and separated, the barrel's progress being arrested while the breech-block continued on its way, an extractor lug in its face taking the spent cartridge case with it and ejecting it. In the process of its motion, the breech-block compressed a spring which acted along its axis of movement. As the pressure forcing it backwards lessened, its motion was in turn arrested and finally reversed. The energy stored in the spring now took over, propelling it back the way it came. It moved forward, stripping a fresh cartridge from the magazine or belt along the way and loading it into the chamber, prior to re-locking itself with the barrel and returning it to battery. The last action was to strike the primer with the firing pin contained within the breech-block, whereupon the whole cycle began

again. Maxim's own guns used rimmed ammunition, and actually pulled the round out of the belt on the rearward stroke. There is another similar method, known as the long-recoil principle. The essential difference between the two is that in the latter the barrel and breech-block stay locked together through the entire rearward stroke before they separate and the recoil spring drives the barrel forward. The spent cartridge is held in the extractor on the face of the breech-block and ejected, whereupon the block starts on its forward journey, picking up a fresh round in the process. From then on the process is similar to that of the short-recoil cycle.

There is a simpler way to achieve the same end. The breech-block can be simply held against the barrel by the pressure of the recoil spring alone, without the assistance of locking lugs. As the pressure in the chamber builds, the projectile leaves the barrel, the spring pressure is overcome and the breech-block is forced back. Now the action reverts to the short-recoil principle, though without re-locking the breech-block and barrel at the end of the former's return travel. This is known as blowback action, and it is sometimes modified or retarded by the introduction of an element of mechanical disadvantage, which has to be overcome before the process can continue, thus slowing it down. This is usually a product of friction or leverage, but occasionally the action of propellant gas, tapped off at a convenient point in the barrel's length.

THE SELF-LOCKING PROCEDURE
Maxim's researches were restricted to what we would now call heavy machine guns, originally in .45 calibre. There is no reason, in theory, why any or all of these essentially similar principles should not be applied to handguns. Indeed, full-automatic pistols have been manufactured occasionally. In reality, however, the amount of energy released in the process requires the gun in question to be both relatively heavy and rigidly mounted if the point of aim is to be maintained with any degree of accuracy. But there is also no reason why the process needs to be full-automatic. By reorganising the trigger mechanism, the sear can be returned to its original blocking position with each round fired. The reloading-and-firing process is thus arrested, with the action cocked each time a fresh round is chambered, and

does not proceed until the trigger is pulled again. This is the way most semi-automatic or self-loading weapons operate. Hiram Maxim himself realised that, and even designed and produced semi-automatic rifles and pistols, though none were taken beyond the prototype stage.

The breech-block in an automatic firearm is not a free agent; it, the barrel and the receiver in which it travels are co-located by a series of interlocking or interacting grooves, lugs, studs, cams, rollers, interrupted screw threads and other fixing devices. They are designed to ensure that the block's relationship with the barrel, their separation and its

■ABOVE: A German soldier photographed during the invasion of Russia in June 1941. He is armed with a Luger, one of the most famous handguns ever manufactured.

motion within the receiver are positively controlled at all times. In general it is the choice and arrangement of these features which differentiate one type and make of self-loading pistol from another, just as they do the different recoil-action machine guns. Even so, other elements, such as the design and layout of the magazine and the trigger action itself, also have their part to play.

Parabellum Pistole

Calibre: 9mm (.35in)
Weight: .96kg (34oz)
Length: 213mm (8.4in)
Barrel Length: 127mm (5in)
Effective range: 30m (98ft)
Feed: eight-round magazine
Muzzle velocity: 351mps (1150fps)
Country of origin: Germany

There is little that is new about the trigger action of the self-loading pistol, since it is basically the same as that in the various types of revolver, except that true hammerless systems, which employ spring-loaded strikers instead, are practical for self-loading pistols where they are not for revolvers. Both single- and double-action systems exist for self-loaders and as is the case with revolvers, both have their merits and disadvantages. The most important difference is that in self-loading pistols, safety interlocks tend to be more comprehensive. The design of magazines or chargers is an area where new ground was broken in the develop-ment of semi-automatic. One of the first attempts at a semi-automatic pistol is found in the origins of Smith & Wesson in the Volcanic Arms Company and the improved 'Volitional Repeater' it was set up to manufacture.

EARLY SEMI-AUTOMATICS
The basic weakness of the 1850 'Volitional Repeater' as developed by Walter Hunt and improved by Lewis Jennings lay in its ammunition, and the design was only made to work satisfactorily by Henry

devising a form of unitary cartridge. Magazine arms in general, both rifles and pistols, and later automatic weapons, only became feasible after the development of the unitary cartridge. Earlier attempts to produce small arms which fed cartridges from charger to breech were doomed to failure, both by the flimsy nature of the cartridges and by their lack of uniformity. Dr Richard Jordan Gatling, found this out: until reliable unitary cartridges became available, his manually operated machine gun, basically sound though it was, simply would not work. As soon as such cartridges were available, Gatling's gun could keep up 300 rounds per minute.

During the 1880s, when the unitary cartridge was freely available, there were many attempts made to devise alternatives to the revolver in the shape of magazine pistols which manually ejected a spent cartridge from the chamber and then transferred a fresh round from the charger to take its place. Magazine repeater rifles had become widely accepted, firstly with their ammunition supply in tubes, either within the butt, like the Spencer of 1865, or below the barrel, as in the Henry of

1860 and then the Winchesters. Recharging and re-cocking was generally accomplished by the forward-and-down/back-and-up action of a lever which also formed the trigger guard. Now these weapons were joined by similarly organised pistols.

PISTOL BOX MAGAZINES
The next step, during the 1880s, was the introduction of box magazines, which could be recharged much more rapidly than tubes. The bolt action – already in wide use, both in single-shot rifles and in tubular-magazine repeaters – was universally embraced to go with them. The Swiss, Frederick Vetterli, who had developed a tubular-magazine bolt-action repeater as early as 1866, is credited with being first to produce a repeater with a box magazine, which sat below and behind the breech. His 1881 rifle followed a design for a magazine produced by a Scots watchmaker who had emigrated to the USA, James Lee (the Lee of both Lee-Metford and Lee-Enfield rifles). Independently, Ferdinand Ritter von Mannlicher invented a box magazine that year, and adapted one of his existing

That same year, one of Hiram Maxim's rivals in the field of machine gun design, Andreas Wilhelm Schwarzlose, also patented a design for a self-loading pistol. This one was particularly unusual in that its cartridges were held vertically, projectile down, in a magazine which lay below the pistol's barrel, and had to be swung through 90 degrees before they could enter the breech. The pistol was put into production, but failed to excite the public's interest.

THE WORK OF HUGO BORCHARDT

The self-loading pistol was an almost solely middle-European invention (if only because America of the 1890s was at home with the revolver), but without American know-how, particularly in production engineering, the first

ABOVE: An Italian Alpini in World War II takes aim with a 9mm Beretta Model 1934, a blowback semi-automatic handgun. Its external hammer could be cocked manually or automatically.

rifle designs to employ it. He then progressively improved his design, taking the final step in 1885 when he devised a clip system, enabling it to be recharged with a full load of cartridges at a stroke.

The designers of the magazine pistols which followed came to grief because the double-action revolver was a more efficient solution to the problem of getting off repeated shots quickly, even if recharging its cylinder did take a little longer. Passler and Seidl, the young Karel Krnka, a Belgian named Counet, Joseph Schulhof and later Joseph Laumann and Gustav Bittner all produced box-magazine pistols which were recharged by the action of an under lever. While most were satisfactory pieces of machinery, they were no real improvement over Colt's, Webley's or even Gasser's revolvers.

STEYR'S GROUND BREAKER

It is no coincidence that most of these men were Austro-Hungarians. The Empire, under Franz Joseph, had suddenly realized an industrial

revolution had taken place, and now embraced it wholeheartedly. Like many latecomers, they had other experts' research to help them. So it comes as no surprise, to find that the first self-loading pistol was designed and made in Austria.

Joseph Laumann, a Viennese gunmaker, filed his first application in 1893 for a pistol to eject a spent cartridge and chamber a fresh one, the reciprocating motion also cocking the action and leaving the pistol ready to fire. Anton Schonberger devised a pistol according to Laumann's principles, which was put into limited production by Joseph Werndl in Steyr; it was never a commercial success, largely due to its own limitations. Its operating principle, rarely seen since, is known as 'primer set-back' and used special ammunition with an extra-deep primer pocket. When discharged, the primer – but not the cartridge case – was forced back by the gas pressure for a distance of about 4mm (.16in), which was sufficient for it to initiate a sequence which unlocked the bolt from the barrel. By that time, the pressure in the chamber had fallen to a safe level, and normal recoil action took care of the rest of the recycling process. John Garand, famous for the self-loading M1 rifle which bears his name, also explored the idea.

Walther P38

Calibre: 9mm (.35in)
Weight: .96kg (34oz)
Length: 213mm (8.4in)
Barrel length: 127mm (5in)
Effective range: 30m (98ft)
Feed: eight-round magazine
Muzzle velocity: 351mps (1150fps)
Country of origin: Germany

commercially successful auto-loader would probably not have appeared when and where it did. Hugo Borchardt first came up with a design for a pistol for the Winchester Repeating Arms Company in 1876, and the following year revamped the celebrated Sharps rifle to accept brass cartridges. In the mid-1880s, Borchardt returned to his native Germany, though he was by then an American citizen. He went to work for the firm of Ludwig Loewe and Co. in Berlin. Loewe started out making sewing machines, having learned how in the USA, but by the time of the Franco-Prussian War (1870-71) was already involved in the manufacture of the machinery to manufacture firearms, according to the American gospel as preached by the likes of Pratt and

Whitney and swallowed whole by Colt and others. He died in 1886, but by then Waffenfabrik Loewe had been established, and was a powerful force in the arms manufacturing business, producing Mauser-designed infantry rifles alongside the old Prussian Royal Rifle Factories.

Seven years later, Borchardt lodged an application for a patent for a self-loading pistol (*selbstladepistole*) in 7.65mm (.3in) calibre, the action of which was similar to that of Maxim's machine guns. It worked on the short-recoil principle from a locked breech, using a toggle joint to lock the breech-block to the barrel. The toggle 'broke' upwards following the passage of enlarged rollers surrounding its pivot over a camming ramp, unlocking the breech-block and allowing it to separate from the barrel. Borchardt produced a

further innovation in that the eight-round removable magazine was housed in the pistol's grip. Magazines for earlier pistols had been fixed and located ahead of the trigger. They had to be recharged from above, while the breech was held open. Borchardt's main rival, Mauser, reverted to the old system for the pistol which relegated Borchardt's design to the history books, as did a number of his contemporaries, but since then, Borchardt's magazine system has become almost universal.

Borchardt's pistol sold in significant numbers until it was discontinued in 1898. But for all that his design philosophy was another wrong turning, even if that is difficult to believe in the light of the enduring success of his literal and spiritual successor, Georg Luger.

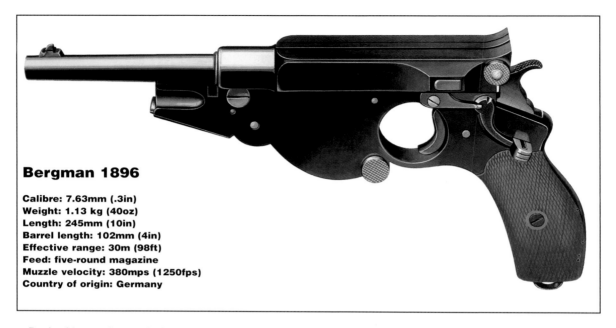

Bergman 1896

Calibre: 7.63mm (.3in)
Weight: 1.13 kg (40oz)
Length: 245mm (10in)
Barrel length: 102mm (4in)
Effective range: 30m (98ft)
Feed: five-round magazine
Muzzle velocity: 380mps (1250fps)
Country of origin: Germany

Borchardt's was a big pistol, almost 350mm (14in) long, and clumsy with it. It came with a shoulder-stock which doubled as a holster, and when that was fitted, transforming the pistol into a carbine, it was more comfortable. Its drawbacks notwithstanding, it sold in small quantities in Europe and the United States, even though it wasn't what the public wanted. Nevertheless, the main contribution it made was in setting the stage for what was to follow.

LUGER'S MASTERPIECE
The years up to and just after the turn of the century were a vital period for the development of the self-loading pistol. Bergmann, the American John Moses Browning, Mannlicher, Mauser, Schwarzlose and the Austrian giant Steyr were all competing with Deutsche Waffen und Munitionsfabriken (DWM), as Waffenfabrik Loewe became in 1896, for domination in the new market. All save the last-named abandoned the Maxim toggle system in favour of actions which if not simpler, were at least neater and rather more compact. But the one that didn't became probably the best-known automatic pistol in the world – the Parabellum Pistole of 1898 onwards, generally known by the name of its designer, Georg Luger. The path DWM took left the mainstream of self-loading pistol development and finally proved to have been a dead end, but the

ammunition developed for it came to dominate the military pistol and submachine gun worlds.

THE PARABELLUM ARRIVES
Luger was born in 1849 in the Austrian Tyrol. He served as an officer in the Austrian Army, where he became acquainted with von Mannlicher, and then, just before the appearance of Borchardt's pistol, joined Ludwig Loewe and Co. in Berlin. He made several trips to the United States over the next few years, one of them, in 1894, to promote the Borchardt. The pistol was tested and turned down by the US Government in 1897, but by that time the inventor seems to have lost interest in it, and the task of developing the design further fell to Luger. In 1898 the original pistol went out of production, and in that year Luger demonstrated what seems to have been a transitional model, the Borchardt-Luger, to the Swiss Army. A year later exhaustive tests of an improved model and improved ammunition, also as developed by Luger, led to the Swiss adopting the Parabellum Pistole in 7.65mm Parabellum calibre as the Pistole 1900, the first time a self-loading pistol received official approval. Compared to the Borchardt, this was 'a much lighter pistol with a safety device', not to mention a much-shortened barrel, 120mm (4.75in) instead of 152mm (6in). From then on the Parabellum pistol (the name

comes from the Latin, and means 'for war') went from strength to strength, as did the 9mm ammunition Luger went on to develop for it.

The pistol appeared in 9mm chambering in 1902 and two years later was adopted, in that calibre, by the Imperial German Navy, with 150mm (6in) barrel and grip safety to supplement the thumb-operated safety catch at the rear of the receiver on the left. Luger had simply removed the 'bottleneck' from the smaller cartridge to bring it up to the larger calibre, which was something of a stroke of everyday genius, for it allowed the existing production machinery to remain unchanged and for the pistol to be produced in either the old or the new calibres side by side, only the barrels – which were screw-in units anyway – being different. That same year DWM began limited production of a carbine model with a 298mm (11.75in) 7.65mm calibre barrel and a detachable shoulder stock, and with a wooden foregrip which housed an additional recoil spring. In 1906, the design underwent its first major changes: a coiled mainspring was substituted for the flat one used up until then in all models; and a new design of extractor was fitted, which also acted as a 'loaded' indicator. The toggles were redesigned to be easier to grip and the toggle-lock on the right-hand side was eliminated. The Swiss Government re-ordered the 9mm version that year, and the Dutch and the Portuguese Governments also adopted the pistol.

THE GERMAN ARMY'S PISTOL

In 1907, following considerable commercial success in the United States, DWM submitted the pistol for official trials there. Informed opinion in the USA had swung back in favour of the stopping power of the heavy .45-calibre round, and two Parabellum pistols were produced in this calibre. The trials were sufficiently successful for the US Government to order 200 more from DWM's New York agent, who accepted the order enthusiastically, only to have to do an abrupt U-turn and decline it soon afterwards on instruction from Berlin. One can only speculate on the reasons why DWM decided not to supply the US Government. One supposition is that it

was reluctant to set up what amounted to a completely new production line for the larger-calibre gun; another, and perhaps more likely explanation is that DWM had been forewarned that the German Army was about to adopt the pistol itself and wanted no obstacle to this step forward. It is certainly true that DWM had very close links with the German military establishment. One authority suggests that the company's senior personnel were better informed about new developments in armaments policy and arms procurement than even very senior officials at the War Ministry were.

THE MODELL 1914

Adopted by the German Army as the Parabellum Pistole Modell 1908 (usually abbreviated to P08), the pistol was fitted with the 100mm (4in) barrel, and the grip

safety was removed. This had the knock-on effect of reversing the sense of operation of the thumb safety, never a sound move. Original production took place at DWM's factory, but by the outbreak of war in 1914 the Royal Rifle Factory at Erfurt in Thuringia had also commenced manufacture. A 200mm (8in) long-barrelled version known officially as the Parabellum-Artillerie-Pistole Modell 1908, but also as the Modell 1914 and colloquially as 'die lange P08' went into production in 1914 and was issued with a detachable shoulder-stock. The only change necessary to the production line was the introduction of the longer barrel at assembly time. At some time before 1914, a spring-operated helical magazine of 32-round capacity known as the 'snail' or 'trommel' (drum) magazine was devised for the pistol by Tatarek and von Benk. The drum was also fitted originally to the Hugo Schmeisser-designed Bergmann Maschinenpistole 18, the first satisfactory submachine gun. The only lasting result of the introduction of this rather cumbersome magazine was a change in the profile of the Parabellum round; the original flattened-nose projectile ('truncated cylindro-conoidal', to give it is correct nomenclature) failed to feed correctly, and was replaced by a round-nosed bullet which has been standard in the Parabellum cartridge ever since.

THE WALTHER P38

After World War I the Treaty of Versailles restricted German pistols to no more than 8mm calibre, with barrels at most 100mm (4in) long. German post-war Parabellum pistols were produced in their original 7.65mm calibre and with 90mm (3.625in) barrels up until the time that Hitler unilaterally rejected the Versailles Treaty in 1936. Needless to say, it took very little to convert guns produced earlier over to 9mm calibre – just the replacement of their barrels by 9mm versions, production of which had never been interrupted. The pistol was also produced by Simson and by Heinrich Krieghoff Waffenfabrik at Suhl, and by Mauser at Oberndorf. Some 6000 examples were even assembled from German components by Vickers-

■LEFT: Two fine examples of the Luger. The Luger was the logical successor to the Borchardt self-loading pistol, the design of which was modified by Georg Luger himself.

Armstrong in Britain, with locally made 9mm barrels, for use by the Dutch. The Swiss Government arsenal in Bern also continued to manufacture the pistol in 9mm calibre for the Swiss Army, and even made some pistols for sale to the public. Production ceased in Germany in 1942, at which time the venerable 'Luger', as it had already come to be called, finally gave way to the Walther P38. In the late 1960s, the pistol as made in 1906 went back into production, Mauser-Werke having restarted manufacture in both 7.65mm and 9mm calibre. Replicas in other calibres were also available as the original design came within sight of its 100th birthday.

By the time Georg Luger had come to re-appraise Borchardt's original design,

Waffenfabrik Loewe was closely linked with Maxim: the company had begun production of Maxim guns under licence, and Ludwig's younger Brother, Simon, was General Manager of the Maxim-Nordenfelt Gun and Ammunition Company in England. Thus, one can imagine that there was a sort of loyalty to the Maxim system, and perhaps it was that which decided the adherence to the toggle-joint system Borchardt had employed. Elsewhere in Europe, where new designs for self-loading pistols were appearing at regular intervals, the unlocking of the bolt or breech-block from the barrel was accomplished by a variety of alternative means, most of them considerably more complicated – where it was necessary at all. The designers of

self-loading pistols realised fairly early on that low-powered ammunition didn't produce the sort of pressures which necessitated locking the two components together, and that a simple blowback system was all that was necessary . Some even tried to employ the unlocked-breech blowback system to pistols chambered for heavier ammunition, but usually came to grief as a result.

BERGMANN'S PISTOLS
One of the pioneers, Thomas Bergmann, went one step further, even dispensing with a conventional extractor for his earliest pistols, produced in 1894 in 5mm and 6.5mm calibres and later in 8mm. Bergmann used quite smooth, entirely rimless cartridges designed by Louis

Bergmann-Bayard Self-Loading Pistol

Calibre: 9mm (.35in)
Weight: 1.01kg (35.5oz)
Length: 251mm (9.9in)
Barrel length: 102mm (4in)
Effective range: 30m (98ft)
Feed: six-round magazine
Muzzle velocity: 305mps (1000fps)
Country of origin: Germany

Schmeisser (father of Hugo), and relied upon the residual pressure in the chamber to blow – quite literally – the empty case out of the chamber as soon as the breech-block was withdrawn. The case struck the next round in the magazine on the way and was deflected upwards and thus away. As one might imagine, the system was erratic, and when re-vamped models of the pistol appeared in 1896, they were fitted with conventional extractors and chambered for conventional 'rimless' ammunition. Bergmann's best claim to fame, as far as these pistols are concerned, is that they were the first self-loading guns to meet the normal criteria for pocket pistols, rather than being strictly military weapons requiring a holster. Although at

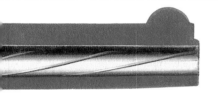

250mm (10in) long and weighing 1.13kg (2.5lb) they were hardly lightweights. Their rather eccentric method of disposing of spent cases aside, the early Bergmann pistols were also notable for their use of a non-removable magazine which was located forward of the trigger and charged from the side. Access to it was by means of a cover secured by a milled retaining catch just in front of the trigger guard, the five fresh rounds being contained in a simple sheet-metal clip which, when empty, dropped out of the magazine as the access plate was opened.

EXTRACTION DILEMMAS

Clearly, the diminutive 5mm and 6.5mm rounds fired by the early Bergmann pistols had no military application and even came in for a certain amount of criticism in the civilian market, while the more potent 8mm Schmeisser round was too heavy for the simple blowback action. Spent cases ruptured as they were expelled too soon, while the internal gas pressure was still very high, leading to frequent stoppages. When Bergmann finally came to attempt a service pistol, in 1897, he recognised the necessity for a thorough redesign of the pistol's mechanism, including in particular a

means of locking bolt and breech together. Bergmann's solution was a simple horizontal slot-and-key, the barrel and bolt recoiling together for a little under 6mm (.25in) before a camming lug on the receiver wall forced the bolt sideways and unlocked it from the barrel. The barrel then stopped while the bolt continued to the limit of its rearward travel, cocking the hammer before starting forward, stripping the next round from the magazine in the process. Encountering the camming lug once more, it was forced to the side again, and when it came back into line was re-united with the barrel, which it pushed back into battery with the last of the energy stored in the recoil spring. The pistol in question, the No 5, also incorporated a removable box magazine, which could also be reloaded in place by means of a charger, still located in front of the trigger mechanism. The No 5 pistol was tested by several countries, including Britain, but was rejected by them all, the usual reason being a lack of confidence in the 8mm round's stopping power.

In the light of this, Bergmann's next pistol was made, at least in small quantities, in a variety of calibres, usually 9mm but also in experimental 10mm and .45 chamberings. The No 6 pistol, often called the Bergmann 'Mars', was first introduced in 1903, and was later manufactured, between 1907 and 1914, by Anciens Etablissements Pieper at Herstal, near Liège, under the name Bergmann-Bayard (Bergmann had over-extended himself by taking an order for the pistol from the Spanish Government and was then unable to fulfil it). It had a different locking system from Bergmann's previous designs, the bolt being locked to a plate extending from below the barrel by a ramp in the floor of the receiver. After initially recoiling together, the plate was allowed to fall, freeing the breech-block to continue on its way. In 1910, by which time Thomas Bergmann had no financial interest in the pistol whatsoever, having sold the rights to it outright to Pieper, a Bergmann design was finally adopted as its official side-arm by a government when Denmark took up the Bergmann-Bayard in 9mm calibre. The Danes put it into local production in 1918 in the state arsenal, and as a result of the investment that required, the Bergmann-Bayard continued to be the Danish armed forces standard side-arm until 1946, when it was replaced by the Liège-manufactured

■ABOVE: Several young members of the Royal Ulster Constabulary hone their shooting skills at their barracks in Enniskillen. The pistols are Webley MK VI revolvers.

Browning Model 1935. Even in its largest calibre, though, it failed to impress the British – who tested it again in 1903 – or the Americans, who tried it against the .45 Parabellum pistol in 1907.

MAUSER'S C96

One might say that Thomas Bergmann was actually rather unlucky, for in 1896, the same year that he modified his pistols to use 'military' ammunition, Waffenfabrik Mauser published details of a self-loading pistol shortly to be put into production, chambered for a powerful cartridge in 7.63mm nominal calibre but similar to that used by Hugo Borchardt. Mauser had been established only 25 years earlier had risen to a position of pre-eminence rapidly, thanks to the adoption of its Modell 1871 bolt-action single-shot rifle by the German Government. Like most Mauser products, the new pistol proved to be superbly engineered and was, in consequence, expensive. Almost from the day of its introduction in 1897, it enjoyed a reputation as a miniature masterpiece, its ungainly lines and complicated operating arrangement notwithstanding.

Bergmann was perhaps doubly unlucky, for at that time, all Peter Paul Mauser's considerable powers should really have been taken up with the Infanteriegewehr Modell 1898, the German Army's new basic infantry rifle which was even then being readied for production in the Oberndorf-am-Necker factory to replace the somewhat unsatisfactory Modell 1888.

The Mauser-Selbstladepistole Construction '96, or C96 pistol, as it is commonly known, was designed by a trio of brothers named Feederle in 1894, and patented in 1895 or 1896 by Peter Paul Mauser. The prototype was completed early in 1895, and was test-fired for the first time on 15 March. Throughout the rest of that year, something over 100 guns were produced in all, most of them in 7.65mm Borchardt chambering with 6-, 10-, and 20-round magazines and some in 6mm calibre with 10-round magazines. In all cases, the magazines were integral with the frame, and were loaded from the top by means of chargers which, when inserted, served to hold the action open.

Production proper began in October 1896, by which time the calibre had been fixed at 7.63mm, though in fact the only change from the larger prototype calibre was a slight reduction in the size of the

neck of the case. Designed to produce a somewhat firmer grip on the round, this change was necessitated by the pistol's action being a little unkind to the ammunition; there was no change to the dimensions of the projectile itself. In its production form, this ammunition, in the 140mm (5.5in) barrel Mauser, produced a spanking 455mps (1490fps) at the muzzle thanks to its eight grain charge and 85 grain bullet; in the Mannlicher pistol of 1903, the almost identical 7.65mm round, loaded with four grains, barely achieved 345mps (1130fps). It was the Mauser's effortless ability to handle that heavy a charge, and produce such a high muzzle velocity as a result, which accounted for much of its popularity. Indeed, so strong is the pistol's construction that a 7.63mm calibre version actually has the capability to chamber and fire a 9mm Parabellum round, though obviously the practice is not to be recommended!

C96 VARIANTS AND COPIES

During the course of a long life very few modifications to the original design were

Bergmann Simplex

Calibre: 8mm (.30in)
Weight: .59kg (21oz)
Length: 190mm (7.5in)
Barrel length: 70mm (2.75in)
Effective range: 30m (98ft)
Feed: six- or eight-round magazine
Muzzle velocity: 198mps (650fps)
Country of origin: Germany

made. Mauser did not take the pistol out of regular production until 1937, though there was a hiatus between 1918 and 1922. In 1902, a form of safety catch was introduced, and its design was altered 10 years later. In 1905 the firing-pin retainer was given a second locking lug, the extractor was shortened and the hammer reduced in size. In 1915, in the midst of a general shortage of small arms of all kinds, a decision was taken to produce the C96 in 9mm Parabellum calibre, and in the three years following

Waffenfabrik Mauser made some 150,000 such pistols. Once again, Georg Luger's intelligent approach to the development of the larger-calibre rounds meant that most components of the two types of pistol were interchangeable. Outwardly, the only immediately obvious difference

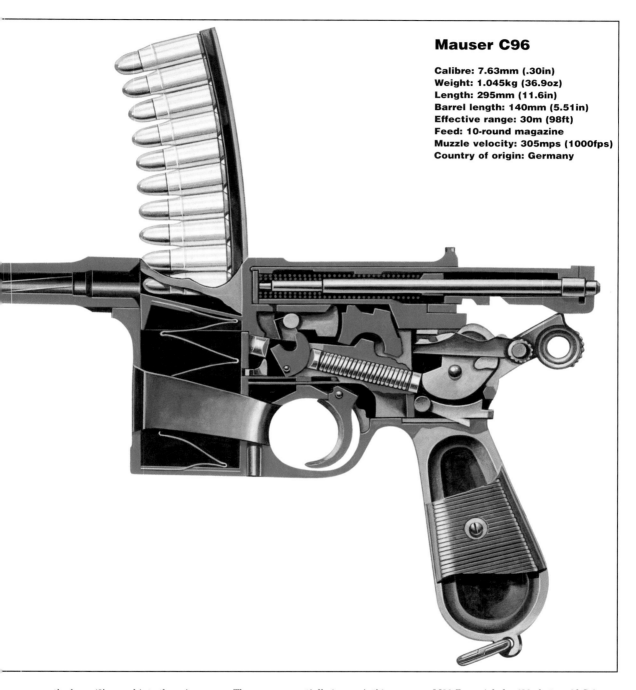

Mauser C96

Calibre: 7.63mm (.30in)
Weight: 1.045kg (36.9oz)
Length: 295mm (11.6in)
Barrel length: 140mm (5.51in)
Effective range: 30m (98ft)
Feed: 10-round magazine
Muzzle velocity: 305mps (1000fps)
Country of origin: Germany

was the large '9' carved into the grips on both sides and stained red.

Between the wars, a large number of 'cut-down' C96 pistols were made, in 7.63mm calibre, for export to the Bolsheviks in Soviet Russia. As a result these became known as 'Bolo-Modellen'.

They were essentially 'neuer Art' (new style) pistols as modified by 1912, but fitted with 100mm (4in) barrels so as not to contravene the Versailles Treaty. That same period saw an aberration in the form of two full-automatic versions of the pistol. The Schnellfeuer-selbstladepistole

M30 Zwanziglader (20-shot rapid-firing self-loading pistol, Model 1930), sometimes known as the M712, was produced in 1931 and sold in small quantities to Yugoslavia and to China. The modifications to produce the M712 were based on the earlier work of Josef

Nickl. Full-auto imitations of the Mauser C96, some made in Spain by Astra, and others of very inferior quality, were also distributed in China. The second version was produced in even smaller numbers. It had a fixed 20-round magazine of the original pattern, as against the M712 and the prototype semi-automatic M711 which had detachable magazines. Known as the Schnellfeuer-selbstladepistole system Westinger, Modell 1936, it was the work of a Mauser engineer named Karl Westinger. Neither was in any way satisfactory as a submachine gun: the combination of a light bolt and a powerful round made for a very high cyclical rate of fire, and the muzzle started to climb alarmingly after only two or three rounds had been fired. Even if the left hand was used to grip the magazine extension in an attempt to hold the barrel down, they were difficult weapons to control. There were other later attempts to produce full-automatic handguns, but all suffered from the same basic problem which afflicted the Mauser.

THE C96'S INTERNAL LAYOUT

The Mauser C96 consisted of four basic assemblies: the barrel and barrel extension, which were forged in one piece; the main frame, including the magazine and butt (the magazine spring and platform being separate); the bolt, square in section, which contained the main recoil spring, striker and striker spring; and the lock itself, from trigger to hammer, including the safety device where it was fitted. Only one screw was used in the entire pistol – and that merely held the two grip-halves together. Otherwise, the pistol went together like a three-dimensional puzzle. The grips themselves were of an unconventional design, perfectly symmetrical all round and swelling out towards the bottom; they soon earned the soubriquet 'broom-handle'. In the rear strap of the frame, a groove was machined to accept a dovetail brass tenon fitted to the shoulder stock-cum-holster which when fitted, transformed the pistol into a carbine.

In operation it was hardly straightforward. The bolt was locked to the barrel extension by means of a separate block fixed to the latter, which was allowed to pivot downwards as the recoil forced the extension to slide back down the frame. Thus unlocked, the bolt continued to the rear, cocking the hammer and compressing the recoil spring in the process. The empty case,

which had been extracted from the chamber by the extractor lug machined into the bolt face, struck the ejector machined into the frame and was thrown upwards and clear. On the bolt's return journey, the mainspring acted on a spur on the bolt lock to force it up, so that lugs on its upper surface could engage others on the lower surface of the bolt. This imparted forward motion to the barrel extension, and an inclined plane machined into the rear of the bolt lock met the upper surface of the trigger lock frame, forcing the two sets of lugs to engage still more firmly and ensuring that barrel and bolt were secured together. A device to hold the action open after the last cartridge in the magazine had been fired was an added refinement. Now virtually universal, but previously unknown, it took the form of a stop on the rear of the magazine platform which rose in front of the bolt when the magazine was empty.

The Mauser C96 was an expensive pistol: around the turn of the century a new gun, complete with a walnut shoulder-stock which doubled as a holster, cost £5 ($25 at the then-current rate of exchange; the Borchardt pistol had been even more expensive, at $30). This was approximately twice the price of a proprietary revolver and the equivalent in terms of purchasing power of perhaps £1000 ($1500) at the other end of the twentieth century. By contrast, in the mid-1990s, a respectable revolver could be bought for $250 and an excellent one for three times that. Aware that the high price limited sales, Waffenfabrik Mauser put a cheaper pistol on the market as the Modell '06-'08. Similar in appearance but with a simplified action based on a self-loading rifle, it had little real success.

Ritter von Mannlicher's contribution to the development of the self-loading pistol has already been mentioned. While it never had the impact that his other work had on the design of the rifle, it was significant, albeit briefly, since the Werndl arms factory in Steyr – one of the first in Austria to be equipped with American-style machine tools – put one of his designs into production in 1894.

Mannlicher's first pistol employed a 'blow-forward' system of operation which was later also to be employed in another pistol designed by Andreas Schwarzlose. The breech-block in this pistol was an integral part of the frame, but the barrel was free to move longitudinally and was thus forced forward by the recoil, leaving

Mauser Model 1912

Calibre: 7.63mm (.30in)
Weight: 1.25kg (44oz)
Length: 298mm (11.75in)
Barrel length: 140mm (5.5in)
Effective range: 30m (98ft)
Feed: 10-round magazine
Muzzle velocity: 427mps (1400fps)
Country of origin: Germany

■RIGHT: General George Smith Patton (left) sporting a pearl-handled Colt revolver, which appears to have attracted the attention of General Bernard Montgomery (right).

the empty case held by the extractor on the bolt face. In the first phase of its movement, the barrel stretched a heavy spring; when its energy was used up this spring reversed the motion. On its return journey the barrel stripped the next round out of the magazine but did not cock the hammer, this being achieved by a standard double-action trigger or by pulling it back manually.

Two years later Mannlicher's next

effort, the Model 1896 pistol, was a
rather more conventional blowback
action, this time with the magazine
situated ahead of the trigger. But it still
did not cock the hammer during the
course of its loading stroke. Like the
earlier model it was chambered for
6.5mm and 7.6mm rounds of
Mannlicher's own design. His first self-
cocking, self-loading handgun firing a
standard cartridge – albeit a relatively
lightly-loaded one – in 7.65mm calibre.
Unfortunately this was almost identical
to the much more powerful Mauser
7.63mm cartridge; the Mannlicher pistol
could chamber and fire the Mauser
round, with often disastrous results. The

Mannlicher Model 1901

Calibre: 7.63mm (.30in)
Weight: .94kg (33oz)
Length: 239mm (9.4in)
Barrel length: 165mm (6.5in)
Effective range: 30m (98ft)
Feed: eight-round magazine
Muzzle velocity: 312mps (1025fps)
Country of origin: Austria

pistol was also apparently designed in 1896, but did not go into production until 1903, and is generally known as the model of that year. In appearance it was somewhat similar to the Mauser C96, with its forward-located magazine, but internally it was quite different, if no less unusual. The breech-block and barrel were locked together by a bolt pinned to the barrel extension, which was separate from the barrel proper. On being fired, the recoil moved the breech-block and the barrel extension to the rear by some 3mm (.12in), the two held together, via the bolt, by a recess in the frame. That cleared, the bolt dropped down, allowing the breech-block the freedom to continue

backwards, ejecting, cocking and reloading in the usual manner before picking up the bolt again and re-locking itself to the barrel extension. It was charged for the first shot by pulling back on a milled knob situated on the top of the frame, and the concealed hammer could also be cocked by pressing down on a large lever situated on the right, above the trigger guard.

The fourth and last of Mannlicher's self-loading pistols was perhaps the most successful – and was certainly the most stylish. It, too, used low-powered 7.65mm ammunition, but this time with a straight-sided cartridge case, and it would chamber no other; Mannlicher

thus felt able to dispense with a mechanism to lock the bolt and barrel together and rely on the simple blowback principle instead. The rearwards action of the bolt was retarded mechanically (by a cam acting against the upper surface of the mainspring) before the spent cartridge case had cleared the breech, allowing the pressure in the chamber to be reduced to a safe level before the case was ejected. Unlike most self-loaders of the period, this pistol – which is somewhat confusingly known as the Model 1900, the Model 1901 and the Model 1905 – had its magazine in the butt in the modern style. Fixed rather than detachable like that employed by

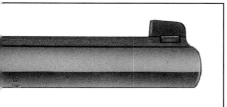

updating of a design Krnka first executed in 1895, which Roth had manufactured and which had previously been improved as the Roth Model 1904. It seems certain that manufacture was moved to Steyr (and to the Empire's other official armoury, Fegyver es Gepgyar Reszvenytarsasag, in Budapest) due to the limited capacity of Roth's own factory. It was later joined by a similar-looking pistol, but smaller and rather different in concept, produced by J.P. Sauer at Suhl, one of the centres of German firearms

Browning Model 1900

Calibre: 7.65mm (.30in)
Weight: .62kg (22oz)
Length: 163mm (6.4in)
Barrel length: 102mm (4in)
Effective range: 30m (98ft)
Feed: seven-round magazine
Muzzle velocity: 259mps (850fps)
Country of origin: United States

manufacture. They are both worth examining because – in conjunction with the better-known pistols described above – they illustrate the many trials and tribulations of the first generation of self-loading pistol designers struggling valiantly to produce reliable semi-automatic handguns.

THE 8MM ROTH-STEYR

Like many of its contemporaries, the Roth-Steyr pistol, in 8mm calibre, employed a mechanism which, to modern eyes, seems vastly over-complicated. Its breech-block – which in this instance is probably better thought of as a bolt – was very long, extending way past the hammer. Solid in the rear (save for the firing pin), it was hollow in front, and large enough in diameter to fit over the barrel. Its interior was machined into a series of grooves which fitted tightly over appropriate lugs on the barrel. When the pistol was fired, barrel and bolt recoiled

together within the receiver for about 12mm (.5in), the bolt progressively disengaging from the barrel and causing it to turn through 90 degrees in the process. The barrel was then prevented from moving any further, while the bolt continued to the rear, cocking the hammer and compressing the recoil spring. On its return, the bolt stripped a cartridge from the magazine, taking it into its hollow forepart via a slot machined into the lower surface, and chambered it. The locking grooves relocated with the lugs on the barrel, pushing it back into battery and turning it back through 90 degrees to 'lock' it again. Strictly speaking, this was not a locked-breech action, but rather a retarded blowback; the bolt and barrel were not locked together, but were collocated by the lugs and helical grooves. Like that of the last Mannlicher, the magazine was also a fixture within the butt, and was loaded from a 10-round charger through the bolt via an aperture in the frame, which also served as the ejector port. Also like some of Mannlicher's pistols, the Roth-Steyr was not self-cocking; instead it employed a spring-loaded striker with a 'hesitation' double-action akin to that found in certain revolvers.

The other pistol bearing Roth's name, the Roth-Sauer, was considerably smaller. Just under 175mm (7in) long overall, instead of over 225mm (9in), it chambered yet another 7.65mm round of unique form. Unusually, particularly for such a small pistol, it used the long-recoil action. The barrel and bolt recoiled together until they reached the rearmost limit, where the bolt was rotated clockwise through a quarter turn by an inclined slot on the actuator, allowing the barrel to return to battery under the influence of the recoil spring. The spent case was ejected from the extractor on the bolt face as the bolt, in its turn, started forward, and a fresh round was picked up from the magazine and chambered. The bolt was re-locked with the barrel once more by being forced anti-clockwise by the slot in the actuator. The Roth-Sauer's trigger action was identical to that of its bigger counterpart, and its fixed magazine was loaded in very much the same way.

STEYR'S 9MM

Though the Roth-Steyr was adopted by the Austro-Hungarian Army, it did not enjoy a long service life. It was

Borchardt and Luger, it was loaded from the top via a charger which held eight rounds. In common with the Mauser C96, the pistol had a hold-open device which came into action when the last round had been fired.

In all likelihood, manufacture of the Model 1901, as the last Mannlicher pistol is most often known, was suspended at Steyr to make way for a pistol designed by Georg Roth and Karel Krnka. Known as the Roth-Steyr Model 1907, the year it was adopted as the official side-arm of the Austro-Hungarian Empire, it was the first self-loading pistol to be so accepted by a major power. The Roth-Steyr had its roots in the previous century, being an

■LEFT: An American security guard of the 1920s proudly shows off his Colt service automatic pistol in its shoulder holster. Such compact revolvers were ideal for undercover or police work.

were simple unlocked-breech pistols, possible with this type of low-powered ammunition, and had no extractors, relying on gas pressure instead, like the early Bergmann designs. Since this method of expelling the spent cases was always somewhat unpredictable – cases were likely to split and jam in the chamber – and there was no means of ejecting a round which had misfired, the pistols were made with very easy access to the breech. Their barrels were pivoted on a pin located just in front of the trigger guard, and secured to the frame by a simple catch; releasing it allowed the pistol to be broken open, and the jammed cartridge or faulty round pried out. This system also permitted the pistol to be used as a single-shot weapon, if the magazine was damaged or faulty.

Before the turn of the nineteenth century, there was very little interest evinced in self-loading pistols outside Germany and the Austro-Hungarian Empire. Even there the revolver was still considered superior, or at least, more reliable, and for service purposes those two terms were congruent. Inevitably, however, there were those elsewhere who became fascinated by the new type of pistol before it became fashionable. One was to become the most celebrated gunmaker of the twentieth century, while another was to sink into obscurity and subsequently vanish without trace: Hugh Gabbett-Fairfax.

HUGH GABBETT-FAIRFAX

Fairfax took out a variety of British patents on the design of self-loading pistols from 1895 onwards, and eventually succeeded in convincing Webley & Scott – which was even then looking to put such a pistol into production – to make up a prototype to his design in 1898. Fairfax worked on the project with Webley's Works Manager, J.W. Whiting (who was later to design Webley's own self-loading pistols) and the two men produced a succession of pistols which more-or-less worked, but none of them satisfactorily. In 1901 Webley lost interest, and Fairfax had to look elsewhere for sponsors.

The Mars Automatic Pistol Syndicate Ltd was formed initially to promote

superseded in 1911 by another Steyr-produced pistol, known as the Steyr-Hahn (The Hammer Steyr) to differentiate it from the hammerless Roth design, but officially as the Repetierpistole Modell 1912. The Steyr-Hahn was made in nominal 9mm calibre, but for a round which was slightly longer than the 9mm Parabellum. Many were re-barrelled for the 9mm Parabellum round after the *Anschlüss*, when the Austrian Army was absorbed into the German Wehrmacht. It also used a rotating-barrel locking system, but this time of rather simpler (and to a later generation, rather more conventional) design. The breech-block was transformed into a heavy slide enclosing the barrel, which was locked to it in battery by the interaction of two pairs of lugs in vertical slots. A further set of lugs on the barrel engaged a helical slot machined into the receiver, and as

the two recoiled together, the turning motion thus imparted to the barrel unlocked it, whereupon it was promptly arrested by a lug on the frame. The slide was free to continue backwards, ejecting the spent round in the process, before it cocked the action and started on its return journey. It stripped off a fresh round and chambered it before mating up with the barrel again, re-locking being accomplished in the course of the remaining forward motion.

UNLOCKED-BREECH PISTOLS

While the Steyr-Hahn was still in the design stage, the company began producing pocket pistols under licence from Pieper of Liège, in both 7.65 and 6.35mm calibres. The latter, in particular, was an early version of the miniature semi-automatic pistol which was to become popular in years to come. Both

Gabbett-Fairfax's designs, but with the intention of establishing a manufacturing facility. To begin with, however, small gunmakers in London and Birmingham were commissioned to produce pistols in very limited quantities for tests and ammunition trials. Fairfax seems to have been obsessed with producing a super-powerful handgun, and most, if not all, the problems with his designs can be traced back to that fixation.

THE MIGHTY MARS

One of the problems he encountered was finding a suitable round, and the prototype Mars pistols were chambered for a variety of cartridges as a result. Rounds of .36 .45, 8.5mm and 9mm were the most common nominal calibres – though the cartridges themselves were frequently not standard military loads. The pistols were conceived with extremely high muzzle velocities in mind, and as a result had actions which simply would not cycle properly with a weaker cartridge. The requirement to contain the effect of an extremely high-powered cartridge also meant that the action itself

had to be very robust, which in turn increased the weight of the moving parts. Fairfax thus set up for himself a vicious circle from which he proved incapable of escaping.

He ended up by specifying a massive pistol – over 310mm (12in) long and weighing 1.35kg (3lb). It fired a severely 'bottle-necked' 8.5mm round which produced no less than 535mps (1755fps) at the muzzle – more than most rifles of the day! As a consequence of its bulk and weight, the pistol was awkward and unwieldly; as a consequence of its power it had a kick like a mule, and in the words of the captain of HMS *Excellent* (the Royal Navy's Gunnery School at Whale Island): 'No one who fired once with the pistol wished to shoot with it again.' Another unfortunate person who had used this gun said 'the Mars is a singularly unpleasant and alarming pistol to shoot with'. And as if its day-to-day bad manners were not damning enough, it also exhibited an unpleasant tendency to eject spent rounds straight into the user's face.

As one might imagine, the Mars

pistol's action was something of a nightmare: it worked on the long-recoil principle, the breech-block and barrel being driven back some 76mm (3in), during this process compressing the recoil spring which was housed under the barrel, and the two lighter springs which acted as independent breech-block return springs. At the limit of their travel they cocked the hammer and then began their return journey.

MECHANICAL DEFECTS

An actuating rod depressed by the barrel acted on a short crank, which in turn forced down a stud which rotated the bolt head through 45 degrees, freeing it from the slots which secured it within the true breech in the rear of the barrel. The magazine – a removable box located in the butt – presented the new cartridge quite some way ahead of the rearward position of the breech. This meant that the fresh round had to be withdrawn backwards during the course of the rearwards stroke of the action, by a carrier which also acted, now, as an ejector, propelling the spent case up and

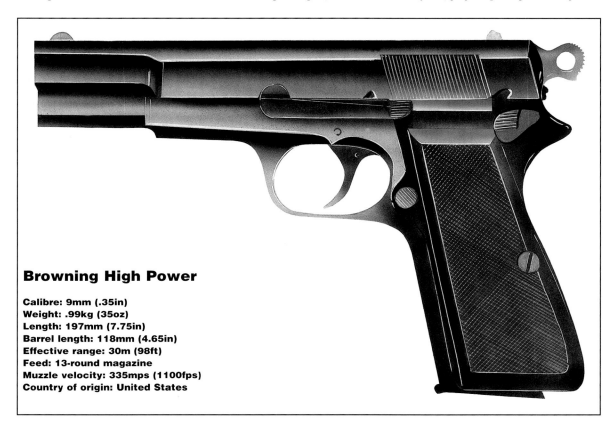

Browning High Power

Calibre: 9mm (.35in)
Weight: .99kg (35oz)
Length: 197mm (7.75in)
Barrel length: 118mm (4.65in)
Effective range: 30m (98ft)
Feed: 13-round magazine
Muzzle velocity: 335mps (1100fps)
Country of origin: United States

away and presenting the fresh round to the breech. The action stayed in this position, with the fresh round poised at an upwards angle of close to 30 degrees, until the trigger was released, whereupon the bolt was freed and forced the new round into the chamber. The bolt's motion turned it through 45 degrees to lock it and the barrel together, before the round was finally discharged.

Thankfully, the Mars quickly sunk into well-deserved obscurity, unlike the work of John Moses Browning.

Browning has been called the finest gunsmith of his own – or any – century. That may be something of an exaggeration, but he did display a versatile inventive genius which has never quite been rivalled. He was responsible for two of the world's most successful machine-gun mechanisms – the recoil system which powered the medium and heavy machine guns which bore his name through two world wars and beyond, and the gas actuation system of the Browning Automatic Rifle (BAR) which was the US Army's standard light machine gun for over 40 years. He also devised semi-automatic rifles and shotguns and the simple locking system which was to make two of his combat-calibre semi-automatic pistols the most prolific sellers in history, as well as a blowback system for lighter-calibre pistols. Even so, Browning's first foray into the field of self-loading weapons was little short of a disaster (at least in its original form), and infringed one of Hiram Maxim's patents into the bargain.

COLT'S 'POTATO DIGGER'

Maxim never pursued the notion of tapping gas off the barrel of a gun and using it to drive a piston to actuate the cycling mechanism – but he did patent the idea, in January 1884. He actually embodied it in two versions of a machine gun and in suitably modified Colt and Winchester lever-action repeating rifles. When Colt took up Browning's first machine gun design and had it accepted as the M1895 'Gas Hammer', Maxim brought (unsuccessful) suit, alleging that it infringed his protection. He was undoubtedly right, but might – that of Colt and the US Army – prevailed

■RIGHT: The Walther PP and its round. This pistol was designed primarily for police use. Its main feature is the double-action lock, which involved the use of an external hammer.

instead. Had the gun in question been a success, one might be able to understand what all the fuss was about, though on reflection its status, as the United States of America's one and only home-grown machine gun was enough to guarantee its survival, (by that time Maxim had long renounced American citizenship and taken out British instead, and had even been knighted). In an attempt to hide the fact that the new gun's operating principle contravened Maxim's patent, Colt fitted the gun with a system of external levers (which gave rise to its nickname 'potato digger'), but all that really achieved was to make it difficult to operate under real combat conditions. The gun only became a success when it was converted to a normally actuated gas piston by Marlin-Rockwell. As the Marlin M1918 it was used in both armoured vehicles and aircraft.

His experiences with the Colt 'potato digger' served one useful purpose – they drove John Browning away from the principle of gas operation, though he returned to the concept soon enough for his light machine gun, the BAR. When he came to consider the design of a self-loading handgun, in or about 1896, he only had eyes for recoil operation, though remained equivocal about the merits of unlocked versus locked breeches. In the event, he was to lodge a variety of patent applications regarding actuation systems for self-loaders, and later exploited two of them. One was for a simple blowback design, a pocket pistol chambered for

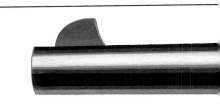

Colt .45

Calibre: .45in (11.42mm)
Weight: 1.02kg (36oz)
Length: 285mm (11.25in)
Barrel length: 152mm (6in)
Effective range: 30m (98ft)
Feed: six-round magazine
Muzzle velocity: 263mps (865fps)
Country of origin: United States

low-powered ammunition, the other a locked-breech system for cartridges with heavier propellant loads, clearly intended for use as a service and police pistol.

BROWNING'S MODEL 1900

For sound commercial reasons, Browning looked outside the United States, where the revolver still dominated, for a market for his self-loading pistols. He found a manufacturer for them, too, in the shape of a new Belgian company, Fabrique Nationale d'Armes de Guerre, of which, incidentally, Waffenfabrik Loewe was a 50 per cent shareholder. The company had been established at Herstal-lez-Liège in 1889, initially to fill an order for 200,000 Modèle 1889 infantry rifles – an adaptation of a Mauser design for a magazine rifle to fire a new 7.65mm round. Browning concluded an agreement in 1898 whereby FN, as the company soon became known, acquired the rights

to manufacture his shotguns, rifles and self-loading pistols under licence. It was the start of a very long-lasting business relationship indeed – one which was strong enough to survive John Browning's death, two world wars and several changes of ownership, the last of which saw FN in the hands of a French Government-owned corporation, GIAT.

The first pistol – styled the FN Model 1900 – was a 7.65mm-calibre hammerless, unlocked-breech design, the recoil spring of which, located in a tube lying along and above the barrel, also served as its mainspring. Its breech-block was secured to its slide by two screws and acted on the spring by means of a long plunger/lever, while the barrel was secured to the frame. Pushing the slide to the rear – either manually or as a result of a round being discharged – resulted in the slide pulling the striker back to full cock and then stripping off and

chambering a round on its return journey into battery. The recoil spring stayed under partial compression so that it could motivate the striker when the trigger was pulled. The eventual production run of this pistol in authorised versions alone is said to have run into the millions, and no-one has any idea how many 'bootleg' copies were made, particularly in Spain and China. This pistol could be said to have started World War I; it was with a 7.65mm Browning Model 1900 that Gavrilo Princip shot the Archduke Ferdinand in Sarajevo on 28 June 1914.

Browning's next pistol – the Modèle de Guerre as it was known – was also an unlocked-breech design, but this time in 9mm calibre, and with an internal hammer. Normally, 9mm would be reckoned too powerful a cartridge for this action, but in this case the round, like the 7.65mm round for which the first pistol was chambered, was one Browning

designed himself, alongside experts from
Winchester. It became known as the 9mm
Long or Browning cartridge, and while it
was not as popular as some other
ammunition types Browning originated,
was adopted for other pistols too, notably
the French Le Français. The pistol was
adopted by the Swedish Government as
the Pistol m/1907, and was subsequently
manufactured by Husqvarna
Vapenfabrik, and adopted by the Serbian
and Turkish armies and the Danish and
Dutch police forces. It was this pistol
more than any other which made

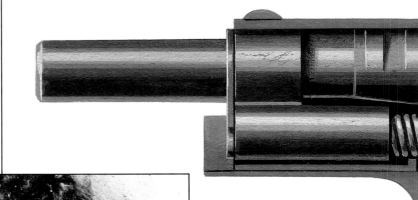

■ABOVE: During the Vietnam war, an
American 'tunnel rat' searches for the
Viet Cong north of Saigon in January
1967 armed with a flashlight and his
trusty Colt M1911.

Colt M1911

Calibre: .45in (11.42mm)
Weight: 1.1kg (39oz)
Length: 216mm (8.5in)
Barrel length: 127mm (5in)
Effective range: 30m (98ft)
Feed: seven-round magazine
Muzzle velocity: 262mps (860fps)
Country of origin: United States

'Browning' a synonym for 'automatic
pistol' in France. In 1906, FN began
production of a 'vest-pocket' pistol, as the
genre was known in the United States, in
6.35mm Browning calibre (which is

synonymous with .25 ACP). This was just
0.4kg (14oz) in weight and 100mm (4in)
long overall. While it may not have been
a remarkable pistol in any real sense, it
deserves mention if only because of its
longevity, as it is still in production as it
approaches its 100th birthday. Colt,
which was looking for a miniature pistol
to put into production itself, bought the
licence and manufactured the pistol as
the Model 1908 until 1946.

Browning's happy association with Fabrique National continued with the introduction of the Nouveau Modèle, or Model 10, another unlocked-breech design in 7.65mm Browning calibre and which supplanted the Model 1900. In 1922, this same pistol was also offered in 9mm Short calibre (.380 ACP), which became known as the Model 1910/22.

By the time of its introduction, John Browning was working on a much heavier pistol for FN – a locked-breech design for the 9mm Parabellum cartridge – a task which occupied him until his death, in Belgium, in 1926. After his demise, the pistol underwent some small modification and appeared, in 1935, as the Modèle de Guerre Grand Puissance, better known to many generations of pistol shooters, soldiers and police officers as the Browning High Power (sometimes rendered as Hi-Power) or GP35.

But before this, Browning was also cementing his links with Hartford, Connecticut, where in the dying years of the old century, Colt Patent Firearms was looking at self-loading pistols.

Colt's association with Browning dated from 1894, when he had put his hand to the 'potato digger' machine gun; soon thereafter he was at work specifying the mechanism for a locked-breech semi-automatic pistol. Once again – as he did

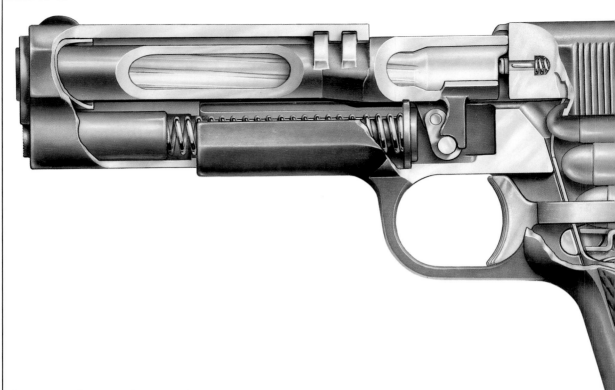

Colt Remington M1911 A1

Calibre: .45in (11.42mm)
Weight: 1.1kg (39oz)
Length: 216mm (8.5in)
Barrel length: 127mm (5in)
Effective range: 30m (98ft)
Feed: seven-round magazine
Muzzle velocity: 262mps (860fps)
Country of origin: United States

with his machine gun designs –
Browning hedged his bets as much as
possible in the patent applications he
made, seeking protection for a wide
variety of different actions. One of them,
for which protection was granted in
Britain and the United States in 1897,
was for the 'parallel link' action which
was, quite literally, to make John Moses
Browning's fortune. In the event Colt
went on to manufacture a range of
Browning-designed locked-breech action
pistols embodying this concept, while FN
produced the simpler, lighter unlocked-
breech pistols, at least up until 1935.
This was not a matter of contractual

Webley Model 1912 Mark I

Calibre: .455in (11.55mm)
Weight: 1.11kg (39.2oz)
Length: 216mm (8.5in)
Barrel length: 127mm (5in)
Effective range: 30m (98ft)
Feed: eight-round magazine
Muzzle velocity: 300mps (984fps)
Country of origin: United Kingdom

little and too late: the US Army's Ordnance Department had already taken to its heart the desperate pleas of the men fighting in the Philippines for a heavier-calibre pistol. Colt reacted by effectively enlarging the Model 1902, and submitted that pistol for trials, too, without marked success, while trying all the while to produce a design which satisfied all the criteria for a service arm.

By the end of 1906, the need to select a pistol – and it was clear, by now, that it would be a self-loading pistol – to replace the .38-calibre revolvers was pressing, and in January 1907 a Board of Enquiry was set up to test the merits of nine rivals. Among them, a new model from Colt. The verdict came down heavily in favour of the Colt. It was duly selected, with a minor caveat in the form of a request for detail changes to the design, which Browning willingly carried out.

THE COLT M1911
In principle, the pistol which resulted, and which was adopted for the US Army, Navy and Marine Corps in 1911 as the M1911, was simplicity itself. The slide, which works backwards and forwards on ribs milled from the frame, extends the length of the pistol and encloses all its operating parts. It is locked to the barrel in the fully forward position by means of two ribs on the latter's upper surface, just forward of the breech, which mate with two grooves in the undersurface of the slide top. The barrel is located at the muzzle end by a bushing held in place by the forward end of the recoil spring and at the breech end by a link extending from the lower surface and pivoting about the slide stop pin in the frame. As the slide is forced to the rear, either manually or by the recoil from a discharged round, the barrel moves with it for a very short distance. It then drops at the rear, the breech actually describing a semi-circular path, as the link moves around its pivot, disengaging the locking ribs and freeing the slide to continue through the usual cycle of ejection/cocking/loading before re-locking with the barrel and returning to battery. Compared to the actions of some of the European pistols of the previous two decades, it was a masterpiece of simplicity, both to manufacture and to operate, and fully deserved the popular acclaim it soon received.

There were niggling complaints, of course, and the hammer spur was extended during the pistol's long World War I production run. It had also become the Royal Navy and Royal Flying Corps/Royal Air Force's official side-arm by then, as well as that of the Canadian Army, in .455 calibre, chambered for the Webley Self-loading cartridge. As a result of combat experience, a variety of further modifications were made, most of them being designed to make the pistol more comfortable in the hand. They were enough to warrant an amendment to the model number, and the M1911A1 pistol went into production in mid-1926. It has remained so ever since, only losing its status as the official US military side-arm to the Beretta Model 92 SB in the mid-1980s.

Norway was the first country to manufacture clones of the M1911, but soon after, in 1916, Argentina adopted the weapon as its official service pistol. Manufacture started there, too, and picked up in the 1930s. Inevitably, unlicensed copies began to appear, too, in a variety of calibres, 9mm being the most common and Spain being the biggest source. Some, like the pistols manufactured by Gabilondo under the trade name 'Llama' and by Echeverria as the 'Star', were – and still are – sound, reliable weapons.

FULL-AUTO M1911
The M1911 clone which Echeverria manufactured as the Star Modello A had one dubious distinction: during the mid-1930s, just prior to the Spanish Civil War, it was manufactured in full-automatic form as the Modello M, in 9mm Largo calibre. Like the schnellfeuer version of the Mauser C96, and the Spanish Astra 902, which was a rather inferior copy of it, the Modello M proved to be entirely unpredictable in use, even when fitted with a shoulder stock, though no doubt its psychological value was considerable under the right circumstances!

The last of John Browning's pistols, the High Power, is very similar in principle to the Colt M1911 save for the substitution of a profiled extension to the barrel below the breech which provided a camming surface to operate against a 'locking shoulder': a lug on the frame. This was used in place of the M1911 link to the slide stop to create the unlocking downwards movement of the breech end of the barrel. It was superior in that it did away with a moving part, and therefore reduced the possibility of wear and eventual malfunction. Being

obligation or obstruction; FN saw a wide market for pistols in lighter loadings, while Colt's customers wanted heavier, more powerful guns. But there was cross-over where there was need, as in the case of the miniature pistol both companies produced, and in the lighter .32 ACP and .38 ACP blowback Colt semi-automatics.

A NEW US SERVICE PISTOL
Colt produced commercial models of Browning's would-be service self-loader from 1900 onwards. They made a first attempt to interest the US Government in 1902, with the Military Model in .38 ACP calibre. It was, quite literally, too

designed for the smaller 9mm Parabellum cartridge, the box magazine in the butt had greater capacity – in fact, by arranging its cartridges in two staggered rows, the pistol held 13 rounds (and one more in the breech, if absolutely necessary) – much more than any pistol seen before.

Such was Browning's influence on the design of the self-loading pistol that many competing products brought to the market in the first quarter of the twentieth century seem to have faded into obscurity, but for all that, they were there, and in considerable numbers.

Having been disappointed in their brief involvement with Gabbett-Fairfax and the Mars pistol project, Webley turned their considerable talents to designing a semi-automatic pistol of their own. It was clear that any pistol which stood a chance of being accepted as a service side-arm in Britain would have to

■BELOW: The Walther PPK, a semi-automatic pistol designed primarily for police plainclothes work. It has an external hammer at the rear activated by a double-action lock.

be in .455 or very similar calibre, and thus would have to be a locked-breech design. It was here that early efforts were directed, though later the company would also turn its attention to unlocked-breech pistols in a lighter calibre.

WEBLEY'S SEMI-AUTO
J.W. Whiting, Webley's Works Manager, executed the designs, and his first effort, patented in 1903, employed a conventional coiled spring lying below and along the barrel, which was locked to the breech at the moment of discharge by two arms on the latter engaging projections on the barrel. Very few examples of this design were ever made up, and it was supplanted almost immediately by a version with a V-shaped recoil spring housed in the right hand side of the butt alongside the magazine. This feature was to endure through all the subsequent Webley automatic pistols and give them their distinctive – and not particularly pleasing – shape.

The second Webley semi-automatic pistol in .455 calibre, known as the Model 1904, utilised a different system of locking barrel and breech-block together.

They were secured by a vertical bolt, which, after it had served its purpose, dropped and allowed the two components to separate. Though the method worked well enough under favourable circumstances, it was complex both to manufacture and maintain, and was said to be susceptible to stoppages if dirt was allowed into the action (a not altogether unlikely occurrence under combat conditions).

THE .455 MARK I
It was also extremely heavy for its size at 1.35kg (3lb); it was hardly in production before work on its successor began. This was produced first of all in 1906, and adopted in 1913 by the Royal Navy as the Pistol, Self-loading, .455 Mark I. It used a locking system which was similar to that which Browning adopted for his High Power. A lug on the barrel engaged in a recess in the under-surface of the upper part of the slide, and was released as the barrel was forced downwards by a camming action. Oblique ribs on the sides of the square-section barrel extension caused this by their movement in matching slots in the slide – after the two

Mauser HSc

Calibre: 7.62mm (.3in)
Weight: .6kg (21oz)
Length: 152mm (6in)
Barrel length: 86mm (3.38in)
Feed: eight-round magazine
Muzzle velocity: 291mps (955fps)
Country of origin: Germany

had briefly recoiled together. A version of the pistol, habitually fitted with a shoulder stock, was issued to the Royal Flying Corps as the Mark I No 2 in 1915, but was soon withdrawn. The pistols made for military issue had a grip safety, and a unique device which could be invoked to prevent the magazine from feeding a fresh round into the chamber. Instead, the slide was held back so that single rounds could be hand-loaded, thus leaving the seven rounds in the magazine in reserve for a time when one-at-a-time loading was too ponderous. Though lighter than the Model 1904, and somewhat simpler, it was still too complex for a service pistol, and too expensive to produce.

WEBLEY'S LIGHT PISTOLS
As well as these locked-breech short-recoil pistols chambered for service cartridges, Webley & Scott also produced a range of lighter pistols from 1905. With external hammers and a simple blowback action, they were chambered initially in

7.65mm and .38 Short calibres and later for the 9mm Long Browning round. Both had barrels locked into the frame by a form of bolt which was actually a lug on the top of the front end of the trigger guard. Made from spring steel, the guard's rear could be disengaged from the butt, and the whole swung forward, releasing the barrel so that the weapon could be stripped for cleaning. Most 9mm Long models were produced with a grip safety like that found on the contemporary military pistols. The smaller-calibre pistol was probably the most successful of all Webley's semi-automatics, being accepted by the City of London and Metropolitan Police Forces in 1911 and remaining in service until 1940. The larger pistol was also adopted for police issue, this time in South Africa.

Webley & Scott also produced a series of 6.35mm calibre 'vest-pocket' pistols, the size of the palm of one's hand and just 0.35kg (12oz) in weight. US gunmakers Harrington and Richardson produced pistols under licence based very

closely on both the miniature pistol and the Model 1905, both of them in .32 calibre hammerless form.

After Webley stopped manufacturing semi-automatics, sometime before 1940, no more such combat or self-defence pistols were to be produced in Britain, though there were later attempts to produce very specialised match pistols. The ways and vagaries of business are unpredictable, however, and by 1990 two of the most important makers of semi-automatic pistols in modern times, both of them comparative late-comers to the genre – Smith & Wesson and Heckler and Koch – had both been acquired by British interests, Smith & Wesson by a privately-owned group in the Midlands and Heckler and Koch by the government, as part of what had originally been the Royal Small Arms Factory.

THE VALUE OF THE AUTOMATIC
World War I saw far-reaching changes in the field of military technology, and that in turn led to the introduction of new

fighting tactics. Thanks to the effective strategic stalemate caused by the terrible trio of artillery, barbed wire and machine guns, hand-to-hand combat took on an importance it hadn't had for centuries. Slowly it became apparent that the extra firepower of the new breed of self-loading handgun gave it a slight edge. An advantage which became much more decisive with the introduction of the submachine gun and the infiltration tactics which it was developed to further, which gave the German Army on the Western Front a late hope of securing if not a victory, then at least a peace on more advantageous terms.

That was not to be, of course, but the lesson of the effectiveness of lightweight, hand-held automatic and semi-automatic weapons was not lost (except on the British Army, which stuck to its revolvers until 1957). Gunmakers in Germany and across what had been the Austro-Hungarian Empire (which was broken up

■BELOW: The Roth-Steyr Model 1907. All Roth-Steyrs fired from a locked breech. The magazine is positioned in the butt, being an integral part of the weapon.

as a result of the war) had by then acquired a considerable body of expertise in the design and manufacture of self-loading pistols. In addition to those already described earlier, Becker and Hollander, Langenhan, Rheinische Metallwaaren und Maschinenfabrik (the successors to Dreyse) and Carl Walther had all been manufacturing semi-automatic pistols in Germany since before the war. Mauser and Sauer also produced designs other than those we described earlier, and all were adopted to some degree or another for military use during the war. This was often with a conspicuous lack of success, the weapons having been designed for rather less rugged conditions and frequently for lighter ammunition than was considered desirable for military use. Defeat for Germany saw to it that much of the country's industrial base was laid waste, and it was some time before even the best-organised of her gunmakers were able to restart their production lines even in a limited sense. Mauser was back in business more rapidly than most, having taken over the manufacture of the Parabellum pistol from DWM. He also

restarted manufacture of a lightweight pistol known as the Modell 1914, to be improved and relaunched as the Modell 1934, a simple blowback design in 6.35 and 7.65mm calibres, and which was later overtaken by the Modell HSc. J.P. Sauer also revamped a pre-war design, the blowback-action 7.65mm Modell 1913 and had it accepted as the official side-arm of the German military and civilian police during the troubled 1930s, before going on to produce one of the best pistols of the interwar period, the Modell 38H. Most important, though, was the contribution Carl Walther made with his Selbstladepistole Modell PP of 1929.

DOUBLE-ACTION PISTOLS
Virtually every self-loading pistol until this time was a single-action handgun – its action had to be cocked by pulling the hammer or the striker pin back, either by manipulating the bolt or the slide to which it was fixed, or, in the case of a pistol with an exposed hammer, by working the hammer directly. Normally, this took place as the first round was chambered, but that left the gun in a precarious ready-to-fire state unless the

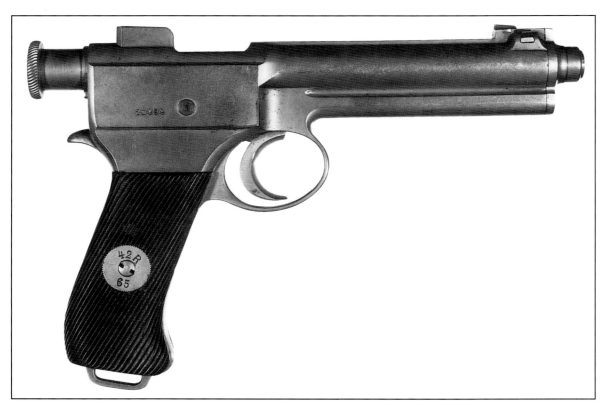

hammer was released under controlled conditions (whereupon it couldn't be fired until the hammer was pulled back again). With a gun with a concealed hammer or a truly hammerless gun, this was simply not possible at all, and led to the incorporation of multiple safety devices; almost all semi-automatic pistols had two safety catches. The introduction of a revolver-type double-action allowed the hammer to be released when a round had been chambered, but readied for action again by the first pressure on the trigger. The hammer was also usually physically prevented from resting on the firing pin, either by being held off the striker by a bar or plate engaged by the safety catch, or by the firing pin itself having been tipped out of the way. Either way, the gun could not be discharged by a blow or if it fell. Walther's Modell PP and later, lighter Modell PPK were the first world-class self-loading handguns to incorporate a double-action lock, though this very desirable feature soon became common as other manufacturers developed new designs. The designation PP stood for Polizei Pistole, the K for Kriminal; the smaller pistol was intended as a concealed weapon for police officers in plain clothes.

GERMAN POCKET PISTOLS

The Modell PP was Walther's 10th self-loading pistol design. The firm's earliest efforts had been 6.35mm 'vest-pocket' pistols to compete with those produced by FN in 1905, and a slightly larger version in 7.65mm followed. In all, the most notable of this series was the Modell 6, a wartime expedient and a handgun to be avoided whenever possible, since it was a simple unlocked-breech blowback weapon yet chambered for the much-too-powerful 9mm Parabellum cartridge. Happily, few were made, between 1915 and 1917, and not surprisingly, even fewer survive. The 7.65mm PPs and PPKs, on the other hand, while they were also simple blowback actions, have always enjoyed a high and thoroughly deserved reputation as a result of the performance of their ammunition being carefully matched to their capabilities.

The other two very successful 7.65mm pocket pistols produced in Germany between the wars, the Mauser Selbstladepistole Modell HSc and the Sauer Selbstladepistole Modell 38H were in no way inferior to the Walther PPK, which they resemble closely. The Mauser HSc had an almost-concealed hammer but could nonetheless be cocked by thumb action. Its safety catch lifted the firing pin out of alignment with the hammer, a feature copied in the post-war Heckler and Koch pistols. The Sauer 38H was a little heavier than the other two, had a somewhat longer barrel, and shot rather better as a result. It had a thumb-operated catch behind the trigger on the left-hand side of the frame which released the internal hammer and allowed it to be lowered onto a loaded chamber. This lever would also re-cock the hammer if one so desired, or the ordinary double-action trigger pull could be employed for the first round, the hammer subsequently being re-cocked by the recoil action. The Mauser HSc went back into production after World War II, but the Sauer 38H never did. However,

■BELOW: The Czech CZ Model 39 was a 9mm blowback pistol which fired a low-powered, and ineffective, round. It was not a great success.

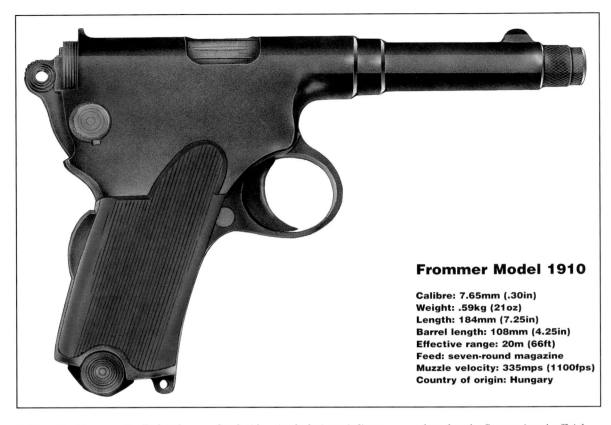

Frommer Model 1910

Calibre: 7.65mm (.30in)
Weight: .59kg (21oz)
Length: 184mm (7.25in)
Barrel length: 108mm (4.25in)
Effective range: 20m (66ft)
Feed: seven-round magazine
Muzzle velocity: 335mps (1100fps)
Country of origin: Hungary

its 'de-cocking' lever eventually found a place in the range of excellent pistols Sauer later began to manufacture in conjunction with Schweizerische Industrie Gesellschaft or SIG.

WALTHER'S P38
In 1937, by which time Germany had unilaterally renounced the Treaty of Versailles, Carl Walther Waffenfabrik began limited production of a locked-breech pistol for the first time, in the 9mm Parabellum chambering which had been the de facto German military standard calibre for 30 years. The Modell AP (for Armeepistole) was, as its name suggests, a contender to replace the expensive-to-produce Luger P08, and was submitted for trials to the Army High Command, the Oberkommando des Heeres (OKH). The single serious reservation OKH had concerned the pistol's concealed hammer, and a revised model with an external hammer, the Modell HP (for Heerespistole) was quickly produced, and adopted as the P38. Like Walther's police pistols, the P38 had a double-action lock, and was

fitted with a simple device to indicate when a cartridge was chambered. The P38 certainly fulfilled the requirement for a pistol simpler in operation than the old Parabellum. Locking of the breech and barrel is accomplished by a wedge-shaped locking block beneath the breech. When the round is discharged, the barrel and slide recoil together until the locking block reaches the end of two recesses, in which its lateral lugs have been engaged, when it is free to drop and disengage the slide and arrest the barrel. Production continued throughout World War II, not just at Walther's own factory in Zella but also by Mauser at Oberndorf and Spreewerke in Berlin (and in Herstal and Brno, in captured factories). Quality in both construction and materials suffered during the latter years of the war, in particular. Walther's original factory was located in what became East Germany, and after the war was over it took some considerable time for the company, by now moved to Ulm, to find its feet again. However, production of the P38 was restarted in 1957, when the pistol, by now known as the Pistole 1, was again

adopted as the German Army's official side-arm. Walther also achieved considerable success in the field of match pistols, having first produced a hammerless, blowback .22 calibre target pistol for the 1932 Olympic Games. An improved version took the first five places in all the disciplines for which it was entered in the following Olympiad, the so-called 'Hitler Games' which took place in Berlin in 1936.

CZ PISTOLS
For the Austro-Hungarian Empire, defeat in World War I had even further-reaching consequences than it did for its ally to the west; Austria, Hungary and what was to become Czechoslovakia suddenly found themselves alone, with no reliable alliance partners to help them through a difficult time of transition. Czechoslovakia proved to be the most able, and in 1919 a small arms factory was established in Brno, Moravia, initially under the name of Ceskoslovenska Zavody na Vyrobu Zbrani, to manufacture first Mannlicher and then Mauser rifles. The Works

Manager was Josef Nickl, who had earlier worked for Mauser, and it was he who put into production at Brno the first indigenous Czech pistol, the Armadni Pistole vz/22. Sometimes called the CZ 22, it had a rather cumbersome and quite unnecessary rotating locking action, and was chambered for the under-powered 9mm Short cartridge. Nickl had actually designed this pistol for Mauser in 1916, but it had aroused little interest at Oberndorf, and in any event had little chance of going into production at a time when every available gun was destined for the armed services. In 1920 the Czech Government tried to rationalise its arms industry, and transferred manufacture of the pistol to a company known as Ceska zbrojovka at Stakonice in Bohemia, run by Alois Tomiska. Some 15 years earlier he had designed a 'vest-pocket' auto-loader known as the 'Little Tom', a 6.35mm double-action pistol. Here the vz/22 was improved somewhat to make it easier to assemble and went into production as the vz/24. The Czech arms industry of the period boasted what has been described as a galaxy of talent in its

design departments. As well as Nickl and Tomiska, Karel Krnka was at work in Prague, and so were Vaclav Halek and his younger brothers Frants and Emanuel, as well as Frants Myska. Vaclav was already employed on the design of a light machine gun, which finally saw the light of day as the ZB vz/26 and later evolved into the Bren, while it was Myska who re-worked the vz/24 into the CZ vz/27, a more manageable 7.65mm design with a straightforward blowback action. A transitional pistol, in 7.65mm calibre but employing the rotating-barrel locking system of the earlier pistols, was also produced, though in small quantities only. The two are very similar externally, the locked-breech version having inclined gripping grooves on its slide, while on the blowback version the grooves are vertical. While it was by no means a military pistol in the accepted sense of the word, the blowback vz/27 proved popular; its production was continued under the Nazis, after they invaded Czechoslovakia, when some versions with a longer barrel to accommodate a silencer were also

produced. Production was resumed briefly after World War II was over by a re-constituted Ceska zbrojovka, and continued under the Communist government which came to power in 1948. Myska was also responsible for a successor to the vz/27, the Pistole vz/38, of which one authority says: 'This is a terrible weapon and there seems to be no good reason for its existence. It is clumsy to hold and point and … accurate shooting is out of the question'. One could say that of many other pistols, of course, but perhaps seldom with as much vigour.

FROMMER'S MODEL 1910

The first semi-automatic pistol produced in Hungary was the Roth-Steyr Model 1907, though the director of the State Armoury in Budapest, Rudolf Frommer, had put forward a workable if unorthodox design based on the long-recoil principle

■**BELOW: The Steyr Model 1911, an efficient and comfortable military self-loading pistol which served with the Austro-Hungarian Army throughout World War I.**

six years earlier, and had it rejected as too complex for military use. Frommer persevered, however, and by 1910 had succeeded in simplifying his pistol considerably, though sticking to the long-recoil principle. With this method the barrel and bolt remain locked together for the entire rearwards phase of the action, only being released as the hammer is brought to full cock. The barrel then travels back to battery, leaving the spent case to be ejected as soon as it clears the chamber, tripping the bolt release and allowing the breech-block to start on its return journey, stripping a fresh round out of the magazine and chambering it in the process. In the case of the Frommer Model 1910, as the pistol came to be known, the locking mechanism itself was by means of a bolt head which rotated through 90 degrees, and was similar in principle to the action of Mannlicher's 'straight pull' bolt-action rifles.

HUNGARIAN SEMI-AUTOMATICS

The process was further complicated by the presence of two recoil springs – one for the barrel and surrounding it, the other for the bolt, and contained within it, surrounding the striker. As the century progressed, there were signs of a large rift between the Austrian and the Hungarian components of the Habsburg Empire. Perhaps for that reason, when Frommer submitted a re-drawn design to the Koeniglische Ungarnische Armee, it was accepted, and went into production in 7.65mm and 9mm Short calibre – but in Budapest only – as the Pisztoly 12M, commonly known as the 'Frommer Stop' model. It was hardly any simpler in concept than the earlier pistol, and still required two recoil springs, but at least now they were carried together, above the barrel, where they gave the pistol, and its smaller brother, the 6.35mm 'vest-pocket' Frommer Baby, their distinctive – though hardly attractive – outline. The Frommer Stop stayed in service with units of the Hungarian Army until 1945, although it had long been supplanted by then, by the Pisztoly 37M, a solid, robust blowback pistol of much more conventional appearance, chambered for either the 7.65mm or the 9mm Short cartridge.

To the north, Poland had relied on Germany and the Austro-Hungarian Empire for supplies of small arms, but by the mid-1930s that policy resulted in a spectacular degree of non-standardisation, not only between units but sometimes

within them. To rationalise this a decision was taken to produce a semi-automatic handgun locally. The design chosen was (almost inevitably) a modification of Browning's Colt M1911A1, the detail changes being the work of Wilniewczyc and Skrzypinski. The pistol in question, the wz.35, was to be manufactured at the Government Small Arms Factory at Radom (Fabryka Broni w Radomiu), and it was the location which gave the pistol

■RIGHT: The Steyr Model 1916 – a variant of the company's Model 1911. Designed primarily for military use, the Steyr 1911 was initially ignored by the Austro-Hungarian Army. However, the outbreak of World War I found Austria-Hungary desperately short of firearms. Any weapon available found its way to the frontline. The Steyr thus entered service, and proved itself a reliable and robust gun.

Steyr Model 1917

Calibre: 9mm (.35in)
Weight: .99kg (34.9oz)
Length: 216mm (8.5in)
Barrel length: 128mm (5.03in)
Effective range: 30m (98ft)
Feed: eight-round magazine
Muzzle velocity: 335mps (1100fps)
Country of origin: Austria

its most common sobriquet. The Radom is also – equally incorrectly – known as the VIS wz.35, the VIS in question (Latin for 'power'), being a play on the initials of the two engineers who modified the design. The multiplicity of names, and the resulting confusion, comes from the original pistols being stamped 'FB Radom VIS-wz.35'. The most important feature Wilniewczyc and Skrzypinski added was a de-cocking lever on the left-hand side of the frame, which allowed the hammer to be lowered safely onto a loaded chamber, having first retracted the firing pin. The secondary safety device on the Colt original was then discarded, and a take-

down latch fitted in its place – a cause of confusion in those who were familiar with the original design. The pistol went into production in 1936, and manufacture continued under German occupation, only the gun's markings being changed.

RED FIREPOWER

Across Poland's long eastern border with the Soviet Union, Browning's M1911 Colt, with its parallel link action, was again taken up to form the basis for yet another successful range of handguns. The Tokarev pistols, named after designer Feodor Vassilivitch Tokarev were produced at the Tula Arsenal. The two

names, Tula and Tokarev, give the pistols their abbreviated designation, 'TT' followed by the year the model was adopted. The first model, the TT-30, was little more than a simplification of the original Browning design, with both the grip safety and the mechanical safety catch removed, but it did have one very useful innovation. In a semi-automatic the lips of the magazine are responsible for positioning the incoming round directly below the bolt, and are often the cause of misfeeding, being susceptible to

damage. In the TT-30 they were transferred into the gun's body proper, where they were machined out of the solid steel and much less liable to distortion as a result. The second important innovation allowed the entire lockwork to be removed as a single unit for cleaning. A major modification introduced in 1933 turned the locking lugs on the barrel's upper surface into rings which were machined right around the barrel. This may not appear to be a significant change, but it simplified

manufacture considerably, for the machining operation could now be consigned to a lathe, rather than to a much slower horizontal milling machine. The pistol, otherwise unchanged, became the TT-33 at that point. The Tokarev pistols are not the most comfortable handguns to fire, since the 7.62mm round for which they are chambered is a very powerful one, producing considerable recoil. Later Soviet designs – the Stechkin and the Makarov – were chambered for a lower-powered 9mm round, but not one which bore any resemblance to existing 9mm ammunition outside the Soviet bloc.

Much of the Austro-Hungarian Empire's war had been fought against Italy, which entered the conflict in late May 1915. In Italy, the tradition of gunmaking in the north, around Brescia in the foothills of the Alps, was already hundreds of years old. And though the Italians were relative latecomers to the self-loading pistol, this actually worked in their favour, since it allowed them to avoid many of the pitfalls along the way to the evolution of a successful design.

ITALY'S SEMI-AUTOMATICS

The earliest Italian semi-automatic pistols were the product of a newcomer to the ranks of Italian gunmakers, Societa Siderugica Glisenti, and were realised in 1905, apparently from a design conceived by two Swiss named Haussler and Roch.

■RIGHT: The Tula-Tokarev 1930, a Russian semi-auto which takes the first part of its name from the state arsenal where it was made. It saw widespread service throughout World War II.

It was accepted by the Italian Army as the Pistola Automatica Glisenti Modello 1906, in 7.65mm Parabellum calibre. It was soon supplanted by the Modello 1910, chambered for the 9mm Glisenti round, a cartridge virtually identical in appearance to the 9mm Parabellum

round, but more lightly loaded; naturally, this gave rise to some confusion later. In outward appearance, the Glisenti pistol resembles the Luger P08, but its workings are actually closer to those of the Mauser C96. While it had a locked-breech action (by a wedge in the floor of

Radom

Calibre: 9mm (.35in)
Weight: 1.05kg (37oz)
Length: 211mm (8.3in)
Barrel length: 114mm (4.5in)
Effective range: 30m (98ft)
Feed: eight-round magazine
Muzzle velocity: 351mps (1150fps)
Country of origin: Poland

the frame), it was not a particularly sound one, a factor which amplified considerably the danger of using 9mm Parabellum ammunition. Perhaps its most unattractive feature was the peculiar method of cocking the action. Like the Roth-Steyr of 1907, it was not self-cocking; instead, it utilised a clumsy form of double action, which led to a long trigger pull and consequent inaccuracy, not just for the first round fired, but for all of them.

ENTER THE BERETTA

In 1915, a competitor for the Glisenti (manufacture of which had by then been taken over by Metalurgica Bresciana ex Tempini, MBT) appeared, engineered by one of Italy's oldest-established gun-makers, Fabrica d'Armi Pietro Beretta of Gardone, founded in 1680 and still going strong. Beretta's first automatic pistol was a blowback 7.65mm chambered for Browning's cartridge, which was unusual only in that its firing pin doubled as the extractor, helped by residual gas pressure in the chamber. It can perhaps best be classed as a wartime expedient. Small numbers of the same pistol (but this time

with a conventional extractor) were also produced in 9mm Glisenti chambering. There was the same danger if 9mm Parabellum ammunition was used as in the Modello 1910 but more problematic, as there was not even a weak locking device in the Beretta.

BERETTA 1934 AND 1935

At the war's end, Beretta made improvements to the basic design of the pistol's lockwork, reducing the trigger pull considerably and incorporating a rather badly designed hold-open device. Renamed the Modello 1922, it sold in small numbers. It was joined the following year by a version chambered for the 9mm Glisenti round, distinguishable by the presence for the first time of a feature which has since become something of a trademark: the ring-shaped hammer spur. It is not unique; the Browning High Power and its imitators have it, too, as do the later Walthers, among others. The Modello 1923 was a better pistol than its predecessors, but it still had one major weakness: it was a blowback pistol which could chamber a round far too powerful

for its mechanism and structure to handle and which, if used consistently, would eventually lead to a very unpleasant accident. The simple answer, and the solution which Beretta adopted, was to re-engineer the pistol so that it would not chamber the too-powerful round, and the new versions produced in 1934 and 1935 were chambered for either the 7.65mm round or the 9mm Short cartridge. The only really valid criticism of them after that was aimed at the ultimate stopping power of the rounds in question. But as far as blowback designs go, the Beretta Modello 1934 and 1935 were as good as any – and a great deal better than most – thanks to the attention to detail which went into their design and the care which went into their manufacture. Even the best organisations have occasional aberrations, however – and Beretta was no exception. During the 1930s a full-automatic version of the Modello 1923 was produced to compete with the schnellfeuer Mauser and its copies and the Star Modello M, but was soon dropped. 'It did not give the type of results we expected,' said Beretta, tongue-in-cheek. 'Firing it on the full-

Tokarev TT-33

Calibre: 9mm (.35in)
Weight: .82kg (29oz)
Length: 196mm (7.7in)
Barrel length: 117mm (4.6in)
Effective range: 30m (98ft)
Feed: eight-round magazine
Muzzle velocity: 411mps (1350fps)
Country of origin: Soviet Union

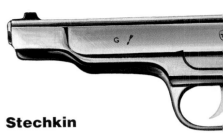

Stechkin

Calibre: 9mm (.35in)
Weight: 1.03kg (36.3oz)
Length: 225mm (8.85in)
Barrel length: 127mm (5in)
Effective range: 30m (98ft)
Feed: 20-round magazine
Muzzle velocity: 340mps (1115fps)
Country of origin: Soviet Union

■ABOVE: The Star Model B, Spanish pistol which entered service in 1928 – a robust and well made weapon which is still in use today. It fires its 9mm round from a locked breech.

automatic setting made aiming it a dangerous and problematic business. Mauser no longer makes (them) either.' Somewhat surprisingly, given that sentiment, Beretta itself was to return to the subject with a full-auto version of the Modello 1951, the Modello 951A, which was produced in small numbers during the late 1950s and early 1960s, apparently at the request of the paramilitary Carabinieri, and again with the more effective Modello 93R, which had a selective three-round burst capability.

SPAIN'S PISTOL INDUSTRY
Elsewhere in southern Europe, Spanish pistol makers – by now concentrated in the Basque country – tended largely to stick to copying successful Browning designs, either the heavy, lock-breech service-calibre pistols manufactured by Colt, or the lighter designs made up by Fabrique National, particularly the Model 1903 and the Model 1910. The most important of them were Gabilondo, with their range of pistols marketed under the Llama name since 1934, and Echeverria, which used the name Star since its foundation in 1919. Both made reliable pistols which were essentially copies, but often with extra more or less desirable features including additional

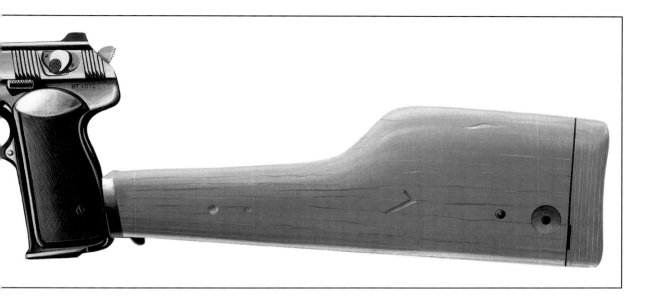

■LEFT: A Soviet officer leads by example during the Great Patriotic War against Germany (1941-45). His weapon is the Tokarev T T-33, of which nearly two million were made.

safety devices. The Star Modello M, which was derived from the very successful Modello A, a Colt M1911 copy in 9mm Parabellum calibre, was modified to enable full-automatic fire – an almost useless option in a pistol. Both manufacturers received a considerable boost from World War I, when they (Gabilondo in particular) contracted to supply large numbers of pistols to the French Army. After the war, smaller Spanish gunmakers started to copy Gabilondo and Echeverria's second-generation designs, and inevitably, some of the pistols produced were of very poor quality indeed, and resembling the originals only very approximately.

Unceta, founded in 1908, concentrated on designs of its own, following its early experience (as Esperanza y Unceta) in producing the 'Campogiro' Model 1910 pistol. The Spanish Government bought this to supersede the Bergmann-Bayard and the French Army to replace the 'Victoria' 7.65mm blowback pistol during World War I. After the war, a series of pistols based loosely on Browning's basic blowback design (but not resembling the FN pistols at all in appearance) were put into production, the best known of them being the Astra 400 of 1921. One of the few blowback pistols chambered for a

powerful 9mm cartridge, it can be reckoned safe to handle by virtue of its heavy slide and a very strong recoil spring – so strong that it requires a very heavy hand indeed to chamber the first round. The nominal calibre is 9mm Largo, as originally designed by Thomas Bergmann – though in fact the pistol's chief claim to fame is its ability to accept virtually any long 9mm round and the .38 ACP). Astra-Unceta also produced copies of the Mauser C96 in both automatic and semi-automatic forms as the Models 900 through 903, and in fact the full-automatic Astra Model 901 actually preceded the schnellfeuer Mauser, and was the reason why Mauser itself began producing a full-auto pistol.

FRENCH BELGIANS

In neighbouring France, the manufacture of semi-automatic handguns destined for the commercial market had begun before the World War I. Even so, it was some considerable time before the 'new' handguns acquired any real measure of respectability or acceptance in government circles, and one would be forgiven for suggesting that was, in part at least, brought about by the truly execrable quality of early French self-loading pistols, both in terms of design and of quality of manufacture. Far more popular were John Browning's designs produced across the border in Belgium (by a company now, ironically, controlled by the French Government). One might further suggest that the only acceptable

home-grown self-loading pistols were copies of those designs, particularly as produced by MAB (Manufacture d'Armes de Bayonne). Certain segments of the French police force, itself composed of many different bodies answering to many different departments, were the first to adopt semi-automatic pistols – Belgian-made Brownings – in the mid-1920s.

FRENCH VENTURES

One of the most distinctive early French-designed automatic pistols was the Le Français of 1928. The Le Français was produced by the Manufacture Française d'Armes et Cycles de St Etienne, a company established in the mid-nineteenth century and later known more simply as Manufrance. The pistol was designed by the company's Chairman and Managing Director, Mimard, as were two pocket pistols with similar mechanisms. The barrel of the Le Français was hinged at the front of the frame; on depressing a catch (or removing the magazine), the breech rose clear of the slide, the barrel tipping down through 15 degrees, giving access to the breech for cleaning or to load single rounds. The magazine held an 'extra' round externally at its base; once the full magazine had been inserted, this round was removed from its spring-clip and inserted by hand into the chamber. The breech was then returned to battery and the pistol was ready to fire, thanks to its double-action lock. Alternatively, the magazine could be held out by just a few millimetres, so that the simple blowback

Glisenti Modello 1910

Calibre: 9mm (.35in)
Weight: .82kg (29oz)
Length: 210mm (8.25in)
Barrel length: 99mm (3.9in)
Effective range: 20m (66ft)
Feed: seven-round magazine
Muzzle velocity: 305mps (1000fps)
Country of origin: Italy

action would not chamber a fresh round; the pistol could then be hand-loaded with single rounds, the eight rounds in the magazine being held in reserve. In common with other 'tip-down' barrel self-loading pistols, there was no extractor fitted. Ejection was accomplished by the residual gas pressure in the chamber alone, and as a result misfires had to be manually extracted.

It was 1935 before the French Army itself tentatively adopted a home-produced self-loading pistol, although it bought such pistols manufactured in Spain in large numbers during World War I. Designed by Charles Petter and put into production first by the Société Alsacienne de Construction Méchanique (SACM) and later by all the major French armaments factories, this was a modification of the basic Browning locked-breech system as used in the Colt M1911. The Pistolet Automatique Modèle 1935 was chambered for an idiosyncrasy – the so-called 7.65mm Long cartridge, which was unknown outside French military circles, and which was also used

in the prototype French submachine gun then under development. Despite their being manufactured at half a dozen different venues, the pistols were never widely issued – or widely popular. It was not until 1950, when the basic design was revamped for the 9mm Parabellum cartridge, that it became an effective side-arm; once again, it was a case of a sound design being rendered ineffective by the nature of its ammunition.

BASQUE FIREPOWER
The commercial manufacture of self-loading pistols in France in the early twentieth century was largely centred in the area across the border from the Basque country of Spain, in Bayonne and Hendaye. The population of that region of France is largely Basque in origin, and it is reasonable to suggest that the siting of the arms industry there is no accident, but that it represents something akin to overspill from Spain. French manufacturers were never as aggressive as their Spanish counterparts in marketing their products. As a result,

French pistols and small arms of all types were (and still are) little known outside their country of origin, the possible exception being the later MAB (Manufacture d'Armes de Bayonne) Modèle P.15.

Rights to the Petter patents involved in the SACM Modèle 1935 were also obtained by Schweizerische Industrie Gessellschaft (SIG), just across the Swiss border in Neuhausen. SIG incorporated them into a version of the Browning GP35 with its fixed cam in place of the parallel link to break the lock between barrel and breech-block. This pistol – which was to be the first in a line of what are generally considered to be the best self-loading handguns in the world – was eventually adopted by the Swiss Government as the Selbstladepistole Modell 49, but long before that went on sale as the SIG P210. Its most notable feature, apart from the high standard of overall workmanship, is the manner in which its slide runs inside its frame, rather than on external rails as is the case with virtually every other similar handgun.

Beretta Modello 1934

Calibre: 9mm (.35in)
Weight: .65kg (23oz)
Length: 152mm (6in)
Barrel length: 95mm (3.75in)
Effective range: 30m (98ft)
Feed: nine-round magazine
Muzzle velocity: 229mps (750fps)
Country of origin: Italy

As stated earlier, the path DWM went down to produce the Borchardt and then the Parabellum pistols proved to be a dead-end, and after Georg Luger, no other designer incorporated Maxim's toggle-action lock into a pistol. But that didn't stop designers from producing pistols which looked very similar to Luger's Parabellum! The Glisenti Modello 1910 was one (and the Le Français also had a passing resemblance), but a pistol made from 1935 onwards by Germany's ally Finland bears the strongest resemblance, though one produced in Japan during World War I is a close second.

FINLAND'S LUGER
Aimo Johannes Lahti was the doyen of Finnish small arms designers, and already had a very successful submachine gun to his credit when he turned his attention to the design of a self-loading pistol in 1935. The Pistooli Malli 35, as it was to become, bears little resemblance to the Parabellum pistol under its remarkably robust skin, even if one could be forgiven for thinking, as one authority suggests, that its designer took the P08 as his starting point and then eliminated everything undesirable in it, starting with the exposed toggle-joint which lay at its metaphorical heart. For this he substituted a closed box, within which operates a simple bolt, breech locking being achieved by a simple vertical block which was cammed up and down as the two components moved backwards and forwards. Very much aware that his country's climate demanded to be taken into consideration, he incorporated an

accelerator not unlike that which Browning used in his recoil-operated machine guns – a curved arm designed to speed up the rearwards passage of the bolt. Browning used his accelerator to speed up his machine guns' cyclic rate; Lahti used his to ensure continued operation under conditions of very low temperature, and it worked perfectly. The Swedish Government adopted the Lahti pistol as the Pistol m/40, and later manufactured it for themselves at the Husqvarna plant when supplies of Walther P38s dried up.

JAPAN'S NAMBU
The Japanese 'Luger-lookalike' was a very different proposition from the excellent Lahti. Designed by an army officer named Kijiro Nambu, and known

officially as the Pistolu Nambu Shiki Jido Kenju 'Ko', or Nambu pistol, Taisho 4th Year, it actually owed rather more to the Glisenti Modello 1910. The Nambu shared its method of locking barrel and breech-block together by means of a floating bolt coupled and de-coupled by a camming wedge in the floor of the frame. This arrangement was satisfactory, but other components of the pistol were decidedly weak. Two versions were made, one in 8mm calibre, chambered for an underpowered round, the other in a diminutive 7mm chambering never seen elsewhere. This latter, known in the West as the 'Baby Nambu', was issued to staff officers; the 8mm version never was officially adopted, but was apparently bought in such quantities by army and navy officers that it achieved a kind of *de facto* recognition.

Ten years later, a much simplified version of the pistol known as the 14 Nen Shiki Kenju or Nambu Pistol, Taisho 14th Year was issued. Similar to the earlier pistol in overall character, it suffered from one potentially fatal design weakness. It could be re-assembled without its locking bolt, and would even chamber and fire a round in this state, resulting in immediate separation of barrel and breech-block and likely disintegration of the gun. It was superseded in 1934 by another Nambu design, the Type 94 pistol. The vagaries of Japanese designation are responsible for the apparently huge jump in type number; in fact, in the interim period the designation system had changed. Where the earlier pistol took as its designator the year of the reign of the emperor in which it had been introduced, the Type 94 was so called because it was introduced in the 2594th year of the Japanese calendar. The Type 94 has been described as the worst service pistol ever issued. Among other 'features' the pistol could be fired when the breech was neither closed nor locked, and its sear bar was external to the frame, so that it could be discharged by a sharp tap on the side, 'without recourse to the trigger'.

LIGHT SAVAGES
In the United States Colt early on established something akin to a stranglehold on the market for self-loading pistols, largely through its prompt connection with John Browning. Before World War I, Colt had just one serious challenger, the Savage Arms Co. (not to be confused with the Savage Revolving Fire Arms Co.), which produced a range of self-loading pistols designed by Major Elbert Searle between 1907 and 1928. The Savage was a contender, alongside Colt, DWM and others, at the US Ordnance Department's 1907 trials, where a prototype pistol in .45 calibre was rated highly enough for its manufacturers to be invited to submit 200 examples for extended testing under field conditions. This proved to be impossible as the trial pistol had been virtually handmade; no production line was in existence. As a result, and since DWM pulled out, the field was left to Colt by default – though the Browning design which ultimately became the M1911 pistol would almost certainly have won the competition anyway.

Savage was actually more at home with lighter-calibre pistols, and over the next two decades produced four slightly

Unceto Victoria

Calibre: 7.65mm (.30in)
Weight: .57kg (20oz)
Length: 146mm (5.75in)
Barrel length: 81mm (3.2in)
Effective range: 30m (98ft)
Feed: seven-round magazine
Muzzle velocity: 229mps (750fps)
Country of origin: Spain

different designs in .32 and .380 calibre, all of which were held in high regard for their quality of finish, but with some suspicion of reliability. There was no magazine safety and thus the pistol could be fired if the magazine had been removed – this being a source of concern because the last round could all too easily lie forgotten in the chamber. Dirty pistols, or those with sear springs weakened by prolonged use, were known to fire more than one round at a single pull of the trigger, despite a flat statement to the contrary in contemporary advertising. Perhaps the weakest feature of the Savage pistols, though, lay at their very heart. They were so-called 'delayed blowback' pistols, which relied on the breech-block having to overcome a mechanical disadvantage before it could cycle the action, rather than being positively locked to the barrel. In this case it had to perform a twist through just five degrees against the influence of the torque imparted by the rifling in the barrel; compare this with the 90-degree twist necessary in the Roth-Steyr Model 1907. Small numbers of

pistols in 7.65mm were supplied to the Portuguese Army before and during World War I as the Pistola Savage do Exercite Portugues M/908 and M/915. It is said that some were also supplied to the French Government, but these procurements must be seen in the light of a desperate need for small arms of any type at the time – particularly in the former case, since Portugal had adopted the German Parabellum and now found itself on the other side, allied with Britain and France.

REMINGTON'S MODEL 51
Savage was rather better known for its rifles, and continued to make excellent examples after dropping its range of pistols. So was another of Colt's early competitors, the Remington Arms Co. of Ilion, NY, which had given up the manufacture of revolvers in the face of competition from Hartford and Springfield in 1894. During World War I, Remington had made large numbers of Colt M1911 auto-loaders under government contract, and this inspired it to produce a semi-automatic of its own, to

a design executed by the well respected John D. Pederson. This, too, was a delayed blowback action, but one which, in contrast to the Savage, worked admirably. On discharge the slide and the breech-block recoiled together over a very short distance, the slide being free to continue (and compress the recoil spring, which was mounted concentrically with the barrel) while the breech-block was mechanically detained. When the slide reached the limit of its travel the breech-block was freed to rejoin it, ejecting the spent case and cocking the action in the process. On the return stroke, a fresh round was chambered in the normal way. A magazine safety catch was fitted, and so, too, were a positive manual safety catch and a grip safety. Despite its virtues, the Remington Model 51, as the pistol was known, was never a great commercial success, not least due to it being some 50 per cent more expensive than a Colt in comparable calibre. Before manufacture was discontinued in 1927, a total of some 65,000 examples were produced in both .32 and .380 calibres. There was also an experimental version

Taisho 14

Calibre: 8mm (.31in)
Weight: .91kg (32oz)
Length: 226mm (8.9in)
Barrel length: 121mm (4.75in)
Effective range: 30m (98ft)
Feed: eight-round magazine
Muzzle velocity: 290mps (950mps)
Country of origin: Japan

in .45 calibre, though there must be reservations as to the ability of delayed blowback action to stand up to the internal pressures produced by a round of that power.

THE SEMI-AUTOMATIC FRAME
The third would-be major force, Smith & Wesson, put its first self-loading pistol into production in 1913. It was based (albeit rather loosely) on a very obscure 'vest-pocket' weapon designed by the Belgian Charles Clement, a curious locked-breech pistol which fired 'bottle-necked' 5mm rimless ammunition originating in Spain. The Smith & Wesson .35 Model of 1913, and the .32 calibre pistol which supplanted it nine years later, were simpler than Clement's, being straightforward blowback pistols with fixed barrels and breech-blocks contained within the slides, which remained stationary in operation.

■BELOW: The Remington Model 51, a delayed-blowback pistol. The top of the slide is milled to reduce glare. The Model 51 was a fine weapon, albeit rather expensive.

Neither pistol was much of a commercial success, once again largely through being appreciably more expensive than equivalent models available from Colt and others. Smith & Wesson discontinued its production of self-loading pistols in the mid 1930s, and did not venture into that area of the market again until 1954, finding considerably greater success the second time around.

Smith & Wesson did make one important contribution to the development of the pistol during that period, however, in the shape of a match pistol which was based on the frame of an auto-loader rather than on that of a revolver, as had been the custom. The single-shot Straight Line Model had a singularly unsuitable action for a target pistol, and this was subsequently modified, but the pistol's greatest contribution to the world of match shooting was its introduction of the semi-automatic frame, with its better balance. And it was in the field of match-shooting that the only other American semi-automatic pistol maker of any note was eventually to make its name. High Standard started life, in the mid 1920s,

Savage 1907

Calibre: 8.13mm (.32in)
Weight: .57kg (20oz)
Length: 165mm (6.5in)
Barrel length: 95mm (3.75in)
Effective range: 30m (98ft)
Feed: 10-round magazine
Muzzle velocity: 244mps (800fps)
Country of origin: United States

as a maker of machine tools, many of them destined for the firearms industry. On its accquisition of the Hartford Arms and Equipment Co. in 1932, it gained a range of handguns, and immediately began to increase it with a variety of simple blowback semi-automatic pistols.

Chambered for all three variants of the popular .22 rim-fire cartridge, these were aimed at the serious match pistol shot and at the growing youth market. High Standard also produced a pistol for military training purposes, and the company became better established in the post war period.

The failure of its three main domestic competitors to produce a satisfactory range of self-loaders left Colt in a dominant position in the United States during the 1930s and through World War II, the heyday of the genre. As well as the Browning-designed M1911 and M1911A1, a variety of smaller blowback-action pistols in .32 ACP and .38 ACP calibre were also produced at Hartford, the most popular of which was one of the earliest. And in fact, this Browning design introduced in 1903, with some modifications, remained in production into the 1980s.

The development of the semi-automatic pistol had one undesirable but probably inevitable side effect. There emerged a plethora of similar-looking cartridges with many different charges and loads, most of them introduced as the result of a particular pistols own strengths or weaknesses. Many were produced with no thought to standardisation whatsoever. It is frequently possible for a pistol to chamber and fire an inappropriately loaded round with disastrous results, and one cannot stress too often the essential need to be sure that pistol and ammunition are 100 per cent compatible.

CHAPTER 5

THE HANDGUN AFTER WORLD WAR II

The last 50 years of the twentieth century has been the era of the semi-automatic with regard to handguns. Light alloys and even toughened plastics, allied to precision engineering, have resulted in ever more powerful and reliable semi-automatic handguns being produced in Europe and the United States.

By the start of World War II all the world's major armies except one – that of Britain and most of her Empire – had already made the switch from revolvers to self-loading pistols, and many were using designs first created by John Moses Browning. As a result of all this copying, imitating and plagiarising, no one has even the remotest idea how many 'Browning' pistols have been manufactured during the course of the twentieth century, but the total certainly runs into tens of millions, and may even approach the next order of magnitude. It can only be said for sure that there were more Browning-designed guns in action than those of any other single gunmaker, giving the Mormon from Utah a particular place in military history which is unlikely to be usurped.

In terms of handgun design, the true significance of World War II was that it changed the face of global manufacturing capacity to a far greater degree than even the previous world war had done, and that nowhere was that change more far-reaching than in the field of arms manufacture. In defeat, Germany temporarily disappeared as an arms

■**LEFT: US Navy SEALs practising ship-boarding drills during the 1991 Gulf War against Iraq. The handgun is a Beretta Model 92F, designated Pistol 9mm M9 in US military service.**

manufacturer, exactly as she had done after World War I, and there was to be no easy return. Many pre-war German manufacturers of quite satisfactory pistols disappeared entirely. A few managed to struggle and fight their way back into production and in the process one new force was formed, a situation which was mirrored later in Austria. It is a tribute to the basic excellence of European engineering practice that by the time World War II had been over for 30 years, Austrian and German pistol makers were once again rated among the best in the world, and their products were very highly sought-after indeed. Britain, for all that she was nominally on the winning side, saw that segment of her manufacturing industry disappear almost completely, chiefly as a result of stricter and ever stricter controls on individual gun ownership.

EUROPEAN MANUFACTURERS
Once again, due to the excellence of its products, Fabrique National in Belgium regained a strong position, and so too, if rather later, did Beretta in Gardone; though neither, it must be said, see themselves primarily as manufacturers of pistols. Almost surprisingly Spain, largely unaffected by World War II but in a state of advanced shock from its own revolution and the civil war which followed, continued to produce small

STAR 30M

Calibre: 9mm (.35in)
Weight: .695kg (24.5oz)
Length: 215mm (8.46in)
Barrel length: 122mm (4.8in)
Effective range: 30.48m (100ft)
Feed: 15-round magazine
Muzzle velocity: 335mps (1100fps)
Country of origin: United States

arms in considerable numbers, though unlike the other two major producers, almost exclusively for commercial, rather than military, markets. Its three major producers – Astra, Llama and Star – went from strength to strength, producing new models of revolver and self-loading pistol on a regular basis. By the early 1980s, Star even felt confident enough to enter the competition to supplant the M1911A as the official US Government self-defence weapon.

The handgun industry in France fared rather better. The country was occupied from mid-1940 through to 1944, and the pistol makers of the southwest, MAB and MAP, in Hendaye and Bayonne, and at St Etienne, carried on as before, but under German supervision. Located where they were, they were safe from aerial bombardment, and when the end of the war came they were able to resume production for themselves quickly, finding customers in the revitalised French

armed forces. MAS at St Etienne began work on an M1911A1 derivative which was adopted for service use, in 9mm Parabellum chambering, as the Pistolet Automatique Modèle 1950. The main difference between it and the original Browning design was the retention of the cross-bolt safety which Charles Petter had introduced in the Modèle 1935. This pistol was superseded by a new design from MAB in the same chambering, one of the few not to be a Browning copy.

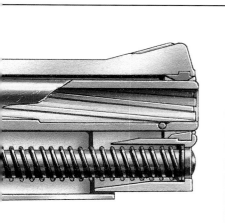

MAB P15

Calibre: 9mm (.35in)
Weight: 1.07kg (37.7oz)
Length: 203mm (8in)
Barrel length: 152mm (6in)
Effective range: 30.48m (100ft)
Feed: 15-round magazine
Muzzle velocity: 335mps (1100fps)
Country of origin: France

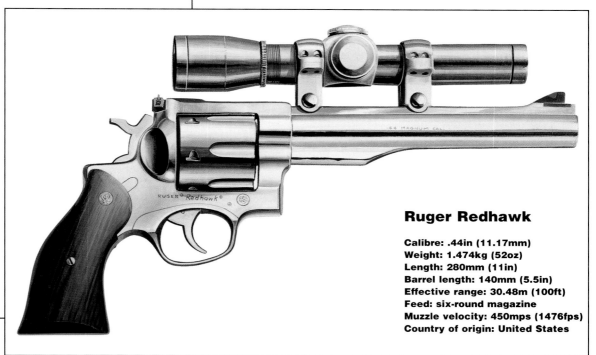

Ruger Redhawk

Calibre: .44in (11.17mm)
Weight: 1.474kg (52oz)
Length: 280mm (11in)
Barrel length: 140mm (5.5in)
Effective range: 30.48m (100ft)
Feed: six-round magazine
Muzzle velocity: 450mps (1476fps)
Country of origin: United States

Instead, locking and unlocking in this pistol was accomplished by rotation of the barrel. The MAB P8 or P15 (the number refers to the capacity of the magazine) was a workmanlike pistol, but was destined never to find wide employment outside France and her states in Africa.

Of all the major producers of individual firearms, only the United States of America remained untouched by the war, her industrial base not just intact but vastly increased in size and capability. One thing remained unchanged: her government's attitude to gun ownership, and that despite a rocketing firearms-related murder rate and even repeated attempts, successful or not, to assassinate national leaders with rifles and handguns. The firearms lobby in the USA proved too powerful to overcome, its efforts secured by the individual's enshrined right to bear arms, contained in the second amendment to the Constitution, which was ratified as long ago as 1791. The industry there went from strength to strength. And in terms of quality of design and execution, its products simply get better and better every year. Firearms manufacturers outside the USA, where the major civilian market lay, were constrained to at least keep abreast of the developments introduced by Colt, Smith & Wesson and others, and that level of competition guaranteed that what might have been a rather stagnant field stayed very active, even – somewhat surprisingly – in the production of new models of revolver.

THE MODERN REVOLVER

If the nineteenth century was the era of the revolver, then the twentieth century can be regarded as being that of the semi-automatic self-loading pistol. By the time World War I engulfed the Western world in 1914, there were very few improvements left to be made to the revolver, which had settled comfortably to being a five- or six-shot pistol. For loading and ejection of spent cartridge cases, the cylinder either swung out on a crane to the left-hand side of the frame, or the pistol broke open about a hinge in front of the trigger guard. The break-open method was perhaps marginally slower in operation than the swing-out cylinder, while its ultimate strength had

always, particularly in the United States, been regarded as somewhat suspect. It struggled on for a while, primarily in Britain, but with the demise of the small arms industry there, soon all but disappeared. Just one model of break-open revolver remained available as the century drew to a close.

From then on, the only real advances came in the materials from which the revolver was fabricated, and in new and more efficient types of ammunition. Stainless steel and light alloys had already been seen, and this move away from 'ordinary' steel became more and more marked as the materials in question got cheaper and more readily available after World War II. Light alloys, in particular, made a considerable difference to the everyday user, cutting the weight of a pocket pistol by as much as 30 per cent – the celebrated Smith & Wesson Model 38 'Chief's Special', for example, weighed 0.57kg (20oz) in steel but only 0.37kg (13oz) as the light alloy 'Airweight', and the price differential was hardly more than five per cent. Often the two materials were combined, with the pistol's frame being in light alloy and the cylinder and barrel in stainless steel,

thus combining the saving in weight of the former with the extra stability, durability and resistance to corrosion of the latter. Some speciality pistols also appeared with frames fabricated from other non-traditional alloys such as manganese-bronze, and even more exotic metals such as titanium and an alloy of beryllium and copper. Nickel plating – long a favourite way of dressing up a pistol – was still widely available, and was joined by a number of other proprietary finishes and coatings, in sophisticated 'space-age' materials such as polytetraflorethylene (PTFE, better known by its trade name, Teflon), though blued steel continued to be the accepted standard finish for most handguns.

NEW HAND GRIPS

The other major change in the appearance of late twentieth century revolvers lay in the shape and constitution of their grips. Finely figured hardwoods, either plain or with more or less complicated chequering, continued to be very popular, particularly for presentation or display pistols. But for everyday working guns, wood gradually gave way to rubber composition and

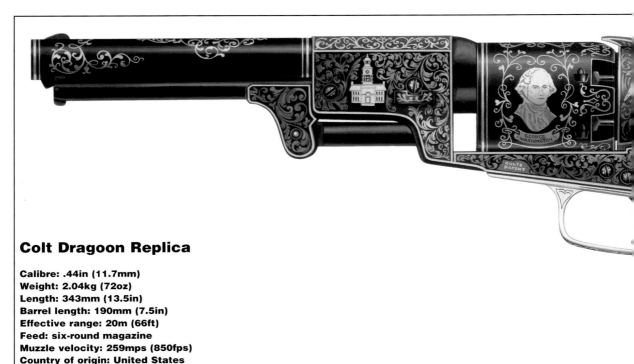

Colt Dragoon Replica

Calibre: .44in (11.7mm)
Weight: 2.04kg (72oz)
Length: 343mm (13.5in)
Barrel length: 190mm (7.5in)
Effective range: 20m (66ft)
Feed: six-round magazine
Muzzle velocity: 259mps (850fps)
Country of origin: United States

polymer grips designed to fit the contours of the hand more closely. They may have appeared a little outlandish, but they were undeniably more efficient and more comfortable, particularly on pistols chambered for heavy, powerful cartridges. The manufacture of such grips became a sub-industry in itself, and many pistol manufacturers routinely offered their customers a choice of independently produced 'custom' grips in place of the ordinary factory variety.

Just as they had all along, new manufacturers continued to spring up, some offering ordinary low-cost weapons but more often producing specialised pistols, finished to a very high standard and with a high price ticket. Not surprisingly, many of the newcomers' products looked like existing designs, especially Colt and Smith & Wesson revolvers. Ventilated barrel ribs and ramp foresights were a prominent feature, for instance, of pistols from as far apart as Brazil, Germany, the Philippines and Spain, and that gave them a strong resemblance to Colt pistols, while other designs showed an affinity for Smith & Wesson, including the adoption of counter-clockwise cylinder rotation. It was

■ABOVE: Hong Kong police officers during an armed robbery call. Their revolvers hold only half the rounds of their semi-automatic counterparts, a grave disadvantage in a firefight.

logical to find that latter arrangement adopted by one of the new American pistol makers – Wesson Firearms – set up by the great-grandson of one of Smith & Wesson's founders after the company's takeover by a British engineering group. Wesson originally turned to the manufacture of machine tools, but it seems that pistols were, metaphorically, in his blood. He began manufacturing a range of heavy frame revolvers chambered for a variety of calibres from .22 LR to .44 Magnum, a common feature being the easy interchangeability of their barrels and grips. As well as supplying 'simple' guns, Wesson offered a 'Pistol Pac' which comprised a complete pistol plus two extra barrels of different lengths and a pair of unfinished grips with their internal machining completed. Depending upon

the model, barrel lengths varied between 64mm (2.5in) and 254mm (10in), and longer versions were available to order.

RUGER'S HAWKS

Sturm, Ruger is probably the best known of the twentieth century additions to the ranks of American pistol makers, and in the early 1970s augmented its range of single-action revolvers with a double-action model chambered for both the rimmed Magnum cartridges and the rimless 9mm Parabellum and .45 ACP rounds, the latter being loaded in half-

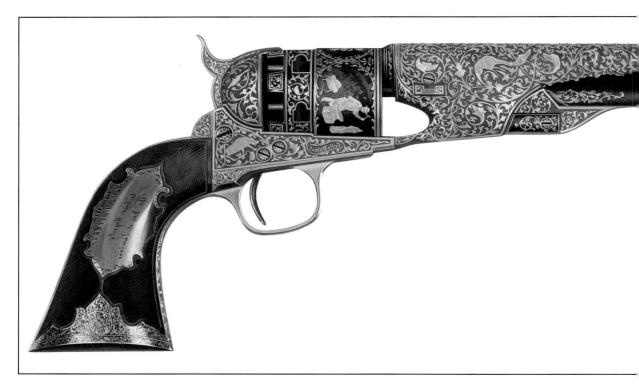

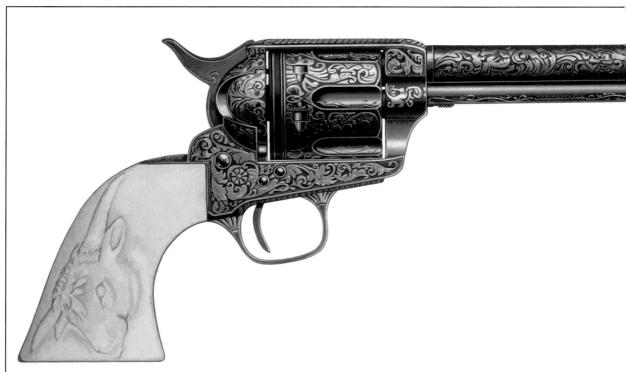

Colt Navy Replica

Calibre: .36in (9.14mm)
Weight: 1.1kg (39oz)
Length: 328mm (12.9in)
Barrel length: 190mm (7.5in)
Effective range: 20m (66ft)
Feed: six-round magazine
Muzzle velocity: 213mps (700fps)
Country of origin: United States

Colt Single Action Army Replica

Calibre: .44in (11.17mm)
Weight: 1.08kg (38oz)
Length: 330mm (13in)
Barrel length: 190mm (7.5in)
Effective range: 20m (66ft)
Feed: six-round magazine
Muzzle velocity: 198mps (650fps)
Country of origin: United States

moon clips. Unlike most contemporary revolvers, the new Rugers had true solid frames, with no side plates. The range was extended by a series of pistols with a new action, and known as the GP-100. Available in a variety of different calibres and barrel lengths, they were later augmented by the lightweight SP-101 series, using the same principles in a much smaller frame. A heavier double-action revolver, the Redhawk/Super Redhawk was added too, chambered only for Magnum ammunition.

BOLT-ACTION PISTOLS

One area of the handgun market where demand grew enormously during the last quarter of the twentieth century was that of replica revolvers. Almost all of these were exact copies of early Colt models, though there were some Remington copies to be found, too. Virtually all the important 'black powder' front-loading Colt pistols were available in their original calibres. Many of the specialist companies manufacturing replica muzzle-loaders also manufactured replicas of early metallic cartridge pistols, as did the original manufacturers. Once again the most popular was a Colt, this time the Single Action Army Model of 1873. New copies of this were available from at least half a dozen gunmakers as well as from Colt itself, while Remington's Model 1875 also came in for its share of attention.

Perhaps more interesting from a purely technical point of view was a range of modern single-action revolvers based very firmly on 'traditional' designs but manufactured from 'new' materials; chrome-molybdenum and high-tensile manganese-bronze were particular favourites for the frame, as was stainless steel. Sturm, Ruger's pistols were the best known in the field, but other companies, like Freedom Arms, also produced interesting revolvers.

Single-shot and multi-barrelled pistols came in for attention from the copyists, too, the most common being more or less exact replicas of the Remington Double Derringer of 1865, using the widest imaginable range of ammunition types from .22 to .45, including the Magnum chamberings. Perhaps the best known producer was the American Derringer Corporation, which not only manufactured replicas but also produced new miniature pocket pistols. They also produced a range of what appeared to be 'vest-pocket' self-loading pistols, but which were in fact either multi-barrelled or manually loaded

from a magazine in the grip by a back-and-fore motion of a slide surrounding the barrel. Self-loaders without the self-loading mechanism, one might say, and a straightforward and handy procedure it was.

Heavier single-shot pistols, such as the Remington Rolling Block, were also available in replica form, but most such guns were new designs. They were often chambered for rounds which are usually associated with long arms (such as the Remington .223) and used actions derived from rifles, too – bolt actions were the most common. Frequently these pistols, which were intended for use by hunters of small game and vermin had barrels much longer than those commonly found in conventional pistols. Remington's four such handguns, for example, had barrels of 368mm (14.5in) and longer. There were multi-barrelled handguns, the most unusual of them being Springfield Armory's M6 pistol, with one barrel in .22 LR calibre and another, below it, in .45 calibre, chambered for the rimmed Colt round, but also capable of taking a .410 shot shell. Such combination guns were well known as long arms but less often encountered as handguns, probably because their real application was minimal and even their novelty value limited. The oddest of them all is a Russian four-barrel pistol in 4.5mm calibre, designed to be used underwater.

MATCH PISTOLS

Handgun hunting is a specialist activity, and so rather more single-shot pistols were produced for match shooting, most of them in .22 LR calibre, but some in heavier chamberings. They varied in character from straightforward-looking pistols to objects which are barely recognisable as handguns at all, with grips (if such a mundane term can be applied to them) which were almost works of art, individually sculpted from single pieces of wood to fit the shooter's hand exactly. These pistols had super-sensitive actions in which a small plunger sometimes replaced the traditional trigger bar and in some cases actuated the pistol electronically rather than by a conventional mechanical linkage. The most exotic – even outlandish – handguns were for use in 'free pistol' competitions, and were single-shot only, often using the Martini action which was also found in match rifles. The freedom in question was from regulations designed to equalise the performance of

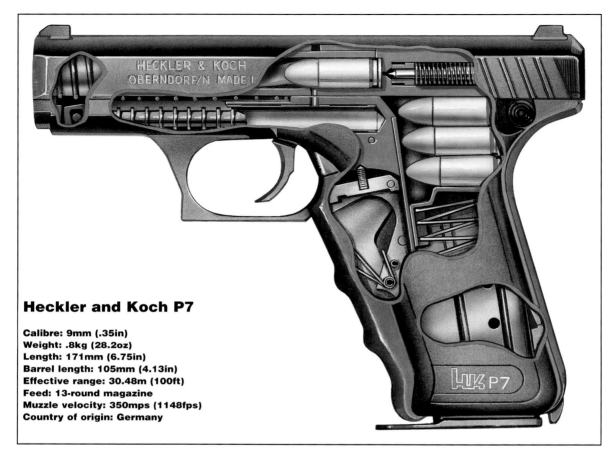

Heckler and Koch P7

Calibre: 9mm (.35in)
Weight: .8kg (28.2oz)
Length: 171mm (6.75in)
Barrel length: 105mm (4.13in)
Effective range: 30.48m (100ft)
Feed: 13-round magazine
Muzzle velocity: 350mps (1148fps)
Country of origin: Germany

different types of pistol, and which covered factors such as barrel length, sight radius and trigger pull. Others, only slightly more ordinary in appearance, were self-loaders, used for standard and rapid-fire matches, and there were even some match revolvers.

Perhaps the best known of the free pistols were those made by Walther, Hammerli and Pardini/Fiocchi. The range of pistols designed by Mikhail Margolin and manufactured at the Tula Arsenal in the ex-Soviet Union also deserves mention, though Margolin's chief claim to fame was probably the celebrated 'upside-down' rapid-fire pistol he produced for the USSR's Olympic team for the 1956 Melbourne Games. It swept the board, but was ruled out for competitive use by the International Shooting Union (Union International de Tir) in 1958, and then disappeared from match events.

There were also pistols specially designed and produced for competitive shooting in disciplines other than free

pistol, and like their more esoteric counterparts tended to betray their purpose by their appearance. The French Unique, produced in Hendaye by MAP, was one such and is the only such pistol produced in France. The German Walther, the Italian FAS and Pardini-Fiocchi and the Swiss Hammerli designs were the other international favourites. In the USA, High Standard was for years a strong contender, but went out of business after 50 years in 1984, while Sturm, Ruger, which started out manufacturing .22 calibre semi-automatic pistols but soon switched its emphasis to revolvers, continued to produce a range of conventional self-loading target pistols.

TREND SETTERS

Purpose-built match pistols are of little more than passing interest to the majority of handgun owners, but they can be compared to single-seater racing cars. Most people who depend on their own automobiles day in and day out have no

interest in racing cars whatsoever, yet many of the products and features which make their cars safer, more economical and more efficient are developed, tried and tested in and for them. To continue the analogy, racing saloon cars and rally cars can be likened to the handguns produced for other classes of competitive target shooting: just as they look much more like the car one drives to work, give or take the odd body panel or aerodynamic spoiler, so these handguns are often much closer to normal pistols, their sometimes rather exaggerated grips notwithstanding. They are usually 'tuned' versions of those sold for general use as self-defence and combat arms, and just as success in rallying and saloon car racing is used to promote road-going models, so successful competitive shooting is used to persuade everyday users of a particular pistol's merits. Thus Beretta, Colt, Glock, Heckler and Koch, Llama, SIG-Sauer, Smith & Wesson, Walther and the other important mass-market pistol makers all produced and promoted selected versions of their standard semi-automatic pistols for use in competition. Most revolvers used in competitive shooting were owner-tuned or customised versions of those used for general purposes, though ERMA produced match revolvers in .22 LR and .32 S&W Long chamberings. They also made a series of blowback-operated self-loading pistols, some of them similar in appearance to the P08 Luger/Parabellum for which the company had long produced .22 LR conversion kits. Compared to the market for general-purpose handguns, the number of specialist target pistols sold each year is minimal – tens of thousands, perhaps, compared with millions.

THE DECLINE OF THE REVOLVER

Military consideration alone meant that by the time the twentieth century was two-thirds through, self-loading pistols far outsold revolvers, and that, in turn, meant that most pistol manufacturers saw self-loading semi-automatic pistols as their main area of development. By then, there were very few companies

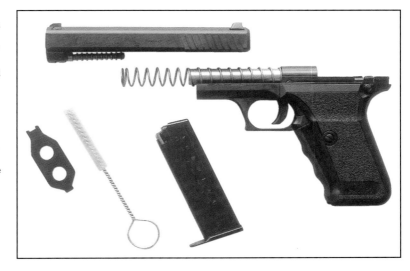

making only revolvers, and most of those, like Uberti in Italy, which ranks among the best, concentrated on replicas.

The majority of newcomers to the small arms industry, post-World War II,

■ABOVE: The 9mm Heckler and Koch P7. It has a unique firing mechanism: a moving grip in the front strap of the butt. As the pistol is raised the hand squeezes the grip to cock the piece.

Heckler and Koch P9

Calibre: 9mm (.35in)
Weight: .8kg (28.2oz)
Length: 192mm (7.5in)
Barrel length: 101mm (3.98in)
Effective range: 30.48m (100ft)
Feed: nine-round magazine
Muzzle velocity: 350mps (1148fps)
Country of origin: Germany

SIG P225

Calibre: 9mm (.35in)
Weight: .75kg (26.5oz)
Length: 180mm (7.08in)
Barrel length: 98mm (3.85in)
Effective range: 30.48m (100ft)
Feed: eight-round magazine
Muzzle velocity: 345mps (1051fps)
Country of origin: Germany

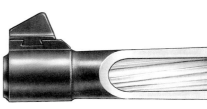

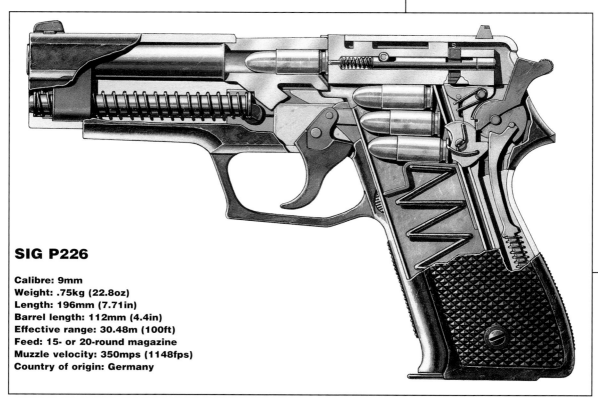

SIG P226

Calibre: 9mm
Weight: .75kg (22.8oz)
Length: 196mm (7.71in)
Barrel length: 112mm (4.4in)
Effective range: 30.48m (100ft)
Feed: 15- or 20-round magazine
Muzzle velocity: 350mps (1148fps)
Country of origin: Germany

certainly tended to concentrate on the more lucrative market for semi-automatics. The most important of them was probably Heckler and Koch. The new company's first production pistol was the

HK4, which was unusual in being delivered in kit form, with four interchangeable barrels and four different magazines, and was thus able to accommodate four quite different

cartridges: .22 LR rim-fire, 9mm Short/.380 ACP, 7.65mm/.32 ACP and 6.35mm/.25 ACP. The frame of this blowback double-action pistol was made from die-cast aluminium, while the slide,

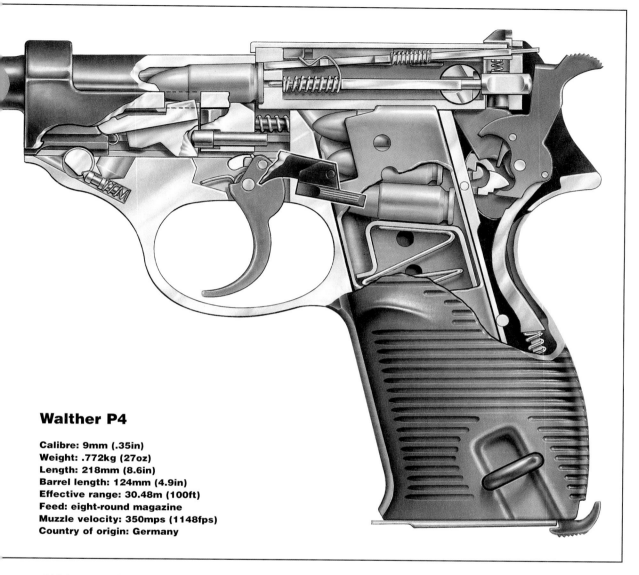

Walther P4

Calibre: 9mm (.35in)
Weight: .772kg (27oz)
Length: 218mm (8.6in)
Barrel length: 124mm (4.9in)
Effective range: 30.48m (100ft)
Feed: eight-round magazine
Muzzle velocity: 350mps (1148fps)
Country of origin: Germany

which incorporated the breech-block, was machined from a steel forging with inserts precision-welded into place. A replaceable plastic pad did duty as a recoil buffer, the plate on which it acted being reversed in order to convert the pistol from centre-fire to rim-fire, that action realigning the firing pin. One of the pistol's strongest features was its safety device which, like that of the Mauser HSc, took the firing pin out of alignment with the face of the hammer, making an accidental discharge virtually impossible.

In the late 1960s, Heckler and Koch developed a service rifle, the Gewehr 3

(G3), from a Spanish design which was itself a development of a concept which originated at Mauserwerke in Oberndorf in the latter part of World War II and resulted in the SturmGewehr 45 (StG45).

HECKLER'S BLOWBACK SYSTEM

The operating principle of this family of assault rifles is unusual. It is a modification of the delayed blowback action more commonly found in submachine guns and in semi-automatic pistols, the modification in question enabling it to handle much more powerful ammunition. The delay in the

rifle's action is produced by projecting rollers on the bolt which engage in recesses in the receiver; a further innovation was the introduction of flutings in the wall of the chamber (a device first employed to solve extraction problems in medium machine guns prior to World War I). Heckler and Koch's G3 rifle proved an almost phenomenal success for the still-young company, and was eventually to be adopted by some 25 countries worldwide in 7.62mm NATO chambering; a modified version, the HK33, chambered for the 'new' 5.56mm cartridge met with less success.

The same system of roller-delayed blowback was used in a 1970s Heckler and Koch pistol in 9mm Parabellum calibre – the Herbert Midel-designed P9/P9S. Additionally, the P9 had a form of polygonal rifling, as originally introduced for the 1888 British Lee-Metford rifle, while it incorporated the side-mounted cocking/de-cocking lever first seen on the pre-war Sauer 38H. The pistol's 'S' variant, which was also manufactured, at least in trial quantities, for the .45 ACP cartridge, appeared with a recurved leading edge to its trigger guard to make a two-handed grip somewhat more comfortable, a feature that was later to appear on other pistols.

THE P7

Firearms specialists in the development department at Heckler and Koch realised that the cocking/de-cocking lever, suitably modified, could be made into a very positive safety feature indeed, and began the development programme that led to the P9's successor, the P7 family of pistols. Now the de-cocking lever was replaced by an extension to the front of the grip, running down its full length and pivoted at the base, in the manner of the grip safety found in many pistols. When the gun was gripped in the hand, the cocking lever was naturally squeezed back into the grip proper, and acted on the hammer to bring the action to the cocked position. While the hand's grip remained unrelaxed, the pistol could be operated in the normal manner, but once the gun was laid down or returned to the pocket or holster, the lever sprang back, automatically de-cocking the action. In the P7 series, the earlier (and rather cumbersome, in a pistol at least) bolt rollers gave way to a gas buffering system to delay the blowback action, which made the pistol smaller and lighter while actually reducing recoil. By the mid-1990s the P7 had become available in a wider variety of calibres, .22 LR, .380 – as the P7K3 (which featured a modified buffering system using an oil-filled shock absorber), in 9mm Parabellum as the P7M8, with an increased-magazine capacity as P7M13, and in the new 10mm/.40 S&W calibre as the P7M10.

THE PLASTIC VP70

Heckler and Koch also developed a family of submachine guns for police and military use, incorporating the same roller-locking system as is found in its rifles. The first and most successful of these, the MP5, chambered, like most of its kind, for 9mm Parabellum rounds, is available in semi-automatic, as well as full-automatic form. It came to be as widely popular as the G3 family of rifles, and was effectively the precursor of a series of unusual high-capacity semi-automatic handguns. These had forward-placed magazines of 15- or 30-round capacity and looked like the submachine guns which inspired them. The SP89 pistol was offered with fitted laser sights as an option – a device which, when correctly aligned, places a spot of bright red light on the point of aim, making it very difficult to miss the target.

Walther P5

Calibre: 9mm (.35in) or 7.65mm (.30in)
Weight: .795g (28.04oz)
Length: 180mm (7.08in)
Barrel length: 90mm (3.54in)
Effective range: 30.48m (100ft)
Feed: eight-round magazine
Muzzle velocity: 350mps (1148fps)
Country of origin: Germany

Glock 17

Calibre: 9mm (.354in)
Weight: .65kg (22.9oz)
Length: 188mm (7.5in)
Barrel length: 114mm (4.49in)
Effective range: 30.48m (100ft)
Feed: seventeen-round magazine
Muzzle velocity: 350mps (1148fps)
Country of origin: Austria

As well as the MP5, Heckler and Koch also came up with a rather different rapid-fire weapon. The VP 70 was a self-loading pistol with the capability to fire three-round bursts with but one pull of the trigger, a feature it shared with the American M16 assault rifle, among others. It was the first pistol to make extensive use of high-impact plastics in its construction, and could be fitted with a plastic shoulder stock which doubled as a holster, just as had the carbine stocks for earlier semi-automatics, but this time with a difference. When the stock was in position, a connection to the pistol's lockwork allowed the firer to select (by means of a lever on the stock itself) between either single round or three-round burst fire. This effectively removed the overwhelming criticism of the full-automatic pistol by limiting the rounds fired in a burst to a number which could be expected to be on or near the target, and stopped the action before muzzle climb set in too far. A similar method was adopted by Beretta later for the Model 93R pistol, and was tried out by Glock in its Glock 18. Needless to say, none of these pistols became available to the casual purchaser. The VP 70 also

incorporated a particularly effective safety device – the striker between the hammer and the round was only brought back to the full-cock position by direct trigger action, with the useful and desirable secondary effect of introducing a distinct first pressure into the trigger pull while removing the heavy pull needed to cock the entire action.

SIG'S MASTERPIECES
Heckler and Koch's is not the only success story to come out of post-World War II Germany. Of the longer-established pistol makers, both Walther and Sauer re-established themselves successfully, the latter in effective partnership with the Swiss arms maker, SIG. SIG had manufactured a 'vest-pocket' semi-automatic in 6.35mm calibre which was better known as the Lignose Einhand (one-handed) model. It was designed by an Austrian named Witwold Chylewski and had been originally produced by Thomas Bergmann. The company's first combat-calibre pistol was a modification of the French Modèle 1935, designed by Charles Petter. A subsequent variant, the SP 47/8, in 7.65mm and 9mm Parabellum calibre,

was eventually adopted by the Swiss Army to replace its ageing Parabellum pistols. In fact, the Petter system was little more than a modification of Browning's locked-breech design, with the locking lugs on the barrel replaced by a simple step which engaged in a recess in the slide. The SP 47/8 was renamed the SIG P210 along the way, and began to acquire an enviable reputation for quality and reliability which subsequent models have only enhanced. It is perhaps worth noting in passing that by the mid-1990s the then-current P210 model, the P216 variant, cost $2500; comparable models from Beretta, Colt and Smith & Wesson were available for around $650, as indeed were the more mundane SIG-Sauer models. In order to circumvent Swiss Government regulations concerning the export of certain types of firearm, SIG formed an alliance with Sauer which, while it stopped short of being an actual merger, linked the two companies inextricably, and their products became known as SIG-Sauer. New models – the P220 and P230 – soon appeared. The former was a lower-cost, double-action combat-calibre (9mm, .38 Super, .45 ACP, and .40 S&W in a later variant) pistol which featured the cocking/de-cocking lever J.P. Sauer had originally devised for its Model 38H pistol. With an aluminium alloy frame, a stamped and welded steel slide, and with its breech-block pinned into place, the P220 was very much a poor relation to the P210, but still managed to find a niche for itself. Its acceptance was increased by the addition of lightweight models, while criticism of its low-capacity eight-round magazine was answered by the P226, P228 and P229 variants, which hold 15, 13 and 12 rounds respectively (the first two in 9mm, the latter in .40 S&W). The smaller, lighter P230, in .32 and .380 ACP chambering, was designed as a self-defence weapon for the civilian market to compete with pistols such as the Walther PPK and the Mauser HSc.

WALTHER'S MATCH PISTOLS

Walther had more difficulty than other German industrial concerns in restarting after World War II due to its original location at Zella, near Suhl, being in what became the German Democratic Republic. Fritz Walther, by then heading the company, fled to the west and started again in the village of Neiderstotzingen in Wurtemburg, manufacturing calculating machines (a Walther product line since the 1920s) to start with. In 1950 the company turned to the production of small arms, starting with an air rifle, in a second factory located in a disused cavalry barracks in Ulm. Between 1945 and the early 1950s, much of Walther's meagre income came from licensing agreements with the Swiss firm Hammerli, to produce the Olympia model target pistol, and with a French company known as Manurhin (Manufacture de Machines du Haut-Rhin) to produce the PP and PPK models.

Eventually, Walther restarted production of the P38. It then designed and produced a new rapid-fire match pistol, the Olympia Schnellfeuer Pistole, and later the Gebrauchs and Standard Pistole. New variants of the PP and PPK followed, as did a composite, the PPK/S, with the slide and barrel of the PPK on the frame of the PP. So did an all-new pocket pistol, the .22 LR calibre Taschenpistole or TPH. At the other end of the scale, the P38 was revamped and produced as the more compact P38K, and a new pistol built around the same action, the P5, was produced with police forces in mind. A wholly new 9mm Parabellum pistol, the P88, this time

using a locking system much more akin to the Browning method, and with more modern lines and a 15-round capacity magazine, was introduced to compete with other combat-calibre self-loading pistols. It found few takers at a price not much cheaper than the SIG-Sauer P210. The Walther design improved on that of the SIG-Sauer in the provision of an ambidextrous cocking/de-cocking lever and magazine release.

THE NEW STEYRS

Not far away, across the border in Austria, was where the world's first-ever self-loading pistol was produced in 1892. The old Steyr-Werke AG, reconstituted as Steyr Daimler Puch AG in 1935 (and eventually as Steyr Mannlicher GmbH in 1986) was also to return to making small arms after World War II. Steyr's first successful new design was the Model GB 80, which was designed and taken to prototype production in the United States as the Rogak P18. The GB 80 was similar to Heckler and Koch's P7 pistols in that it used 'waste' propellant gas to retard its blowback action, but it was essentially rather more sophisticated, with gas seals at the muzzle and halfway down the barrel, the port which provided the retardant gas being located between the two. The great advantage of this type of action is the savings in size and mass it permits, principally in the moving parts but also in the constitution of the frame itself. Like most modern combat pistols, the GB 80 was chambered for the 9mm Parabellum round, and its magazine held no less than 18 rounds in two full rows. Even so, the gun was still comfortable in the hand thanks to the use of sheet metal stampings for the frame and thin, high-impact plastic grips, something quite unthinkable in a pistol of similar power employing a mechanical locking system.

GLOCK'S LIGHTWEIGHTS

The other Austrian pistol manufacturer of note also produced lightweight weapons by revolutionary means. Glock GmbH came into being a little later than Heckler and Koch, but with no original intention to produce firearms; instead, Gaston Glock set out to produce metal and plastic furniture. It was only after

■RIGHT: A stripped Browning High Power. The parts are, from top to bottom, the slide, breech-block, recoil spring and main frame. The slide locking lever is to the left of the spring.

securing a government contract for the supply of bayonets and general-purpose knives for the Austrian Army that his thoughts turned to weapons at all. Glock produced his first pistol in 1980, and his use of plastic mouldings for the frame and magazine of the handgun he called the Glock 17 set the arms world on its ears. This new 'plastic' pistol stirred the imagination, however, not least of numerous thriller writers who could not resist weaving improbable plots around the existence of a handgun which was invisible to the sort of metal detectors used at security checks. In fact, that was never Glock's intention, and was certainly not the case; the pistol's slide, barrel assembly, lockwork and recoil spring alone, being of high-grade steel, were more than sufficient to set off even a relatively insensitive alarm system, to say nothing of the 17 rounds of 9mm Parabellum ammunition contained in the magazine! The other main technical innovation in this otherwise standard locked-breech pistol was its employment of a novel polygonal rifling system, this

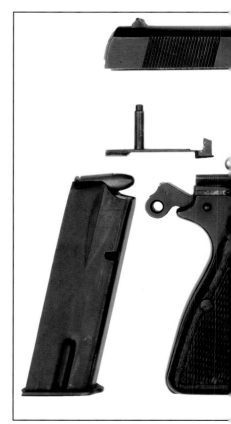

Glock 18

Calibre: 10mm (.39in)
Weight: .75kg (26.5oz)
Length: 210mm (8.25in)
Barrel length: 114mm (4.5in)
Effective range: 30.48m (100ft)
Feed: 19-round magazine
Muzzle velocity: 375mps (1230fps)
Country of origin: Austria

Beretta Model 81

Calibre: 7.65mm (.30in)
Weight: .67kg (23.6oz)
Length: 172mm (6.77in)
Barrel length: 97mm (3.82in)
Effective range: 30.48m (100ft)
Feed: 12-round magazine
Muzzle velocity: 300mps (984fps)
Country of origin: Italy

time a modified form of Whitworth's hexagonal system, rather than Metford's. The firing pin was also held off after the cocking process has been completed, a feature which permitted the safety catch to physically intervene between it and the round in the chamber. The pin is fully retracted only by the action of pulling the trigger, which has a desirable secondary attribute: the pull on the trigger is exactly the same for each round fired. The excellent Glock 17 was adopted with some alacrity by the Austrian armed forces; those of Norway soon followed, and the pistol obtained the coveted NATO approval in 1984. Standard and compact versions chambered for alternatives to the 9mm round were also produced, in .40 S&W, 10mm and .45 ACP calibres. The essential ordinariness of the Glock range of pistols is betrayed by just one thing: their price (fine engineering does not come cheap). They sell for no more than comparable products from Beretta, Colt or Smith & Wesson, still the most reliable standards by which to judge other mass-market pistols.

Beretta entered World War II quite literally fooling around with a full-automatic version of a pistol which had been designed as far back as 1915, and successively – and successfully – modified thereafter. With the war over, and its enterprise in ruins, the company took time to recover. But within six years it had produced a prototype of a new pistol in 9mm calibre, first chambered for the Short cartridge, rather than for the 1910 Glisenti the company had previously employed, and later for the Parabellum cartridge. Thus Beretta brought itself into line with most of the rest of Europe.

BERETTA'S COMEBACK
The new pistol, known as the Modello 1951, was to have had a light alloy frame, but at prototype stage it became clear that the resulting weapon was unpleasant to fire and inaccurate to boot. It was re-engineered and appeared as an all-steel pistol in 1957. Its action had a certain resemblance to that of the Walther P38, locking being achieved by a vertical wedge and a pair of lugs on the

barrel which engaged in recesses in the slide. They were unlocked on their rearward journey by the wedge being tripped loose when it encountered a shoulder on the frame. Updated versions of the old blowback-action Modello 1935 became known as the Series 70 pistols, and were available as both small-calibre pocket pistols and as match pistols, with longer barrels and improved sights, a trend continued by the Model 80, designed for rapid-fire courses and available in .22 Short chambering only. In 1977 the Series 70, which was now beginning to look a little long in the tooth, was supplanted by a range of double-action blowback pistols initially in .32 and .380 ACP chamberings, characterised by their much greater magazine capacity and simplified construction, and these were joined in 1982 by an improved version of the Modello 1951, the Model 92. By now, with improvements in methods and technology, the original plan to furnish the combat-calibre pistol with a light alloy frame had become realistic. The weight-saving thus achieved was promptly applied to increasing the capacity of the magazine from eight to fifteen rounds, but otherwise the pistol was basically unchanged. In its final form, as the Model 92F, it weighed 0.95kg (34oz), slightly more than the contemporary version of the Browning High Power but less than the Colt M1911A1. The Model 92 was to announce its capabilities in spectacular style, when it won the bitterly contested mid-1980s competition to replace the M1911A1 as the standard US Government and military side-arm. To give some idea of the scope of Beretta's coup, and of rival US manufacturers' chagrin at seeing such a prestigious order leave the country, one only need look at the US Government's requirement for handguns: the initial order for the new pistol (designated the M9) totalled 315,930 units, to be delivered over a five-year period starting in January 1987.

■RIGHT: A US Marine fires his Beretta 92F during the 1991 Gulf War. This model has been replaced in US military service by the Model 92FS, with a slightly extended hammer axis pin.

As early as 1936, Beretta set up a subsidiary company in Brazil to produce revolvers under the name Taurus. It achieved considerable success, not just locally, but in North America, too, and by the 1980s had become more and more openly acknowledged as Beretta's US

subsidiary, with a large production plant, even though Beretta also had one of its own, where the Model 92s destined for the US armed forces were first assembled and then produced. Taurus still continued to manufacture revolvers, but also produced a range of self-loading pistols

Beretta Model 92SB

Calibre: 9mm (.35in)
Weight: .99kg (35oz)
Length: 216mm (8.5in)
Barrel length: 127mm (5in)
Effective range: 30.48m (100ft)
Feed: 13-round magazine
Muzzle velocity: 335mps (1100fps)
Country of origin: Italy

which were clearly Beretta-designed, among them the PT 58 in .380 ACP, the PT 92 and PT 99 in 9mm Parabellum and the PT 100 in .40 S&W.

FIERCE COMPETITION

As well as Beretta, some of the other notable European manufacturers competed for the US Government side-arm contract. Heckler and Koch submitted both the P9S and the VP 90; SIG-Sauer entered – and was almost successful with – the P226; Star submitted its Model 28; and FN put up the venerable but still enormously popular Browning High Power. Local contenders included a stainless-steel pistol from Colt and a double-action Browning, which was a considerable improvement on the original design. It had a cocking/de-cocking handle, and could be switched over to single action mode; it was actually the SIG-Sauer P220 by a different name. Also competing was the Smith & Wesson 459, a 14-shot capacity version of the Model 59 which

had appeared in 1974 and had been the company's first serious entrant into the combat-calibre self-loading pistol market. The Ruger P 85, which many people considered to be a superior pistol, was not entered for the trials after its manufacturers concluded that its development programme was not sufficiently far advanced.

SMITH & WESSON'S PISTOLS

The Smith & Wesson 459 was only one of what, after only 40 years in the semi-automatic pistol business, had become a massive range of pistols from the company which became the most significant manufacturer of handguns in the United States and thus, probably, in the world. As well as the wide variety of revolvers, there is a bewildering range of semi-automatic pistols available from Springfield. The smallest is the diminutive Model 2214, an eight-shot .22 LR pistol with an aluminium frame and steel slide, just 150mm (6in) long overall and weighing 0.5kg (18oz). There is then

Smith & Wesson 469

Calibre: 9mm
Weight: .735kg (26oz)
Length: 175mm (6.89in)
Barrel length: 89mm (3.5in)
Effective range: 30.48m (100ft)
Feed: 12-round magazine
Muzzle velocity: 350mps (1066fps)
Country of origin: United States

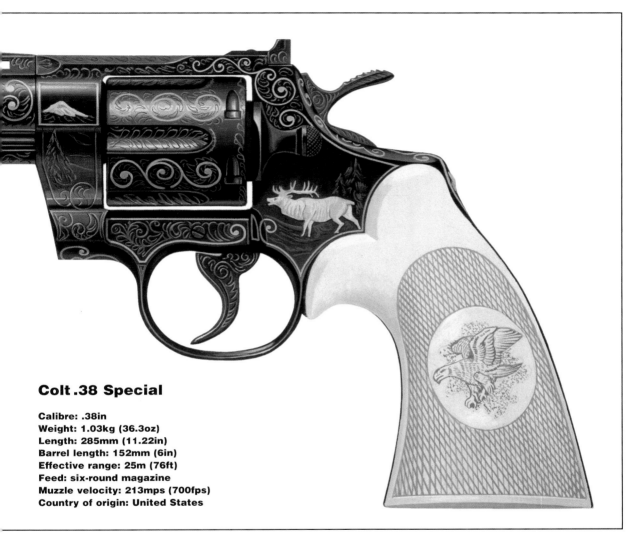

Colt .38 Special

Calibre: .38in
Weight: 1.03kg (36.3oz)
Length: 285mm (11.22in)
Barrel length: 152mm (6in)
Effective range: 25m (76ft)
Feed: six-round magazine
Muzzle velocity: 213mps (700fps)
Country of origin: United States

a wide variety of 9mm, .40 S&W and 10mm calibre pistols up to the Model 4506, in .45 ACP calibre. The Model 4506 alone has a dozen slightly different variants, with basic construction material, barrel length, magazine capacity and the choice of single- or double-action being the most significant differences between them. Smith & Wesson also produced self-loading target pistols in .22 LR and .38 Special calibre.

THE 2000 DA

Smith & Wesson's biggest rivals, Colt, which enjoyed dominance over the US semi-automatic pistol market for many years, reached its 150th birthday with very few models in production. But over the 15 years which followed, Colt steadily produced new pistols in both combat and self-defence calibres. They even began manufacturing one with a polymer frame, the All American Model 2000 DA, in 9mm calibre, which, with a 15-round magazine, still weighed less than 0.85kg (30oz). Most other models were produced in 9mm calibre, too, but many were available in .38 Super, .380, 10mm and .45 ACP.

Their position in the market and their reputation notwithstanding, both the giant US pistol-makers had to withstand great competition from small companies, usually with just one or two models in production. They split into three main groups: those producing cheap pistols for self-defence; those producing expensive,

hand-finished versions of classic designs; and those which produced odd-looking pistols of their own conception. These often had very large-capacity magazines, such as the Calico Model M-950 9mm pistol with a choice of 50- or 100-round helical-feed magazines. Many of the pistols which fell into this latter category had an unmistakable resemblance to a submachine gun, and there can be little doubt that they were designed that way primarily to frighten or impress, whatever claims their manufacturers might make. They only qualify as pistols because there is no more appropriate classification to put them in; most had a below-barrel foregrip (the Uzi pistol was an exception) and are gripped two-handed.

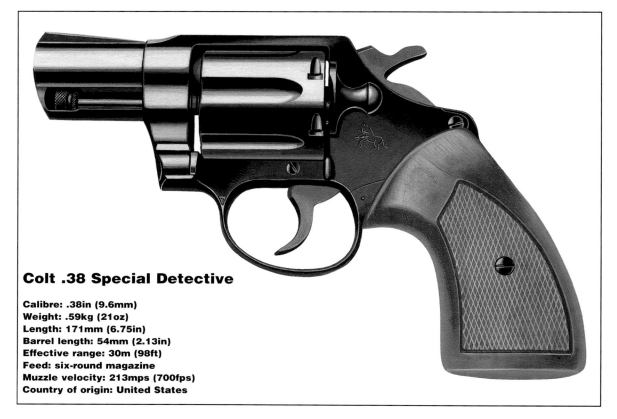

Colt .38 Special Detective

Calibre: .38in (9.6mm)
Weight: .59kg (21oz)
Length: 171mm (6.75in)
Barrel length: 54mm (2.13in)
Effective range: 30m (98ft)
Feed: six-round magazine
Muzzle velocity: 213mps (700fps)
Country of origin: United States

The domestic US pistol makers also faced stiff competition from foreign newcomers, particularly from the Far East. During the 1980s, self-loading pistols were manufactured in Korea, the Philippines and the Republic of China, where a copy of the 1930s-vintage Soviet Tokarev, re-chambered for the 9mm Parabellum round, was manufactured by Norinco. The collapse of communism in Eastern Europe and the Soviet Union brought a number of newcomers to the international small arms market, mainly in the form of the Czech CZ range and copies of Czech originals manufactured in Yugoslavia in 9mm calibre. These arms were generally cheap and surprisingly well made, as was the Russian Pistolet Makarova. The Makarov, as it is known in the West, was a design which owes a great deal to the Walther PP, but uses its own idiosyncratic 9mm Russian chambering. Other Russian pistols that began to appear include the Gyurza, also in 9mm but with a more powerful cartridge designed to pierce most types of body armour at ranges of up to 50m (164ft), and the diminutive 5.45mm PSM

pocket pistol. One thing which all the contenders for the US Government contract had in common was their calibre: they were all chambered for the 9mm Parabellum round in its heavier-projectile guise as the NATO ball cartridge, which the US military designates as the M882. However, many experts on both sides of the industrial fence had already begun to question the efficacy of that round for military purposes. More and more targets appeared to be protected by new light-weight forms of body armour which the 9mm projectile could not penetrate.

FN'S FIVE-SEVEN
One manufacturer with a respectable track-record in introducing new types of ammunition to solve fresh tactical problems was Fabrique National. FN had both brought in the 7.62mm rifle round, and had later took over development of the military 5.56mm round from the commercial .223 cartridge and made it work properly. The company soon announced that it was to give up Georg Luger's hasty expedient in favour of a

much smaller 5.7mm calibre, known as the SS190 round, and would produce both a submachine gun, the P90, and a pistol, the rather awkwardly-named Five-seveN, to accommodate it. The P90 submachine gun was first shown to the public in 1990, and went into limited production two or three years later; the new pistol was unveiled in 1996 and scheduled for production before the end of the century. The new round they were both designed to fire showed particularly good penetrating power out to 200m (650ft), where it was able to perforate 48 layers of Kevlar and all other high-mobility body armour. Its light (31 grain, as against the 124 grains of the NATO 9mm round) projectile had a muzzle velocity of almost 762mps (2500fps), more than

twice that of the 9mm round. Like the SS109 5.56mm round, the new projectile was designed to tumble on hitting its target, thereby greatly increasing the damage it does. As the cartridge is physically slightly smaller than the 9mm round, a pistol of normal size chambered for it could carry more ammunition than the same gun in 9mm. The FN Five-seveN, which was just over 200mm (8in) long overall and 0.6kg (1.33lb) empty – a little less than the slightly smaller Glock 17 – could carry 20 of the new rounds.

Not all firearms users accepted the assertion that large, blunt and comparatively slow projectiles were less effective than full-jacketed high-velocity rounds much more akin to those fired from military rifles. Some maintained

that the kinetic energy delivered by a very large, heavy projectile was equally effective, if for rather different reasons and generally in different circumstances. The result was a huge increase in the popularity of Magnum loads as originally developed for heavy frame revolvers in the 1930s, and that popularity resulted in the appearance of self-loading pistols to accept them. The best known of these was perhaps the Desert Eagle, developed in the United States and then put into production in Israel, but it was not the first. That honour fell to Harry Sanford's Auto Mag pistol, first seen in 1968 in .44 Magnum chambering. AMT, the company which acquired the rights to, and parts of, the original pistols, later successfully manufactured and sold more conventional

Colt Python

Calibre: .357in (9.1mm)
Weight: 1.08kg (38oz)
Length: 235mm (9.25in)
Barrel length: 102mm (4in)
Effective range: 30.48m (100ft)
Feed: six-round magazine
Muzzle velocity: 325mps (1066fps)
Country of origin: United States

■LEFT: A New York detective shows off his Colt revolver in the 1960s. It is probably a Police Positive Special Model. As it was the first small-frame swing-cylinder revolver capable of firing powerful ammunition it soon became a very popular police handgun. Over 750,000 were made.

semi-automatic pistols in a range of calibres from .22 WMR to .45 ACP, but there has been no sign of the original Auto Mag resurfacing. More recently, other comparatively small American manufacturers began producing standard recoil-action, locked-breech pistols based on Browning's designs in a variety of Magnum calibres from .357 to .45 Winchester Magnum, as well as versions which fire .30 carbine rounds.

THE WILDEY AUTOMATIC PISTOL

Another early Magnum-chambered self-loader, the Wildey Automatic Pistol, was developed in the mid-1970s by Wildey J. Moore from a Swedish design. The pistol was still in production 20 years later, even though it too went through a few changes of manufacturer along the way. Available in a range of heavy calibres, some of them unique to it (10mm Wildey, 11mm Wildey, for example) and on up to the later .45 Magnum which Winchester developed, the Wildey Automatic pistol shared one other important feature with the Israeli Desert Eagle: it was gas operated, with a rotary three-lug bolt. Up until then, self-loading pistols were

recoil-operated, most of them with either simple blowback actions or variants on the short-recoil theme, though there had been pistols which made use of propellant gases to both delay the blowback action and to soften the recoil. The Wildey and the Desert Eagle broke new ground, for these pistols were actually gas operated, and thus, in technical terms, were closer to modern self-loading rifles and machine guns than they were to other semi-automatic handguns.

To operate the Desert Eagle – which was offered in .357 Magnum, .41 Magnum, .44 Magnum and .50 Magnum – a portion of the propellant gas was bled off through a port just ahead of the chamber into a transfer cylinder underneath the barrel and parallel to it. Here it exerted pressure on the face of a piston, which in turn moved the slide to the rear, unlocking the bolt in the process. The spent case was ejected and the hammer cocked on the rearward journey, and as the (decreasing) pressure on the piston and the (increasing) pressure on the recoil spring came into equilibrium, the slide's direction was reversed, a fresh round chambered and the bolt and barrel

CZ 75

Calibre: 9mm (.35in)
Weight: .98kg (34.6oz)
Length: 203mm (8in)
Barrel length: 120mm (4.7in)
Effective range: 30.48m (100ft)
Feed: 15-round magazine
Muzzle velocity: 350mps (1150fps)
Country of origin: Czechoslovakia

Calico Model M-950

Calibre: 9mm (.35in)
Weight: 1kg (35.3oz)
Length: 365mm (14in)
Barrel length: 152mm (6in)
Effective range: 30.48m (100ft)
Feed: 50- or 100-round magazine
Muzzle velocity: 393mps (1290fps)
Country of origin: United States

relocked into battery. Because the barrel did not move relative to the frame of the gun, the pistol was remarkably accurate; because some, at least, of the gas was bled off to cycle the action, the recoil was tolerable. Quite what purpose there is for a handgun firing rounds of this dimension and power is not clear, but the Desert Eagle was a moderate commercial success. Israeli Military Industries, which manufactured the Desert Eagle, also produced a range of more conventional combat-calibre self-loaders. The Jericho 941 was available in five different models and three chamberings (9mm Parabellum, .40 S&W and .41 Action Express), and was based on a Browning design. The Jericho pistols were usually provided with two barrels, recoil springs and magazines – all that was necessary to switch between different chamberings which use almost identical cartridge cases. The changeover could be carried out as part of the normal stripping routine, with no special tools needed, a definite advantage under combar conditions. IMI also produced a high-capacity semi-automatic

handgun based on a stripped-down, miniature Uzi submachine.

If military theorists were starting to see the 9mm Parabellum round as deficient, civilian users, and particularly police forces, were increasingly concerned about the penetrating power of full-metal jacketed rounds. Known in civilian circles as jacketed hard point (JHP), their heavy cartridge loads gave them a 'shoot through' potential, where they might pass right through the target and hit a bystander. Their answer was to formulate a requirement for projectiles which spread open upon impact and remained within the target, rather than exiting the other side with their potential to inflict damage almost undiminished. The result was the so-called jacketed soft point (JSP) bullet, with sufficient initial penetrating power to go through relatively thin, hard material – glass, wood planking or the flimsy sheet metal of a vehicle body, for example – but spread out upon impact with flesh. This would also increase the potential wound size substantially as a result of the

phenomenon known as hydraulic shock. These 'new' rounds came into the public eye in the late 1980s, when apocryphal stories about 'cop killer' bullets, designed to penetrate body armour and then expand within the body itself, started to surface. In actual fact, expanding, exploding and fragmenting projectiles had been around as long as the unitary cartridge. All the main ammunition manufacturers have produced such rounds at one time or another, and only the technology behind them was new about this latest crop.

A trend could be seen, beginning in about 1975, towards the use of hollow point ammunition for law enforcement purposes. Not unnaturally, ammunition suppliers responded rapidly in what is, after all, a very important market, and began to develop new products based on applying the twin technologies of metallurgy and dynamics. A good example is the case of Winchester, by then a division of the Olin Corporation, which first entered the ammunition business in the early years of the

Makarov

Calibre: 9mm (.35in)
Weight: .66kg (23oz))
Length: 160mm (6.3in)
Barrel length: 93mm (3.66in)
Effective range: 30.48m (100ft)
Feed: eight-round magazine
Muzzle velocity: 315mps (1033fps)
Country of origin: Soviet Union

PSM

Calibre: 5.45mm (.22in)
Weight: .46kg (16oz)
Length: 160mm (6.26in)
Barrel length: 85mm (3.34in)
Effective range: 30.48m (100ft)
Feed: eight-round magazine
Muzzle velocity: 292mps (960fps)
Country of origin: Soviet Union

■BELOW: The 9mm Heckler and Koch VP-70. The weapon can fire three-round bursts, having a magazine which can accommodate 18 rounds. However, because of this the butt is rather bulky.

twentieth century. The first step towards the development of a satisfactory JSP round was the Silvertip, a lead projectile with a tapering cavity in its nose, the external walls of which were jacketed in aluminium. Seen in profile, the Silvertip and other commercial JSP rounds looked much like any other projectile, an essential attribute if they were to feed correctly in self-loading handguns. In order to ensure that the round mushroomed on impact, rather than collapsing into the cavity, the aluminium jacket was serrated around its rim. The next stage was to replace the aluminium jacket with one of rather more malleable copper, and this intermediate step resulted in the subsonic round.

INCREASING STOPPING POWER
The testing of such rounds is routinely performed by firing them into blocks of what is known as 'ordnance gelatine', a transparent substance derived from animal tissue in which both the passage of a round and the resulting rupture and internal damage can be traced visually. Modern high-speed photographic methods

allow ammunition technologists to trace the projectile every step of its way through the gelatine, and determine exactly how it reacts and changes its form between penetrating the test block and coming to rest. This is usually over a distance of between 300-450mm (12-18in) with a combat-calibre round. Such photography revealed that the expansion of 'conventional' JSP rounds, the cavity of which was V- or Y-shaped, was effectively retarded by the hollow point becoming plugged with material from any 'hard' layer (or even clothing) which the round had to pass through before it made contact with soft tissue. This led to the introduction of both cylindrical sump-type cavities, which were harder to plug, and changes to the profile of the jacketing itself, which now became thicker towards the 'point'.

DEADLY PETALS
It also became obvious that the serrations in the nose of the jacket actually caused the reinforcing to peel back as segments or 'petals', forced outwards and back by the presence of the material driven into

Desert Eagle

Calibre: .357in (9.1mm) or .44in (11.17mm)
Weight: 1.76kg (62.1oz)
Length: 260mm (10.25in)
Barrel length: 152mm (5.98in)
Effective range: 30.48m (100ft)
Feed: seven- or nine-round magazine
Muzzle velocity: 455mps (1493fps)
Country of origin: USA/Israel

■RIGHT: FN's latest recruit, the 5.7mm Five-seveN. Its round can supposedly penetrate up to 48 layers of Kevlar armour and all other types of body armour currently in use.

the hollow cavity. The thickening of the jacket material towards the nose had the unlooked-for (but, in the ammunition technologists' eyes, desirable) effect of allowing these 'petals' to remain intact. They also retained their recurve (formed where they had gripped the rim of the cavity) throughout the bullet's passage through the target, finishing up in the shape of an open flower with recurved claws. Rounds of this design reached the market as the 'Black Talon'.

'BLACK TALON'
They should probably have been on sale only to law enforcement agencies right from the start, but Winchester made them available to the general public for 'defensive and hunting purposes', an apologist adding, by way of explanation: 'After all, more criminals are confronted by private citizens than by police officers'. The Black Talon round, a bullet 'designed to rip your guts out' (as described by one noted US legislator), came under such concerted attack that the company

withdrew it from sale in November 1993, while continuing to insist, perhaps somewhat ingenuously, in view of its decision to put it on the open market, that it had only been developed in the first place in response to demand from law enforcement agencies. Eventually the round, now known as the Ranger SXT, was re-instated, but only for sale to law

enforcement agencies while a modified 'de-clawed' version named Supreme SXT was made available to the public.

The development of the JSP round clearly has little to do with handgun design; ammunition manufacturers actually rarely interact with gunmakers, and though the development of the Magnum rounds tells a different story, that can be seen as an isolated case. There has never been much attempt made by either party towards the elimination of the plethora of different calibres and cartridge forms, even though the dangers of being able to chamber and fire a powerful cartridge in a gun designed for something less potent are obvious. It would surely be advantageous to both industries to pursue a policy of closer co-operation, and could only enhance their respective products. There are currently 85 commonly listed cartridges available for handguns, in 30 different calibres and dimensions; with a longer list for rifles. This lack of cooperation was not always the case, in the early days of the handgun and the unitary cartridge, there was much more, largely because two interdependent industries were emerging concurrently. In modern times, one can point to the success of both Fabrique National and the massive state arsenals of the ex-Soviet Union in developing weapons in new calibres and producing matching ammunition. However, it is neither accidental, nor coincidental, that the ex-Soviet arsenals are still state-owned, and that FN could

only survive by being swallowed by the French government, and that thus both have exclusive access to huge captive markets for their guns.

THE GYROJET

The question as to whether either the French or the Russian Governments can actually create a market for ammunition in new calibres is moot; the calibres which dominate came about largely by accident and tend to be self-perpetuating. Even when a new type of cartridge does take hold, its appearance has only served to increase the number available, not to set any useful new, widely adopted standard. It will probably take a complete and revolutionary technological departure to change things, and this looks extremely unlikely.

There was an attempt to introduce a new technology into the field of small arms during the 1960's. Two Americans, Robert Mainhardt and Art Biehl, convinced that the conventional unitary cartridge and the handgun that fired it had reached the limit of their development, produced the MBA Gyrojet pistol. Looking like a conventional self-

loading handgun, it was in fact, a miniature rocket launcher. The 'round', 13mm (.5in) in diameter and 38mm (1.5in) long overall, was composed of two parts – a solid 'warhead' and a tubular body containing a propellant charge. The base was closed save for four thruster jets, with their apertures angled tangentially to impart stabilising spin . The pistol's 'hammer' worked on the nose of the rocket, driving it to the rear were a static firing pin struck a conventional percussion primer located between the jets, so igniting the propellant. The passage of the rocket down the barrel reset the hammer, while the next projectile simply popped up out of the magazine and into place in the 'breech'. The pistol was neither accurate nor powerful, and the project was terminated. In technical terms the principle of the Gyrojet pistol was actually no different from that of the light anti-tank rockets that have been in use since World War II, and there is no obvious reason why it should not be successfully applied to the handgun. To many, however, the real question is: why bother, when the unitary cartridge works as well as it does?

MBA Rocket

Calibre: 13mm (.51in)
Weight: .98kg (34.5oz)
Length: 234mm (9.2in)
Barrel length: 127mm (5in)
Effective range: 50m (164ft)
Feed: six-round magazine
Muzzle velocity: 274mps (900fps)
Country of origin: United States

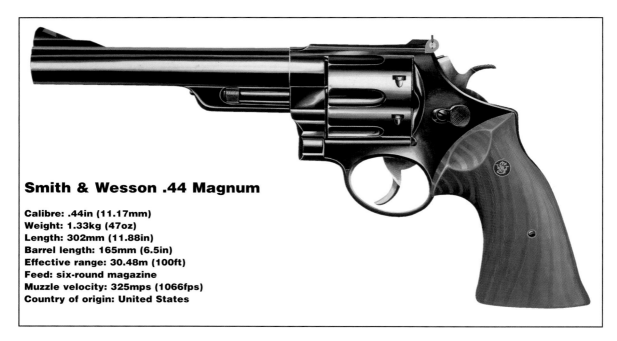

Smith & Wesson .44 Magnum

Calibre: .44in (11.17mm)
Weight: 1.33kg (47oz)
Length: 302mm (11.88in)
Barrel length: 165mm (6.5in)
Effective range: 30.48m (100ft)
Feed: six-round magazine
Muzzle velocity: 325mps (1066fps)
Country of origin: United States

The only satisfactory answer to that is that the 'conventional' gun has reached the end of its development cycle, at least until radical improvements are made in the field of propellants – unless, perhaps, something can be done to eliminate the cartridge case. That would cut out the need to extract and eject the empty case before a fresh round could be chambered, which in turn would remove the current obligation to stay with quasi-cylindrical rounds symmetrical around their long axis. Triangular or square-section 'rounds' would take up much less space in the magazine; liquid propellant would be even easier to store. The projectile itself could be encapsulated within a solid propellant charge, or fed separately in the case of liquid propellant, and could actually be of any shape and cross-section, as long as it was aerodynamically sound. A square or triangular-section barrel, for example, is perfectly feasible, though there is little reason beyond economy of projectile storage to think it desirable. There is a major problem facing developers of the caseless round, however. The cartridge case is not simply a container for the propellant and a way of linking it to the projectile; it is also an essential disposable heatsink – a way of taking excess heat out of the gun itself. It is the researchers' inability to tackle this aspect of the problem in a different way which has been one of the major factors

which has brought the various 'caseless round' small arms projects to a halt. As far as the handgun alone is concerned, this is less of a problem, but until it can be solved for other types of small arms, and a new form of widely compatible ammunition can be produced, there is no good reason to introduce a new element into an already confused situation.

A HEALTHY FUTURE?

As the twentieth century draws to a close, the days of the handgun as a military weapon seem to be numbered – though we would probably do well to remember that no less a soldier than Wellington himself suggested the same, well over a 150 years ago. Equally, as a non-military weapon, it seems to have taken on a new lease of life as the restraining bonds of society weaken and man's readiness to harm, maim and kill his fellows comes to the fore again. Combine the two, and we can perhaps begin to perceive a very good reason for banning the manufacture of handguns entirely, no matter how unpopular such a move might be in certain circles.

It is impossible to separate the purpose from the object. Guns are intended to wound or to kill and in the wrong hands they are widely abused for this purpose: they have no other real purpose. Handguns, which have only very limited value as hunting weapons, have no other

role than to wound or to kill our fellow human beings. That the best of them, after half a millennium of development, are miniature masterpieces of engineering technology, matters not at all when measured against that fact; neither does the craftsmanship and artistry which went into the best of such weapons during an earlier stage in their development.

EQUALISERS

During the nineteenth century, when the world as we know it was in the process of rapidly industrialising and the great urban conurbations were becoming established and lawless, the practical pistol was hailed as the great equaliser at a time when the forces of law and order were next to non-existent. They were carried as a matter of course by outlaws and men of good character alike. Alongside the steamship, the steam train, the telegraph, and all the other essentials that contributed to our civilisation, the handgun should probably have passed into the museum case decades ago, but instead they are still with us, carried in the car or on the body, openly or concealed, and to hand in the home. Their deadly power for good and evil is graphically demonstrated every day in our cinemas, on our television sets and in our newspapers. In real life and in the creations of the media the handgun remains a potent symbol.